Talking to Children About Responsibility and Control of Emotions

Michael Schleifer, Ph.D.
and
Cynthia Martiny, Ph.D.

Calgary, Alberta, Canada

Talking to Children About Responsibility and Control of Emotions
© 2006 Michael Schleifer and Cynthia Martiny

Library and Archives Canada Cataloguing in Publication

Schleifer, Michael
    Talking to children about responsibility and control of emotions / Michael Schleifer and Cynthia Martiny.

Includes index.
Includes some text in French.
ISBN-13: 978-1-55059-321-1
ISBN-10: 1-55059-321-8

1. Emotions in children. 2. Responsibility in children. 3. Children – Conduct of life. I. Martiny, Cynthia II. Title.

BF721.S288 2006   649'.7   C2006-904755-3

Detselig Enterprises Ltd.
210, 1220 Kensington Road NW
Calgary, Alberta T2N 3P5

www.temerondetselig.com
temeron@telusplanet.net
Phone: (403) 283-0900
Fax: (403) 283-6947

All rights reserved. No part of this book may be reproduced in any form or by any means without permission in writing from the publisher.

We acknowledge the support of the Government of Canada through the Book Publishing Industry Development Program (BPIDP) for our publishing program.

We also acknowledge the support of the Alberta Foundation for the Arts for our publishing program.

SAN 113-0234
ISBN 1-55059-321-8   978-1-55059-321-1
    Printed in Canada   Cover Design by Alvin Choong

Contents

List Of Contributors 5
Introduction by Cynthia Martiny and Michael Schleifer 7

Part I: Educating The Emotions
Chapter 1: Critical Thinking and the Education of the Emotions 13
    Sharon Bailin
    Discussion 21
Chapter 2: The Siblings of Cinderella and Joseph: What Should Educators Say
    about Jealousy and Envy? 29
    Michael Schleifer
    Discussion 37

Part II: Victims And Violence
Chapter 3: Happy Victimizers and Moral Responsibility: Sociocultural and
    Developmental Considerations 49
    William F. Arsenio
    Discussion 65
Chapter 4: When Adults Lose it, Do Children Catch it?: What to Say to Children
    Who Witness Inter-Adult Violence 71
    Cynthia Martiny
    Discussion 81

Part III: Development
Chapter 5: Understanding The Flow of Thoughts and Feelings 95
    Paul L. Harris and Suzanne Duke
    Discussion 107

Part IV: Classroom Discussions
Chapter 6: Emotion Recollected in Tranquility? Learning the Emotions Through Art:
    Aesthetics and Philosophy for Children 121
    Wendy C. Turgeon
    Discussion 143

Chapter 7: Introduction to Ann sharp's Paper 147

How to Educate the Emotions in the Context of the Classroom
Community of Inquiry 151

Ann Sharp
Discussion 161

Part V: General Discussion

Topic 1: Emotion and the Arts 167
Topic 2: Developmental Considerations 175
Topic 3: Research and Educational Initiatives 179

List Of Contributors

William F. Arsenio is Associate Professor of Psychology at the Ferkauf Graduate School of Psychology, Yeshiva University (New York City). His research focuses on children's and adolescents' emotions and emotion understanding in relation to several areas, including: social competence; risk for psychopathology; and school-related performance. Dr. Arsenio's research has been funded by the National Institute of Mental Health. He is a Fellow of the American Psychological Association (Division 7, Developmental Psychology), and an advisory and editorial board member of several developmental journals. Along with his students and colleagues, he has written a number of recent reviews and theoretical articles on the role of emotional processes in children's aggression and moral development.

Sharon Bailin is a Professor in the Faculty of Education at Simon Fraser University. Her research, which is philosophical in nature, addresses issues relating to creativity, critical thinking, argumentation, and arts and drama education.

Paul Harris, professor at the University of Harvard, is interested in the early development of cognition, emotion and imagination. His most recent book, *The Work of the Imagination*, gathers together several years of research carried out at Oxford University, where he taught developmental psychology. Currently, he is conducting research in two areas. First, he is studying whether children rely on their own first-hand observation or alternatively trust what other people tell them – especially when they confront a domain of knowledge in which first-hand observation is difficult. For example, many aspects of history, science and religion concern events that children cannot easily observe for themselves. How far do children believe what they are told about these domains? When and how do they become aware of the conflicting claims made by science as compared to religion? Second, he is studying children's understanding of mental states, including emotional states. He is particularly interested in the extent to which children's access to conversation about psychological matters influences their understanding of emotion.

Cynthia Martiny is a Professor in the Faculty of Education at the Université du Québec à Montréal (Section Counselling). Her published articles concern the verbal and non-verbal manifestations of empathy. She leads counselling groups for men who have committed conjugal violence. Her professional experience includes therapeutic foster care with children, mediation between parents and children, group home care for delinquent adolescent girls, and counselling for victims of sexual assault. She is a mother of four children with whom she discusses emotions and morality.

Michael Schleifer is a Professor in the Faculty of Education at the Université du Québec à Montréal (Sections Foundations, Epistemology, and Educational Psychology). He obtained his B. Phil. in Oxford (Philosophy) and his Ph. D. at McGill (Psychology). He has taught Ethics at McGill University (Philosophy Department) and worked as a Clinical Psychologist at the Montreal Children's Hospital (Department of Psychiatry). He has published numerous articles in Educational, Philosophical and

Psychological journals. He has also edited books on Identity, Cooperation, and the Development of Judgment. He is a grandfather of three children with whom he enjoys conversing about feelings and values.

Ann Margaret Sharp is Associate Director of the Institute for the Advancement of Philosophy for Children and Professor of Education at Montclair State College. She is also the coauthor (with Matthew Lipman and Frederick S. Oscanyan) of *Philosophy in the Classroom* (Temple). She is author of the early childhood philosophy program The Doll Hospital and a philosophy program for middle school children focusing on philosophy of body and prevention of child abuse entitled Hannah.

Wendy Turgeon teaches philosophy at Saint Joseph's College in New York and also teaches philosophy for children courses at Stony Brook University. She has worked in the area of philosophy for children for a number of years with teachers and students. Her major areas of interest are aesthetics and the history of philosophy. Newly engaged by Icelandic sagas, she is beginning to explore the ethical systems within this form of mediaeval literature.

Other participants whose questions and comments were recorded at the end of each chapter and at the end of the book included: professors Jean-Claude Brief, Gerald Boutin, Pierre Lebuis, and Catherine Meyor; and educators and counsellors Lee Londei, Leonie Richler, Alexander Herriger, Pierre Laurendeau, and Phil Guin.

Introduction

Cynthia Martiny and Michael Schleifer

This book is the result of a symposium held at the Faculty of Education of the Université du Québec à Montréal from May 9 to May 11, 2006. We asked a number of invited speakers to address the topic of "Talking to children about responsibility and control of emotions." The presenters included developmental psychologists and philosophers of education. In addition to the texts, we have included samples of the questions, exchanges, and debates from the participants after each paper was presented, as well as at the end of the book. In this introduction we provide an overview of some of the major themes including the major agreements and controversies.

Control

Not one of the participants chose to speak directly about control. An emerging consensus seems to be that we still have much to learn about the comprehension of emotion, which is in any case a crucial factor in regard to control. This agreement is consistent with recent positions both within psychology (Campos, Frankel, and Camras, 2004) and philosophy (Gazzard, 2000) that we cannot talk of the control of an emotion as separate from the emotion itself. Control of emotions develops over time. Regulation and management of one's emotions (terms often preferred to "control") focus on behavior which typically concerns interactions with others. (Eisenberg and Spinrad, 2004). The discussions in these meetings – whether about anger, frustration, jealousy, or any other emotion – always included questions about what the child understood about the emotion, in addition to questions about his behavior and his interactions. Reason and emotions are intimately interconnected. What a child understands is a function of development as well as interventions of an educational sort. Most of the papers refer to the importance of conversations about emotion, whether with parents (Harris, Schleifer), professionals (Martiny, Arnsenio) or teachers in the classroom (Sharp, Turgeon) These conversations and dialogues, which include the important ingredient of linguistic labelling, will aid the child in progressing in the development of emotional understanding. (For more on control of emotion, see Saarni and Harris 1989, part IV).

Responsibility

A second emerging consensus concerns being responsible for emotions. This theme was explicit in several papers (Bailin, Schleifer, Sharp) and features prominently in the general exchanges and discussions. The idea is that we must take responsibility for our emotions much the same way as we take responsibility for our actions and their consequences. One can find this argued long ago by Aristotle in the Nicomochean Ethics. More recently it has been revised in the work of Martha Nussbaum (2001) for whom emotions are a form of judgment, tied to our beliefs (see also Solomon 1980, Adams 1985, Fisher and Ravissa 1998, Smith 2005, Campos et al 2005, p. 392, Schleifer and McCormick, 2006).

Sharon Bailin (Chapter 1) sees emotions as fundamentally rational, part of our critical thinking and moral discourse: As she puts it: "Emotions are neither dichotomous nor in opposition to reason." Her philosophical viewpoint follows that of Nussbaum (2001) and Solomon (1995) and the earlier tradition of Aristotle which highlights emotions as primarily cognitive, as a form of judgment, and indispensable to moral reasoning. Reflecting and conversing about emotions presupposes some version of this cognitive perspective.

Michael Schleifer (Chapter 2) accepts this view of emotions and applies it to the complex set of jealousy/envy. He analyzes the concepts and also refers to empirical research on children's understanding from ages 2 to 12. Although children at age 2 have a good inkling about these feelings, they cannot be said to understand the emotions until age 5. Further development allows for more sophisticated linguistic articulation.

William Arsenio (Chapter 3) presents his observational data of children's and adolescent's behaviors associated with harming others and their conceptualizations of the emotional outcomes in terms of moral development. He finds that many young children (4 to 6 year olds) expect victimizers (both themselves and others) to feel happy following acts of victimization that produce material gains until the age of 8. After that age, he attributes this type of reaction to a developmental lag. According to his findings "aggressive preschoolers are more likely to be happy while aggressing than their peers, and are more likely to be disliked by their classmates as a result. " He discusses "how some aggressive children's happy victimization expectancies may play an adaptive (or at least coherent) role in helping them cope with maladaptive environments that may be characterized more by power relationships than by moral and empathic reciprocity."

Cynthia Martiny (Chapter 4) addresses the effects of children witnessing conjugal violence, the function of anger and its characteristics. She explores some of the emotional motivational reasons of inter-adult violence. After describing treatment strategies, she finishes her paper by presenting what children who witness conjugal violence should know in light of the topics addressed. Although powerless to change aggressive behaviors between their parents, children need to stay safe, can adopt effective coping skills and develop emotionally healthy relationships.

According to Paul Harris and Suzanne Duke (Chapter 5), preschool children as young as 4 understand that the emotional intensity linked to either a positive or negative event diminishes with time and that remembering the episode re-activates the original emotions. Further Harris and Duke research has demonstrated that 8 year olds were able to conceptualize how intrusive thoughts could be kept at bay while 5 year olds showed only an emerging grasp of how to control cognitive intrusions. These findings suggest that children gradually become aware of their ability to regulate intrusive and unwanted thoughts in spite of their involuntary flow into consciousness.

Ann Sharp (Chapter 7) offers an example of discussing the emotions with very young children (at preschool) through the use of stories. Some of these stories have been produced recently exploring abuse, violence, inappropriate touching and similar topics (Schleifer 2006). Sharp, one of the principal founders (with Matthew Lipman) of the Philosophy for Children approach and curriculum stresses that these new materials are consistent with the original theoretical concern. From the outset doing philosophy was not only meant to help reading and thinking skills (which many results have shows it has), but to instill a form of caring thinking.

Wendy Turgeon (Chapter 8) combines philosophy and music to provide material for reflection about emotions. She presents a theoretical thesis about the use of art for exploring emotions, returning to Aristotle. She also provides a practical demonstration of the use of musical pieces to elicit reactions from the listeners and provoke discussions about these emotions. These topics are explored not only in her paper, but also in the general debates between participants.

References

Adams, R. (1985). Involuntary sins. *Philosophical Review, 94*(1) 3-31.

Campos J, Frankel, C. and Camras L. (2004). On the nature of emotion regulation. *Child Development, 75*(2) 377-394.

Eisenberg, N. and Spinrad, T. (2004). Emotion-related regulation: sharpening the definition. *Child Development 75*(2) 334-339.

Fischer, J. and Ravizza, M. (1998). *Responsibility and control,* Cambridge UP.

Gazzard, A. (2002). What does Philosophy for Children have to do with emotional intelligence?. *Thinking 15*(1) 39-45.

Nussbaum, M. (2001). *Upheavals of thought: The intelligence of emotions,* Cambridge UP.

Saarni, C. and Harris, P. (1985). *Children's understanding of emotion.* Cambridge UP.

Schleifer M. and McCormick, M. (2006). Are we responsible for our moods and emotions?. *Thinking 18*(1) 15-21.

Schleifer, S. and Martiny, C. (2006). *Talking about feelings and values with children,* Detselig Temeron Press.

Solomon, R. (1980). Emotions and choice. A Rorty (ed.) *Explaining Emotions,* Berkeley: University of California Press.

Solomon (1995). Some notes on emotion, east and west. *Philosophy East and West,* 45(2), 171-202.

Smith, A. Responsibility for Attitudes: Activity and Passivity in Mental Life *Ethics, 115* 236-271.

Part I

Educating the Emotions

Chapter 1
Critical Thinking and the Education of the Emotions
Sharon Bailin, Simon Fraser University

Introduction

Although emotions constitute an extremely important aspect of our lives, their centrality as a topic of philosophical examination has waxed and waned. And although the nature of the relationship between emotion and reason has been treated variously by philosophers in the Western tradition, nonetheless the image persists, in western cultures, of the irrational passions set in perennial opposition to a bloodless reason. I shall argue in this paper that this image is far from the reality, because the two are not strictly dichotomous nor in opposition, but rather intimately intertwined. I will contend that this interconnection is central to our mental operations. I will also explore some of the implications of this stance for educating the emotions and for the possibility and fruitfulness of thinking critically about our emotions.

History

The subject of the emotions has been treated by many classical philosophers from Plato to Hume, and, although there was a waning of interest in much of earlier twentieth century philosophy, interest in the topic revived in latter part of the century (de Sousa, 2003). The popular view is that, within the Western philosophical tradition, emotion is viewed as irrational and in need of governance by the steadying force of reason. Yet, in actual fact, the nature of the relationship has been conceived in a variety of diverse ways. It is true that for Plato, emotion is in the part of the soul to be controlled by the reason. Nonetheless he holds that emotion can be an ally of the rational part (de Sousa, 1980). Emotion plays an even more important role for Aristotle, who argues that a capacity for the moral life is largely a result of learning to feel the right emotions in the right circumstances, and failing to feel an emotion in a certain circumstance is a ground for moral criticism. Hume famously asserted that reason is and ought to be the slave of passions. Thus the picture of irrational passions in need of restraint by reason is not an entirely accurate portrayal of the way the issue has been treated in the Western tradition.

Connections between Emotion and Reason

The role of reason in emotion

Although philosophical theories about the nature of emotion are diverse in their conceptualizations, some degree of consensus exists amongst contemporary philosophers regarding some features of emotions. To begin, most current philosophical theories view emotions as intentional; they are about something and have some object. In addition, there have been widespread objections to theories which conceptualize emotions strictly in terms of feelings. Such theories are thought to be inadequate in terms of differentiating between emotions (for example, the difference between pride and admiration does not seem to lie in the physiological sensation, but rather in the attitude to the object (i.e. whether one takes responsibility for the achievement under consideration). It is also argued that feeling theories are unable to explain the fact that emotions can be explained and justified. The neglect of the connection between an emotion and its intentional object is seen as another shortcoming of feeling theories. In addition, some philosophers argue that not all emotions are primarily about feelings, for example trust or courage, which may be characterized more by a particular frame of mind or pattern of attention and action than by particular feelings (Elgin, 1996). As Elgin puts it:

> This is not to deny that feelings of trust and feelings of courage exist. But it is to suggest that the relation between having an emotion and feeling it is more complicated and less direct than it first appears. (Elgin, 1996, p. 149)

The problems with feeling theories centre on the realization by many theorists that emotions are, in some manner and to some degree, thought-dependent. They have a cognitive dimension, although how to conceive of this cognitive dimension is the subject of some debate. It has been variously conceptualized in terms of beliefs combined with desires (Marks, 1982), normative judgments (Solomon 1980), systems of judgments or scenarios (Solomon, 1995), and cognitions which may or may not be conceptual (Elgin, 1996). Moreover, some emotions may be more thought-dependent than others.

It is also commonly believed that emotions are learned, at least to some extent. Many emotions require the ability to manipulate concepts, and, as individuals develop, they learn occasions for their appropriate use and attribution.

That emotions have a cognitive dimension also means that they can be explained and justified. Emotions can be assessed for their rationality, as demonstrated by the fact that we do hold people responsible for their emotions.

The role of emotion in reason

Another important connection between emotion and reason lies in the role played by emotion in enabling rational assessment and action. Emotions function as ways of seeing, serving to constrain and direct attention, thereby rendering salient certain aspects of our experience. They provide cues regarding what to inquire about, what to attend to, and when we might be on to something, directing us to salient alternatives in rational deliberation. Without such direction, rationality would be impossible since the number of possibilities for attention and investigation is virtually infinite (de Sousa, 1987). Moreover, emotions seem to be vital for the conduct of a rational life. Individuals with impaired emotional capabilities, for example, have been shown to have difficulty in making intelligent practical decisions (Damasio, 1994).

Another role played by emotions in reasoning is in terms of the 'rational passions.' Inquiry is not a dispassionate activity, disassociated from emotion. Rather, people can be emotionally committed to the search for truth and care passionately that the outcome of an inquiry be the best justified. Such 'rational passions' as love of truth, repugnance of distortion and evasion, and respect for the arguments of others are essential to critical thinking (Peters, 1972). In addition, emotions such as curiosity, surprise and the joy of verification all play a significant role in the conduct of inquiry (Scheffler, 1991).

Educating the Emotions

There are several senses in which one might view the education of the emotions: developing appropriate emotions, and critiquing and altering emotions.

Developing appropriate emotions

The first of these has to do with the learning of emotions. Although babies do appear to exhibit feelings, the initial identification of emotions, and the acquisition and refinement of a complex emotional repertoire take place through participating in a form of life. Through daily activities and the learning of language and concepts, and through exposure to the narratives and stories of the culture, children learn what de Sousa has termed 'paradigm scenarios,' which are situations that provide the characteristic objects of an emotion as well as a set of the characteristic, or 'normal' responses to the situation (de Sousa, 1980, p. 142).

Such learning involves the internalization of the concepts of culture, and is a public enterprise. Although the physiological basis of emotions may be universal, emotions do seem to vary culturally. The emotion of anger, for example, which is displayed with considerable frequency in the U. S., appears to be a rarity among the Utku Eskimos, and the concept is all but unintelligible for them (Solomon, 1995). There does seem to be significant cultural variation in terms of what causes particular emotions, the ease with which certain emotions are triggered, the context in which they are thought appropriate, how they are described and embellished, and how and whether they are acted upon (Solomon, 1995). Solomon points out that, although it may be the case that we are hard-wired to feel an emotion such as panic, significant differences seem to exist, from culture to culture, as to what are the circumstances which evoke it, how much panic is appropriate in particular circumstances, to what extent certain displays of panic are seen as acceptable by the culture, and whether it is considered surmountable by education or experience (Solomon, 1995). He puts the point thus:

> The language of emotions, the way they are talked about, and the ways in which they fit (or do not fit) into a culture's ethics and customs may vary enormously, and there will be any number of encouraging or discouraging features of the culture and the environment that will provoke, support, excite, suppress, or possibly even extinguish certain emotions or types of emotions (Solomon, 1995, p. 172).

Thus, although children are likely genetically programmed to respond in certain ways to at least some scenarios, de Sousa summarizes an important role played by education:

> An essential part of education consists in identifying these responses, giving the child a name for them in the context of the scenario, and thus teaching it that it is experiencing a particular emotion (de Sousa, 1980, p. 413).

Elgin elaborates thus:

> Learning to identify emotions thus involves learning what sorts of situations typically elicit a particular emotion, what saliencies it gives rise to, what range of verbal and nonverbal behaviors generally manifest it, and what sorts of defeaters undermine the foregoing context (Elgin, 1996, p. 163).

It can be seen, then, that naming emotions and talking about emotions and their appropriateness in specific contexts is important in terms of the acquisition by children of a rich and appropriate emotional repertoire. Moreover, it might be desirable to highlight those cases and expose children to those stories which exemplify the emotions and emotional connections that we think are educationally valuable. I think here, in particular, of putting deliberate emphasis on the rational passions, as these are frequently under-emphasized in education and in life in general (Bailin & Battersby, in press). By modeling such rational passions as intellectual curiosity, a love of truth, the joy of verification, and a respect for the arguments of others in their interactions with children, educators can provide them with the paradigms to develop these important emotions.

As individuals mature and become more discriminating, their emotional ascriptions tend to increase in complexity, sophistication, and interrelation, and this process may be aided by exposure to new paradigm scenarios, particularly through literature and the arts. Works of art, and literature in particular, explore in evocative detail human situations, interactions, motivations, and emotions. They present us with a range of problems, issues and contradictions with which human beings struggle and have struggled, thereby giving us access to ways of being which go beyond our own experience, and to the thoughts, motivations and feelings of diverse individuals. Barrow makes the point thus:

> Novelists and poets enrich and illuminate our understanding of love, jealousy, hate, envy, etc., by their detailed exploration of particular instances. A novel such as Arnold Bennett's *Riceyman Steps* is, for example, a sustained study of the emotional state of miserliness. The reader is led into the mind of the miser and brought to understand what it is like to be a miser (Barrow, 1990).

Many authors have pointed out this role of literature in providing models of human emotion, models which can serve to help bring more breadth, depth, sensitivity, and sophistication to our emotional reactions.

Critiquing and altering emotions

Given that emotions are intentional and have some cognitive content, the possibility exists that they can be assessed for their appropriateness, critiqued, and altered. Elgin points out that the judgments at the heart of emotions can often be accurate and need not distort perception or derail reason. On the contrary, emotions can serve as early-warning systems. Some emotions are information-sensitive, and it is not a coincidence that much of what we fear is in fact dangerous, much of what we cherish is in fact valuable, and so on (Elgin, 1996).

Goodman argues, in fact, that we are likely to be better off if we are skilled in fearing, wanting, braving, or distrusting the right things, animate or inanimate, than if we perceive only their shapes, sizes, weights, etc. (Goodman, 1976, p. 251). Emotions may provide useful cues for future assessments and can provoke discovery. Thus they can be viewed as initially tenable hypotheses, providing resources to investigate further (Elgin, 1996).

Although emotions need not distort perception or derail reason, we are all painfully aware of the fact that they often do. They may lead us to misread evidence, give undue prominence to certain factors, and engage in irrational behaviors. Thus it is important to try to distinguish credible emotions from non-credible ones by attending to the warrant of the judgments inherent in our emotions, and correcting them as necessary. This includes critically scrutinizing our intuitions in the context of inquiry. Intuitions may provide accurate clues to discovery or problem-solving, but it is equally possible that they will not.

Thus they must be subjected to testing and verification (Bailin, 1991). The emotions we experience in the context of human interactions require similar critical scrutiny to determine their accuracy and appropriateness. The possibility of such an enterprise is demonstrated by the fact that we do commonly subject emotions to public evaluation.

We regularly criticize one another for being unjustifiably angry, overly optimistic, or needlessly concerned. We credit one another for being rightly resentful, justifiably proud, or entitled to grieve. And we often achieve consensus about such matters (Elgin, 1996, p. 159). Such a consensus presupposes the existence of standards of assessment; these criteria, although perhaps tacit, are frequently shared, challenged, and defended by argument. Moreover, as Elgin further argues: "the fact that resolution of such arguments often turns on correct characterization of relevant circumstances indicates that our standards measure the appropriateness of emotions to context" (Elgin, 1996, p. 159).

As a consequence, critically examining our emotions, as well as the judgments underlying them, can play a role in making them more appropriate to the circumstances. Recognizing the inappropriateness of the emotion or the inadequacy of the beliefs and judgments that underlie them can often result in a change in the emotion itself. For example, if Bob is angry at his Department Head for making a preemptory decision, and Bob subsequently learns that the decision actually emanated from the Dean's Office, then his anger at his Department Head should vanish.

We know, however, from leading human lives, that our emotions do not always change when we learn that the belief or judgment at the base of the emotion is not true. The fear of flying, for example, is notoriously resistant to information regarding the safety record of airplanes. Such emotions may not even change if, at some level, we realize that they are irrational. Instead, they are often conserved, redirected, or rationalized. The problem of the intractability of some emotions seems to show, that connection between emotion and beliefs described above does not tell the whole story. One problem may be that the connection of an emotion to its underlying judgments is not always easily accessible, and may be difficult to formulate. A number of theorists (e.g. Rorty, 1980; Solomon, 1980) draw a distinction, which may be helpful here, between the reasons for and causes of an emotion. Although the reason for an emotion may be immediate and simple (the Department Head made a peremptory decision), the causes of the emotion may have a lengthy and complex history, relating to the actual situations in which one initially acquired the emotion as well as the contexts in which it subsequently developed. Rorty (1980) emphasizes the importance of early, even prepropositional, patterns of salience, organization, attention and interpretation, patterns, which easily become habitual. Thus we may really be reacting to the significant events that formed our habits of response and only minimally to the present situation. So, for example, if Bob was raised by a domineering father, he may react negatively to an action of someone in authority even when the person's action is shown not to be authoritarian. Another cause of the intractability of some emotions may be emotional investment, including the cost of giving up certain emotions. Thus, for example, if Richard has been angry at his brother Jim for many years over some alleged wrong-doing of Jim's, Richard might not be willing even to consider the possibility that Jim's action was not culpable because of the potential weight of guilt at having harbored an unjustified anger for so long.

We have seen that emotions can change with assessment of their underlying judgments. So thinking critically about beliefs and judgments, being willing "to search out, and challenge the normative judgments embedded in every emotional response" (Solomon, 1980, p. 270) can be helpful in altering inappropriate emotions. We may be unable to stop a certain emotion, but we can "open ourselves to argument, persuasion and evidence" (Solomon, 1980, p. 270) that may affect if, and when, we feel something. Thus the activity of emotional examination and critique is one which is undertaken, to some extent at least, in interaction with others.

But our emotions can also change with our understanding of their causes and purposes. Thus being self-reflective and attempting to become aware of the causes and purposes of our emotions also has an important role to play in changing our emotional reactions. So, for example, if Bob's colleagues succeed in demonstrating to Bob on a number of occasions that the actions of the Department Head and of other persons in authority are not, in fact, peremptory, then Bob may come to consider the possibility that the cause of his anger in these cases is something other than the reasons he has given himself, and to attempt to understand their causal history, possibly including his relationship with his father. This process may require the aid of a psychotherapist since connections may not always be direct nor causes and purposes easily and painlessly accessible (de Sousa, 1980). De Sousa argues, in fact, that the possibility and efficacy of talk therapy itself presuppose the thought-dependence of emotion.

Such self-awareness involves being alert to instances where we seem to hang on to an irrational emotion and to situations which tend to trigger inappropriate emotions in us. It also involves a willingness to think about our judgments in new and different ways, to restructure and revise our emotional repertoire, and to try to change emotional habits. If de Sousa is correct when he suggests that shifts of emotion are primarily shifts of salience, then becoming willing and able to see situations in different ways (which will alter the habitual patterns of salience) becomes crucially important. Let us take the case of Sally, who is envious of her husband's opportunity to spend several days in Paris after his conference. Perhaps, with some effort however, she can manage to see the situation not in terms of someone who is getting something that she can't have, but rather in terms of a person whom she loves and whose happiness she genuinely cares about having a pleasant experience. If she manages this shift in perspective, then the envy may turn into satisfaction, or at the very least, the feeling of envy may be reduced or countered. Thus, although emotions tend to determine patterns of salience, a deliberate attempt to change the way a situation is viewed can shift the patterns of salience and thus result in a change in the emotion.

Such self-awareness and willingness to critique must, by necessity, extend beyond particular judgments embedded in an individual's emotions to systems of judgments, since our emotional repertoire is tied to a whole cultural world-view. We learn emotions through the paradigm scenarios of our culture, but this does not mean that we cannot be critical of some cultural paradigms and the emotions they engender (de Sousa, 1980). For example, Nussbaum (1997) makes reference to the Stoic belief that, since emotions such as fear and anger come from the habits and conventions of the surrounding society, they can be altered through a critical examination of those beliefs and practices. In this context, she cites the following example drawn from Seneca:

> an average Roman male is likely to get very angry indeed if his host seats him in a low place at the dinner table. Challenge the culture's obsession with these outward marks of status, and you have effectively challenged the person's basis for anger (Nussbaum, 1997, p. 29).

As a more contemporary example, someone who was raised in the southern United States pre 1960, might have learned to feel indignation at the sight of a black person trying to sit at the front of a bus. Nonetheless, he can, through education, become aware of the injustice of the racism which underpinned the situation and thus become critical of the 'paradigm scenario' in which his emotion was learned. This opens up the possibility of a change of the emotion experienced in this situation.

An even more radical type of shift of salience is proposed by certain philosophical theories which have a very different perspective regarding the role of emotion. The Stoics, for example, held the view that emotions are judgments regarding the value that their objects have for us, but from this starting point they drew the conclusion that we would be better off if we did not experience emotions. Emotions set us up for unhappiness because, as the result of our susceptibility to emotions, our happiness ends up depending on factors which we cannot control. What they advocate, then, is not simply that we alter particular emotions by altering particular judgments, but that we detach ourselves from emotions altogether by correctly judging that the contingent matters of life are unimportant. A similar detachment from the contingent attachments of life is advocated by Buddhist philosophy. Whether such a complete detachment from emotion is either possible or desirable is a fascinating question, but one which I shall leave for another time.

Conclusion

Rather than being totally dichotomous and in perennial opposition, it appears that emotion and reason are intimately interconnected and jointly necessary in the conduct of life. On the one side, emotions enable, and are indispensable to, rational assessment and action, because emotions make salient particular aspects of experience as a basis for rational deliberation. Certain emotions, such as the rational passions, also play a central role in rational activity by fuelling inquiry and motivating its virtues. On the other side, emotions have a cognitive dimension and thus can be evaluated as to their appropriateness. They can also be altered (to some degree and in some contexts) with an alteration in the judgments that underly them, by gaining critical purchase on their causes, and/or with a reconceptualization of the situation which gave rise to them.

As a consequence, in opposition to the view that we are hopelessly in the thrall of our emotions and are helpless victims of their vagaries, there seems to be good reason to believe that conversation of various sorts can broaden, deepen, and hone our emotional reactions, and that critical reflection and dialogue can give us some critical purchase on our emotional lives. Solomon makes the point, worth noting here, that talking about emotions plays back into the language of emotion and into the emotions themselves: "Talk about emotion is not just commentary on emotions. It is also, in part, constitutive of emotion" (Solomon, 1995, p. 194). This observation underlines the importance of critical exchanges, and of ongoing conversation, for the education of the emotions.

References

Bailin, S. (1991). Rationality and Intuition. *Paideusis*, 4(2) 17-26.

Bailin, S. & Battersby, M. (in press). Reason appreciation. in H. Hansen & R. Pinto (Eds.) *Reason Reclaimed*.

Barrow, R. (1990). *Understanding skills: Thinking, feeling and caring*. London, Ontario: Althouse Press.

Damasio, A. (1994). *Descartes' error: Emotion, reason and the human brain*. New York: G. P. Putman's Sons.

de Sousa, R. (2003). Emotion. *The Stanford Encyclopedia of Philosophy* (Spring, Edition), Edward N. Zalta (ed.). http://plato. stanford. edu/archives/spr2003/entries/emotion/

——. (1980). The Rationality of Emotions. in A. Rorty (Ed.), *Explaining Emotions*. Berkeley: University of California Press, 127-151.

——. (1987). *The rationality of emotion*. Cambridge, MA: MIT Press.

Elgin, C. Z. (1996). *Considered judgment*. Princeton: Princeton UP.

Feldman, N. (2001). The link between our minds and emotions. *Chicago Tribune*, November 18, 2001.

Goodman, N. (1976). *Languages of Art*. Indianapolis: Hackett.

Marks, J. (1982). A Theory of Emotion. *Philosophical Studies*, *42*, 227-242.

Nussbaum, M. (1997). *Cultivating humanity: A classical defense of reform in liberal education*. Cambridge: Harvard UP.

Peters, R. S. (1972). Reason and Passion. in R. F. Dearden, P. H. Hirst, & R. S. Peters (Eds.), *Education and the development of reason*. London: Routledge & Kegan Paul.

Rorty, A. (1980). Explaining Emotions. in A. Rorty (Ed.), *Explaining Emotions*. Berkeley: University of California Press, 103-126.

——. (Ed.) (1980). *Explaining emotions*. Berkeley: University of California Press.

Scheffler, I. (1991). *In praise of the cognitive emotions*. New York: Routledge.

Solomon, R. (1980). Emotions and Choice. in A. Rorty (Ed.), *Explaining Emotions*. Berkeley: University of California Press, 251-281.

——. (1995). Some notes on emotion, east and west. *Philosophy East and West*, *45*(2) 171-202.

Discussion Regarding Sharon Bailin's Presentation

Phil Guin: Sharon I really enjoyed your paper. Earlier, you said we hold a person responsible for their emotions, did you mean that in some kind of legal sense?

Sharon Bailin: No. I meant it in an everyday sense, such as *your anger is not justified*, or *that person really didn't do anything bad*, or *get over it.*

Phil Guin: So by the same token, would you say, then, if the person lacks an emotion that we would hold them responsible?

Sharon Bailin: Yes, I think we do that as well. *Why aren't you feeling grief with this? You should be indignant at this.* I think you are responsible for not holding an emotion. It would be inappropriate.

Phil Guin: So, if an adult says to a child "you ought to be grateful for all I have done for you," and the child is not moved, is the onus on the child or on . . .

Sharon Bailin: It depends on the situation. Because the problem is that the adult's appropriateness of emotion may or may not be justified as well; the adult is not always right. So, it is complicated. What the educator is saying and doing has to be justified as well. That may or may not be an appropriate kind of response to the child.

Phil Guin: So in a sense, if the adult is saying: Well, if you believe the way I do, then you are grateful.

Sharon Bailin: And then you can go further . . . Elgin makes a point that it is part of the whole justification, because we might go further with the child or interaction, where both people can engage in that discussion. The child may ask "why?" so the adult will have to answer what is it about that situation that the child should be grateful for? So we try to characterize the situation in more detail, to try to discover whether the emotion is justified or not.

Michael Schleifer: This question that Phil has asked is one of the fundamental ones that I would like to consider: In what sense we are responsible for emotions? An article which is now online in *Paideusis* (the Journal of the Canadian Philosophy of Education Society) by Schleifer and McCormick, is entitled "Responsibility For Emotions and Moods." Also *Thinking*, the Journal for Philosophy for Children, has our article on "Responsibility For Beliefs and Emotions" in their latest edition. This is an important issue and I tune in on Sharon's side. It is a very complicated matter in what way we are responsible. As for the gratitude example, perhaps we can come back to that as well.

Jean-Claude Brief: I am happy you just mentioned responsibility, because the question I had earlier was: when you talk of a connection between reason and emotion, I never saw in your paper the notion of decision, which I see as a link between emotion and reason. And the notion of responsibility comes in very strongly. Although, another one, which you can comment on, is that if you look at decision as being important, then you have to look at the context as being important. And then you have to look at, if you put in the context, the corporal involvement. So I see all those things being linked to connect emotion and reason. So if you could comment on how you could bring all these notions together. It should take another half an hour . . .

Sharon Bailin: First of all, on the context, I absolutely agree. And I think that an important factor is how we describe, how we conceptualize the situation and the context. As I said in response to Phil, we would in the kind of discussion earlier on whether emotion is justified, we would probably describe the characteristics of the context in the situation, *no, this person did that, not that*. Try to be clear on the context, I think that is crucial.

In terms of decision, I think it depends on whether we are talking about action or just judgment. That is, certainly if we hold people responsible for an action based on emotion and there I think might be a decision, that is, you decide to act on your anger and do something and responsibility certainly comes in with that kind of decision to act.

In judgment, I am not so sure. I don't think that when we decide to feel an emotion that we make a decision. And I don't think that decision is necessary for rationality; that is that we have reasons all the time when we don't decide. I don't think it's that we see a certain way, we make a decision to feel an emotion and then we feel the emotion. So I am not sure the decision is necessary for judgment but certainly for the level of action.

Jean-Claude Brief: The decision was brought in order to link emotion to reason.

Sharon Bailin: Yes. I think it links emotion to action. I don't think it is necessary to link emotion to reason. I don't think we make a decision to feel an emotion.

Michael Schleifer: Let's put that as another question for reconsideration, decision as a possible notion not as a link.

Ann Sharp: We should also highlight what Sharon said that we don't make a decision to feel a certain emotion.

Michael Schleifer: On the question of being responsible for an emotion, gratitude as one example (or grief or regret), we can say that whatever responsibility for action or consequences of action are, in the legal sense and in the moral sense (let's take for the time being that we know what that is and it is complicated), I would say with Sharon too, that we can be responsible for our emotions in the same way, whatever that is. But the question is whether we need a link like decision or not.

William Arsenio: A question come out of Phil's observation, talking about gratitude, because I thought that was interesting. For me, in order to deal with that immediate situation of what is going on, whatever the age of the child, I would want to know something as a developmental psychologist. What are the roots, the trajectory for that particular parent and child over time, because I think that one of the things that we want to deal with a little bit over the next couple of days is: there has to be a point below which children are not responsible for their emotions. What is involved in that transition from a stage in which they really have no active kind of control or volition in terms of emotions and regulations and how adults interact with them to help them hopefully effectively – but sometimes not so effectively – develop that kind of control of emotions. So really to know the situation that you are describing, if you would like to know what is the history of this dyad over time and you will also want to know something developmental: how old is this child and what would you expect for where this child will be at.

Paul Harris: I am not quite sure how to introduce this point, but I felt that your paper was a long meditation, and specifically a long meditation on the relationship between reason and emotions. But 95% of the time, you imply that in the end emotion is dependent on some kind of a judgment, appraisal, and reason and if things are to change, with respect to one's emotional stance, it is probably due to some reappraisal or psychotherapy and so forth might help them. And indeed these notions of responsibility might kick in there, because you could reconsider the judgments you made, the appraisals you have made and so forth. And that seems to me all perfectly reasonable, but there are one or two places in the paper where you imply and raise the possibility that it's one's emotions which drive one's appraisals or judgments. And yet, you don't actually analyze that or give us very convincing examples. When you do give some examples, they are actually, as far as I can see, the opposite or the reverse.

So, on the other hand, if you look at the psychological evidence – there is quite a lot of evidence, in fact – depending upon rather transient moods that people are making when they have gone to a sad film or happy film or more permanent moods, be they depression or anxiety. People's appraisals are in fact shifting. And that seems to me to raise the dilemma for educators because it could be the case that a particular emotion you feel should be reconsidered is in some sense grounded in a particular judgment that you can get at. But it could also be, that the particular emotion and its deleterious effects are in some sense not something you could target by asking a person to reappraise, it is just that the emotion happened to be there. And that it led to these various other incendiary effects which have nothing to do with the particular grounds of the emotion. The grounds of the emotion, that for all one knew, could be inappropriate and so forth. So, whilst I sympathize, as it were, with the general stance you are taking, I have certainly been more cognitivist in my discussion on how we come to understanding emotion. It does seem to me this beast, so to speak, going around in a pattern which we are not really dealing with.

Sharon Bailin: Yes, certainly having one's appraisal shifted by a transient emotion is a real and important phenomenon. Although, I wonder if it is one that can't be dealt with along these lines by looking at both reasons and bases of judgments and also possibly causes and of course in discussion with others. If one's judgment, one's emotion, seems inappropriate and one is in a discussion, other people will say: "why do you feel that way?" And what led to the conclusion that in fact the emotion isn't appropriate, one may then start looking at the causes and one may realize that: "I must be in a bad mood because I just saw that film." Or those kinds of emotional impacts on one's appraisal would come in. So I still think this is kind of what one could get at in the course of that kind of discussion with others.

Paul Harris: I think that would help to illuminate the particular distortion of the general mood it introduced. But it would not necessarily help to alter the emotion/mood, because it is leading to a variety of distortions. So if somebody is depressed or chronically anxious, it's not that you are going to help them get over that, to get out of those particular unjustified emotional reactions that they happen to have. I don't think it works like that.

Sharon Bailin: But again, I think that is where the issue of the causal history comes in. Because, in the case of Bob who is perennially angry at authority figures, that might be the kind of case you are talking about, so that is distorting his judgment in particular cases. But if in the course of his colleagues continuously showing him: well look in this case there is no grounds for anger, and in this case there is no grounds for anger, and so on and so on. If Bob is self reflective, he may start to say "no, I am pretty angry at these folks, maybe I should look into why." These are some of the kinds of the reasons why people shift here.

Paul Harris: But you shifted the grounds of the argument. You are reintroducing a case where the emotion itself is triggered by an unjustified appraisal.

Sharon Bailin: I nonetheless want to use my analysis. Bob is chronically anxious, but, again, if friends keep pointing out that *there is no ground for anxiety* in a range of cases, then perhaps that will cause self-reflection. He will think "I am chronically anxious maybe I should try to get at why that is and get some help with this."

Michael Schleifer: This is another fundamental issue: the question of moods. The issue is complex, because we're talking about emotion but we are also talking about moods. Martha Nussbaum, for example, makes a fundamental distinction between them when talking about depression. She will talk about endogenous depression and general anxiety. These are moods and they are very different, they don't have the cognitive aspect. I have criticized that in another place, I think they overlap more. But I am taking seriously Paul's example, because we have introduced things which we would call moods, and maybe they are simply that. If somebody becomes severely depressed, the challenge will be, well no amount of cognition or working on it, or even working in Philosophy for Children is not going to help, maybe it is just medication or something more fundamental.

Wendy Turgeon: Paul, I am struggling to make sure I understood what you were saying. But I am thinking that you were raising the question about the dichotomy and the privileging of reason versus emotion. I listened to Sharon's paper, I am thinking if there isn't some amount of privileging of reason, then we are left in a place where emotion is so strong that it can't be overcome or be shaped or reparadigmed or whatever that is. I am wondering if consciousness might be some sort of middle term here, where it's not reason in the classical sense, but it is also not mood or emotion. It is just a suggestion and I haven't fully fleshed it out. I think I see what you are concerned about, and yet I'm not sure how we get out of that. That sense in which the emotion or mood would define my world to the point where I couldn't be self reflective

Paul Harris: There is no reason to suppose we can get out of it.

Catherine Meyor: Voila, et le commentaire par rapport à la question et d'après tout ce qui est dit. Il y a l'émotion d'un côté et il y a l'expression de l'émotion, et toust ce qui concerne l'émotion approprié, etc. Est-ce qu'il n'y a pas quelque chose qui reste tout à fait particulier aux émotions, dans le sens où il y a effectivement un vécu émotionnel ou affectife, et un vécu aussi de jugement ou de raison mais qui n'arrivera jamais totalement à rejoindre l'émotion.

Michael Schleifer: Is there not part of an emotion that is not going to be reduced in any sense to judgment, reason or cognition which could, we might say, be the part of the emotion which is experienced? Is there not part of that which is therefore not going to be susceptible to education?

Catherine Meyor: Et je rajouterai pour terminer, que quand on parle de l'émotion, l'on parle toujours après l'émotion, l'émotion a toujours déjà fait son œuvre, il a déjà apparu. Donc c'est un commentaire, ou expression qu'on fait sur quelque chose qui prècède, qui est déjà accompli. Il me semble qu'il y a toujours ce type de dynamique.

Michael Schleifer: She just wants to add the point that we seem to, when discussing emotions, and maybe we are making the mistake here as with everyone else, we talk about an emotion which is past. We are reflecting about the emotion completed, as opposed to the emotion during, it is always afterwards that we talk about the emotion. So we may be missing this ingredient.

Sharon Bailin: I think sometimes we do reflect on emotions when we are having them, I think those are the interesting cases, working through some of these issues. Those are the times that are illuminating, when I am having an emotion, I think "why am I so upset?" You can do it while you are in the throes of it. And I think that adds something that reflecting on it post facto doesn't do. I think one of the things that it points out is the conservation of emotion that they don't always go away that easily. I know X, Y, Z, but I am still upset. I think we can do that as well while we are in the throes of the emotion, and I think it is kind of helpful. Also I am not wanting to reduce emotion to cognition, and I am not wanting to deny the feeling. I want to say there is a cognitive dimension. I am not trying to reduce, it isn't all just judgments.

Gerald Boutin: When you use the words 'education of the emotions,' in what sense do you mean? Is there a difference for you between to educate the emotions or to teach the emotions?

Sharon Bailin: Of course, a lot hangs on the difference one sees between teaching and educating. I don't think we teach emotions in the sense that babies come without any and we give them to them. Babies have feelings, they cry and seem to be angry, they smile, there seems to be some genetic basis for feelings. So I think what we do is educating in the sense of identifying, conceptualizing, learning appropriate circumstances, learning control and so on, increasing sophistication. I think those are the ways in which they get educated.

Michael Schleifer: Can we tune in and make a link between Gerald's question and Bill's challenge as a developmental psychologist to a philosopher. At what age? Is there a lower level in your view where you wouldn't want to talk about education of the emotions?

William Arsenio: I will give you a short version. I think that we talk about norms, there is something about early attachment relationships, and that kind of interaction that goes on between parent and child I think that it is the root of the subsequent emotion regulation and also emotion understanding. What is the nature of that relationship, how much can you talk about emotions and a whole bunch of other pieces that go with it? That's the short version and the long one is too long.

Michael Schleifer: So that question is hanging here, what age? A child of two is more or less talking with us, but long before that we are certainly talking to the child and the roots are there. So the question at what point we are going to talk about education.

Paul Harris: Can I just follow up on this point? One of the things that attachment theory implies, perhaps wrongly, is that when you are nurturing a child with a sense of emotional security, and allegedly some caregivers are more or less successful at nurturing that sense of security, that will have wide ranging repercussions on the child's emotional life, as if it were going well beyond that feeling of security. So in some ways, that is an example I think, of the way in which "the education of the emotions" could be directed at some sense the elicitation of a particular emotion, which would then have repercussions for the child's emotional life in all sorts of domains. But it wouldn't be something that was done, so to speak, by educating the child on the grounds for which a particular emotion was appropriate. It would be the nurturance of this pervasive sense of well being and confidence. That speaks to my point earlier about the way in which there seem to be these two somewhat distinct channels for altering the child's emotional trajectory, one by getting the child to think, the other getting the child to feel, I suppose.

Michael Schleifer: We have another huge issue. This is an interdisciplinary conference as everyone has gathered, in which we have leading psychologists in the field, developmental psychologists, Bill and Paul, and others around the table, and there are philosophers, and I happen to wear both hats you know. We have two solitudes that we talk about in Canada. As philosophers, generally speaking, we talk about education, we talk about dialogue, we talk about conversations, as Sharon did. We do not talk about these parts: with ages, making a child feel more secure and attachment theory. Are we in two solitudes here? On one hand we have the philosophers talking about education and emphasizing how to think about the emotions, while, on the other hand, the psychologists are saying that perhaps the most important thing is getting a child to cope later on with anger. You mentioned envy, is it a matter of getting them to feel it which would be giving them a certain sense of security, which then would have to bring us to attachment theory. So is there a link?

Ann Sharp: Wouldn't that imply that we should be concerned about the education of the caregiver in those very early formative years. In other words, are there things that I can do that can possibly help the child to have the kinds of experiences that will nurture security and confidence?

Wendy Turgeon: I think Ann was addressing that issue that Paul raised, even with older children and adults. If I am in a community where I am enjoying it, and am even surprised that I am having pleasurable feelings, even as I am talking. That's in essence doing the same type of thing we want a parent to do with their child, so the child has a kind of emotional education there. So I don't think it is necessarily something you do at the beginning of life and later on it becomes completely cognitive. I don't think you can separate things out like that.

Sharon, there are some wonderful ideas in your paper that were so provocative, and one of them was naming emotions', the act of naming emotions, and that just entranced me because it is quite different from naming objects, or naming colors, because I have to internalize. It seems to be involved with facial expressions, but it is more than that. I don't know if you wanted to comment on that.

My second question, another topic to think about, was the culture piece. I am wondering if there are universal emotions, or whether they are all situated within a culture in terms of appropriateness, or a commonness or even experienced. I don't know if either of those sound interesting for you to comment on?

Sharon Bailin: I am not sure what else I would say about the naming, it seems important in terms of individualization and getting the concepts and gaining the sense of appropriateness of the emotions for the context. I mean the culture piece is fascinating, I would love to hear other people on that because I sort of just started getting a little bit into that, this issue of universality. From what I understand from the little literature I have looked at in that area, there seems to be consensus about some universals, and it's the facial expressions that are universal, but also various degrees of cultural variations, in terms of how they are played out. I have done that example of the Utku that I found fascinating, I mean the research that I have seen referred to. I would like to look at it more carefully to see how they arrived at that. The Utku have nothing much in the way of displays of what we would call anger in the culture, it seems kind of amazing from our perspective. I would love to know more about what's going on there. Did the culture eradicate it, this universal emotion, or the expression of it? I don't know.

Michael Schleifer: There is a book, which I have reread for the eighth time, Martha Nussbaum's book, *Upheavals of Thought*, has a huge section on these examples and among other things the notion of universality. Paul Eckman is one of the ones looking at the question of the non-verbal expression of emotions. Martha Nussbaum, who is aware of Eckman's research and the notion that there are universal emotions that transcend culture, says she has looked at them and she raises doubts about the universality of emotion. So there are another two issues you have raised about culture and naming emotions that we might get back to.

Wendy Turgeon: What triggered that in my mind was autistic children and their inability to recognize and name the emotions and what a disconnect I saw.

Ann Sharp: And not just autistic. I had a friend who was thirteen and she didn't have the word to put to this, all she could describe was a physical something in her stomach, vague like that, and a tensing here of the shoulders, but she had no name to put to it. At thirteen she realized it was jealousy, at thirteen.

Michael Schleifer: That is a good lead into my talk on jealousy and envy coming up after the break.

Ann Sharp: Because you see, if I can't name it, then I can't deal with it, I can't talk to you about it, I can't analyze it, I can't look for the underlying belief. This thing just makes my stomach turn, in a sense it cripples me if I can't name it, which is so important in terms of self correction.

Cynthia Martiny: Well I liked your comment earlier, where the parents can take a role in educating. However, the problem is when you have dysfunctional parents who misname the emotion. As a practitioner working with violent men, some of their descriptions of what happened are so distorted that the child will be confused about what he actually feels because of parents misnaming and misunderstanding what the child feels. I was thinking also as a parent, when my daughter was two years old, she ran into the door, she hit her head and was crying. I asked her what she was crying about, and she said "I am angry, at the door. " I could have said to her that you are sad, because you made a mistake and walked into the door. But actually she was angry, because for her, the door wasn't supposed to be there and it was the door's fault. This was just to give an example of how we have to be careful about how we name emotions. Mislables can be carried onto an adulthood. Sometimes when I listen to violent men, I am thinking that their descriptions resembles that of a two year old.

Leoni Richler: I also believe in the importance of naming emotions. What I found working with adolescents is not so much that they make a mistake in it, it is just that they have, what I call, an umbrella emotion like anger and then underneath that are the other layers related to the context of like what you are bringing up. Kids especially can learn about identifying their emotions through their body because they are more connected to their feelings in their body, which is really interesting. The other important thing about naming emotions is, because even the person who is having the dialogue with them, as a professional, or as an acquaintance, or as friends, it almost doesn't matter, because it seems to, I believe, trigger in the other person, it is like when you go to a therapist, it is not even so much what they have to say, it is like a sounding board which you can't always do by yourself. It isn't the same as talking to yourself or to the wall. It is in that connection with another human being, so when you have that dialogue, it seems to help the person, that if they are stuck in their emotion, it is like pain pills, even if they don't understand all of it. So the naming is really important and crucial and I think it is really the root at helping educators educate children at whatever age level that they are working.

Paul Harris: I sort of agree, but on the other hand, I do think this is an enormous truism that people kick around but never really analyze. So you walk into any preschool and children are told to use their words as opposed to express their emotions in non-verbal, perhaps less restrained ways. We all have the assumption that when people are in therapy, in some sense identifying their emotions helps them. If you look at the evidence it is pretty thin. There is a huge tradition in psychology that's thinking about the relationship between language and thought, Vygotsky, Piaget, and onwards. Most of it is pretty cautious in claiming any benefit from putting, as it were, concepts into words. And yet this is the assumption that I am tempted to make, you are tempted to make and most of us are tempted to make. I just wanted to put that on the market there and say, okay, let's live with that assumption and expectation, but the evidence for that is thin.

Michael Schleifer: You know that's probably a good note to take a break . . . (laughter)

Chapter 2
The Siblings of Cinderella and Joseph:
What Should Educators Say About Jealousy And Envy?

Michael Schleifer, Université du Québec à Montréal

Jealousy is almost as inevitable a part of being hurt by life as are guilt and anger. How can the injured person not feel jealous of people who may not deserve better but have received better? . . . It serves no purpose to try to moralize against jealousy and talk people out of it. Jealousy is too strong a feeling. It touches us too deeply, hurting us in places we care about . . . perhaps the only cure for jealousy, is to realize that the people we resent and envy for having what we lack, probably have wounds and scars of their own. They may even be envying us.

– Rabbi Harold Kushner

We are currently undertaking a study on the development of the emotions to see how they are understood by children as young as 2 years old until adolescent years, and then as young adults. We are examining some of the more complex moral emotions like jealousy and envy. In order to develop the instruments to administer in our research, our team of professors and students have been brainstorming about what these emotions mean to us. We share examples from our personal lives, when we have been jealous or envious, and discuss whether jealousy and envy are bad or good emotions, whether they can be eliminated, or are "just part of life." Finally, we want to see what our educational aims are in our philosophical discussions with children in regard to these feelings.

My professional and personal life have both contributed to me thinking hard about jealousy and envy. I have come to some tentative conclusions. First of all, envy and jealousy are two separate emotions. Secondly, envy is a worse one than jealousy. Thirdly, many languages do not make a distinction between the two emotions, so that we must restrict ourselves in discussion to one word. I propose "jealousy" to be used in two different senses, one of which will capture the idea of "envy," the second to refer to classical jealousy. Fourthly, jealousy in both of its senses is part of human life and cannot be entirely eradicated. Fifthly, education and reflection should concentrate on understanding these emotions. There are several aspects which must be studied. These include the causes of jealousy and envy (primarily insecurity, lack of love or unequal love), the consequences of these emotions (hate and violence) and the components (anger, sadness and fear) which blend together to make up the more complex emotions. Finally, jealousy and envy, like the basic emotions, can be controlled to a certain degree. Also like the basic emotions, whether or not they can be controlled, we must take responsibility for them.

Envy and Jealousy Are Not the Same

Envy is not jealousy, although most people use the two terms interchangeably (Anderson, 2002; Salovey & Rodin, 1988; Parrott & Smith, 1993). In short, jealousy is about what one has, envy about what other people have. The etymology of the two words is quite different. The word "jealousy" was originally used in a good sense as equivalent to "zeal. " This should be contrasted with the entomology of the word "envy," which had from the outset a hostile force, based on "look at" (with malice). Jealous is related to the latin root "zelus", which became "zealous" and then later "jealous. " Envy is from "invidia," literally "to be looking at, with an evil eye."

Another way people have contrasted the two emotions is to point out that jealousy involves three actors, envy only two. Typically, person A is jealous of person B who may be flirting with person C. With envy, person A only needs one other person to be envious. In Shakespeare's *Othello* we see both jealousy and envy. There is the well known jealousy of Othello, who imagines that Desdemona is unfaithful with Cassio. We also have envy, the feeling of begrudging another person's success. It is the villain, Iago, who envies both Othello and Cassio because they are successful generals, popular with friends, and the women. Iago's envy leads to hate and violence, even more surely than Othello's jealousy.

Yet another way to contrast jealousy and envy is in terms of their causes in infancy. Here is an account, as told by Martha Nussbaum, inspired by John Bowlby, Melanie Klein and David Winnicott:

> In the life of the infant, if things go well, the child's emotions evolve in relation to an environment which is relatively stable, which provides space for the development of wonder and joy, as well as stable love and gratitude. But of course, no such environment is completely stable. Caretakers must come and go, support the child and allow him to fend for himself, so that, he will learn how to get around in the world. The infant is always inhabiting a world that is both safe and dangerous, both able and unable to rely on receiving nourishment and security from his caretakers.

Before long, the child recognizes that the very same objects, who love and care for him, also go away at times and attend to other projects, heedless to his demands. He realizes that he depends on caretakers or parents, who are not in his control. This means that love and anger come to be directed to one and the same source. Thus love, anxiety, anger, and sometimes hatred, come to be aroused by one and the same person. This anger is itself ambivalent, for it is mixed up with the wish of love to incorporate and possess the needed object, and the anger itself may be used as a device of control.

This synopsis shows that from early infancy we have the roots of the emotion of jealousy, the wish to possess the good object more completely by getting rid of competing influences. The emotion of jealousy is a judgment (yes, it is a bit strange to talk about an infant having "judgment") that it is very bad that there should be these competing influences and that it would be very good for them to vanish from the earth. This is the essence of "hate, " namely the wish that the other person disappear or die.

We also see the close cousin of jealousy, namely envy. Jealousy, as we have seen, has the caretaker as its focus; envy takes as its focus the competing objects who for a time enjoy the caretaker's favor — especially other siblings, and the lover or spouse of the primary caretaker — or their love for one another, if both caretakers are primary. In envy, the child judges that it would be a good thing for him to displace the competing objects from their favorite position.

Although jealousy and envy are separate emotions, they nevertheless often overlap in real life. For example, when a younger sibling throws a tantrum when his mother is paying attention to his older sister, he is probably experiencing both jealousy and envy. He is envious of the sister, whom he does not want to have the mother's affection: Why her, why not me? He is also feeling jealousy because of what he thinks is his due; namely, his mother's attention is now shared with another. Another example is the envy and jealousy felt by Joseph's ten older brothers. Directed at their father Jacob, was first-level jealousy; against Joseph, leading to hate and violence, we could call it envy. For those who haven't read the Bible lately, here is a synopsis:

Jacob had twelve sons, the eleventh being Joseph, the twelfth Benjamin (these last two with Rachel, the others with other wives). Joseph was smart, cute, and very much liked by his parents, and particularly his father. The ten older brothers, were very unhappy (jealous!) about the situation, They were particularly offended when little Joseph (about 3 or 4 years of age) reported to them about his vivid dreams. These dreams invariably involved the theme of Joseph being rich and famous, and the 10 older brothers being less rich, less famous, and usually Joseph's servants. Joseph was thrown into a pit by the brothers, who decided to kill him. They relent at the last moment, because of the pleadings of one brother, and sell him as a slave into Egypt. There, we have a series of dramatic events, which include his getting thrown into prison for the crime of flirting with the wife of another man (not clear if he was guilty). His talents as dream interpreter and economic manager are recognized by the prison warden (who also becomes his friend and buddy), and by others, including finally the Pharoh (Joseph becomes his friend and buddy too). Joseph becomes the most powerful person in Egypt next to Pharoh. The ten brothers find themselves needing grain because of the famine which Joseph foresaw; they come to Egypt from Israel, Joseph recognizes them; there is a reconciliation, some apology, some forgiveness, and a tearful reuniting with younger brother Benjamin.

Envy is Worse Than Jealousy

Of the seven deadly sins, only envy is no fun at all.

– Epstein

In the misfortune of our best friends, we always find something that is not displeasing to us.

– La Rouchefoucauld

Because they feel unhappy, men cannot bear the sight of someone they think is happy . . . . A human being, at the sight of another's pleasures and possessions, would feel his own deficiency with more bitterness. Hatred always accompanies envy.

– Schopenhauer

The first recorded case of envy is that of Cain killing his brother Abel. When God found Abel's offering to him of the first of his flock of sheep acceptable and Cain's offering of the fruit of the ground less acceptable, it was too much for Cain, the older brother, to bear. A second famous example is that of Joseph and his brothers.

Envy involves malice. It is not enjoying another's success or happiness; it is petty, small-minded, and often secretive. One may not be aware of envy, which is there eating one up. It often leads to hatred. No one likes this emotion, and invariably, when thinking of an example of feeling envy, one is not proud of that emotion. Some people admit readily to being envious, others find it hard to think offhand of examples (although they always will in the end have one or two examples, which they will also regret).

I am convinced that the philosophers quoted above (Epstein, Schopoenhauer and La Rouchefoucauld) are correct in their affirmation: Everyone experiences envy; nobody likes it. Perhaps the only exceptions may be saints like Mother Theresa and the Dalai Lama. A few of my friends and relatives have trouble conjuring up envy. As I mentioned, however, everyone invariably remembers situations where they experienced this feeling. Invariably, they are not proud of this. Envy clouds one's judgments, stops one from being compassionate and leads one to be irritable and angry.

If one knows that a colleague is applying for a book award, or a research grant, one should without hesitation, doubt, or exception, wish them well. If it is a friend, all the more so. But we all know the feeling: Why him? Why not me?

A student recently offered an interesting personal example. She has a best friend, who on a canoe trip successfully navigated the rapids in the river, while she was too afraid to do it. She was happy for her friend, but could not bring herself to be 100% happy. Even thinking about it long afterwards, it was difficult for her to rid herself of that petty malicious idea: Why her? Why not me? She remembers thinking to herself: "Why couldn't my friend's canoe have tipped over?" (Although she didn't want her to hurt herself or drown). She also remembers thinking: "I will be happy for her to succeed, but only after I succeed, not before."

There is a flip side to envy, which is quite positive, which we might label "yearning" or "emulation." For example, a female colleague has told me how she feels a bit sad because her best friend is pregnant with her first child. She is happy for the friend, but a little bit "envious" because she too would like to have a child. She may in fact decide to become pregnant, partly inspired by her friend's experience. This is very much like envy except for the absence of malice. A third example from my own experience is in regard to my admiring the success of some bridge playing friends, particularly a married couple. I watched them work hard at the technical and the emotional aspects of their partnership, and this helped my resolve to work in the same way with my bridge partner/spouse. I had the emotion of yearning but none of the negative envy. I was 100% happy for the success of these friends. My thoughts were: Good for them! Why not us also, one day!?

It is important to highlight that the productive nature of envy gives it a positive side. As illustrated above, the person who envies someone can use them as a role model, or motivating agent to achieve or reach his/her desired goal. If someone hears about another person winning the lottery, and feels envious, this will inevitably be a negative feeling: Why him? Why not me? There is no positive aspect to this, because there is nothing one can do to try to succeed. The lottery is simply a matter of luck, so it is classic envy. The feeling is that these people didn't really deserve to win the big money: What an unjust world!

There is another emotion which is similar to envy, where we wish the other person did not get what he got; as he does not deserve it. We may not want it for ourselves but we just can't bear the idea of them having it. We have the "malice. " without the coveting.

Envy is a real problem for me, and I want to continue eliminating it if possible. I know, furthermore, that envy, in my case, comes in part from pride. I believe in pride, the good kind, not the excessive or bad pride. Therefore, all I can do to control this emotion is to be aware of my tendency to envy, to remind myself of its existence, to think hard about the good points about friends and colleagues, and wish them well, with the most sincere feeling I can muster. By thinking about them, by reminding myself of their friendship, good gestures, by being compassionate, I can work bit by bit on diminishing this ugly emotion.

The only upside that I see in regard to envy is that by thinking about it, I can try to change. As with all other emotions (the basic ones like anger or the complex moral ones like pride) the element of self-knowledge, or self-awareness is always positive. So just as I can work on my feelings of anger or moderate my emotion of pride, I can also think about (and somewhat diminish) envious feelings when they occur.

A Proposal About Language

Some languages such as French do not use "envy" as a term to refer to the sin or vice, but rather to what one wants, as in " j'ai envie de. " French speaking colleagues and friends have explained to me that they will consciously avoid the word "envieux" or "envieuse" because of its religious connotation. They would prefer to use the expression "je suis jaloux, je suis jalouse" because these are secular terms. There is a parallel here to people avoiding the use of the word "orgeuil" and preferring the word "fierté" for pride. "Orgeuil" refers to one of the cardinal sins as does envy.

In Hebrew, the word which is translated by either jealousy or envy is *keenah*. The Second Commandment says "I am a jealous God, " the Tenth Commandment says "do not covet or envy. " The Hebrew word in both cases is the same. German uses the word *neid* for envy or jealousy.

Italian and English have retained two words, *gelosia/invidia* and jealousy/envy respectively. Italians (including children) do use both words I have been told. In English, however, almost everyone uses the word "jealous' these days, and certainly it is the only word we use with young children. Epstein (2003), in his book "Envy" is obliged to constantly correct various authors who use the word "jealousy" adding: "They really mean 'envy.'" In the quote by Rabbi Kushner at the beginning of this paper, he uses the word "jealousy" but clearly means "envy. "

Whatever the linguistic situation of any particular language, whether or not there are two words, or only one, we recognize the feelings whatever they may be called. We understand the emotion of wanting what the other has (envy), and wanting to keep what we already have (jealousy).

My terminological proposal stipulates that we only use the word jealousy when talking to young children. However, we can retain two senses of jealousy: Sense one, being jealousy of, for example, one's boyfriend being with another girl; sense two, jealousy as meaning envy Since. I have already discussed sense two (jealousy/envy), I will now turn to the classical jealousy – sense number one.

Jealousy

I used to believe, as Bertrand Russell did, that one could eliminate jealousy. The Buddhists still preach this philosophy, I now think that it is part of life, and it may be built into intimate exclusive or romantic or sexual relationships. I do not agree with those who want to classify jealousy as a basic emotion (Sabini & Silver, 2005). Unlike the basic emotions (joy, anger, fear and sadness) jealousy has no specific facial expression. In addition, jealousy is too complex an emotion involving at least anger, fear, joy and sadness, as well as complicated appraisals and judgments.

In my first marriage (in the 1960s) we thought jealousy was old fashioned, and experimented with various combinations of relationships. My current marriage is based on an exclusive relationship. Intimacy (including sexual intimacy) is defined and discussed by my partner and myself. In both my marriages, of course, there is also a special intimacy, not defined sexually, of being parents and grandparents, the sense of being "mates" or "life partners."

I can and do acknowledge jealousy in regard to my wife, but try to curb that where it is unreasonable, and expect her to do the same. We have a pact about what is acceptable in regard to romantic involvements with others: candlelight dinners are out, but lunches at work acceptable, bicycle excursions alone in the woods for my wife with a male friend or a lesbian one are allowed, meetings by me with female students as well. In all this there has to be some element of trust.

If one feels no jealousy, then perhaps the thing one has is not considered valuable. It is also possible that some people cannot imagine their partner betraying them. This may be because of trust or because of a lack of imagination. Jealousy, like every other emotion, has its limits. One must be aware of it. It can become too intense, too unreasonable, can cloud someone's judgment, and can lead to violence and hate, and ugly words. Jealousy is linked to a sense of insecurity and mistrust. So if we build the trust and security, jealousy in its ugly or extreme form can perhaps disappear. But let us keep a little of it, why not?

I accept the analysis of philosophers, like Nussbaum (2001), Rabbi Harold Kushner, author of *When Bad Things Happen To Good People* (1981), and psychologists, like Bowlby (1973, 1980, 1982), Klein (1984) and Winnicott (1965), that jealousy is an inevitable part of the emotional development of the human child. That is also the view of the novelist Marcel Proust (1982). It is interesting to note that Proust tells us that it is only toward literary characters that one can have love without jealousy and envy. Proust's narrator can love real people without jealousy only when they are asleep. Jealousy, may, indeed, be a destructive emotion, as Goleman (2003), Ekman (1999), Russell (1929), the Dalai Lama and Saint Paul have pointed out, but I do not agree with this latter group that it can be eradicated.

There are those who theorize (e. g. Barash 2005) that jealousy has an important evolutionary function. These same theorists affirm that males are especially vulnerable to sexual jealousy simply because of their biology. According to these psychologists, whereas women can rest serene in their confidence that they are genetically related to any offspring that emerges from their bodies, men have to take their mate's word for it.

Whatever one wants to believe about these theories concerning jealousy, it is important to stress that they do not talk about the emotion of envy. Of course, we can speculate that envy may also have an evolutionary source. If my co-hunter is eating the meat of the animal, and I, as his competitor, have no food, I may likely feel the first stirrings of envy. This speculation can extend to seeing envy as more part of the male psyche, where competitiveness was important in the role of hunter, whereas women may have been involved in more shared activities, with less competitiveness and therefore less envy.

There are non-human animals who exhibit jealousy in much the same way as human beings. This is probably restricted to those species where mates are in long-term relationships. Rats, as far as I have gathered, are promiscuous; we can assume they have no jealous feelings.

Education and Reflection About These Emotions

Let us assume that jealousy, in both senses, is part of life. Our task in education is to talk about it, acknowledge its existence, clarify it, and help young children to anticipate the consequences of the emotion. So, just as we must sometimes say "you are angry," "you are sad," "you are happy," or "you are a little bit happy and sad," to help a child understand his emotions, we must also say, "you are jealous" at the appropriate occasion. A parent, about to give birth to a younger sibling might consider not only saying the usual "you will soon have a cute little brother to play with." One might also say something like "when your little brother arrives, this will take a lot of my time and you may feel a little sad and a little angry. You will feel jealous."

Kieran Egan (1987) has argued that children as young as two years of age already understand about jealousy. He points out that these very young children readily follow the story of Cinderella and her jealous stepsisters. Egan says:

> If we tell a child the story of Cinderella, we presuppose that for the story to be meaningful, the child, in some sense, has available concepts of love, hate, greed, fear jealousy and so on. These, of course, are some of the great abstract organising concepts which we use to make sense of our experience. I do not mean that young children necessary know these *terms*, or how to define them, but rather that in some sense they must know them and use them for the story to be meaningful.

Our research with young children has undertaken the task of testing Egan's claims. Our preliminary results show that although it is true that the two year old can understand something of the feelings, it is clear that they do not yet have a concept of jealousy, in either of its two senses. Sometime between the ages of two and five a comprehension of the complex emotion will begin to appear. The feeling of jealousy/envy is no doubt quite strong (as we have argued above) from earliest infancy. This does not mean, however, that the child understands the emotions.

Understanding jealousy and envy takes a great deal of reflection, discussion, and dialogue. Not only preschoolers are confused about the meaning of these emotions; older children and many adults are not clear about them as well. Part of the educational job is to look at some of these classical stories – including Cinderella and her sisters, Joseph and his brothers, and even Anniken Skywalker in Star Wars – and ask the difficult questions concerning why the ugly step sisters, Joseph's brothers, and Skywalker develop such intense jealousy and envy. We can begin to think about the link between their feelings and the insecurity they also felt, because of a lack of love, or an unequal love.

It seems clear that jealousy and envy can only be controlled and regulated up to a point. Independently of the question of control, we need to take responsibility for these complex moral emotions much the same way as we must take responsibility for the basic emotions like sadness, fear and anger.

References

Anderson, R. (2002). Envy and Jealousy. *American Journal of Psychotherapy, 56*(4), 455-479.

Barash, D. (2005). *Madame Bovary's Ovaries: A Darwinian Look At Literature.* New York: Bantam Dell.

Egan, K. (1987). The Other Half of the Child. *Thinking, 7,* 2-5.

Ekman, P. (1999). Basic Emotions. T. Dalgleish and M. Power (Eds.) *Handbook of cognition and emotion.* New York Wiley.

Epstein, J. (2003). *Envy.* Oxford: Oxford UP.

Goleman, D. and the Dalai Lama (2003). *Destructive emotions: How can we overcome them.* New York: Bantam Press.

Klein, M. (1984). *Envy and gratitude.* Delaware: Hogarth Press.

Kushner, H (1981). *When bad things happen to good people.* Avon Press.

Nussbaum, M. (2001). *Upheavals of thought: The intelligence of emotions.* Cambridge: Cambridge UP.

Parrott, W. G. & Smith, R. H. (1993). Distinguishing the experiences of envy and jealousy. *Journal of personality and social psychology, 64*(6), 906-920.

Praust, M. (1982). *Remembrance of things past.* (3 Volumes), New York Vintage Press.

Russell, B. (1929). *Marriage and morals.* New York: Norton Press.

Sabini, J. & Silver, M. (2005). Ekman's basic emotions: why not love and jealousy. *Cognition and Emotion, 19*(5), 693-712.

Salovey, P. & Rodin, J. (1988). Coping with envy and jealousy. *The Journal of Social and Clinical Psychology, 7,* 15-33.

Schleifer, M. & Martiny, C. (2006). *Talking about feelings and values with children.* Calgary: Detselig.

Winnicott, D. (1965). *The maturational process and the facilitating environment.* Madison: International UP.

Discussion after Michael Schleifer's Presentation

Phil Guin: All the discussion, Michael, seems to deal with dyadic and triadic relations among persons. But sometimes we hear about, say, the terrorists groups with religious zeal. These emotions are more general as the whole cultures, whole societies . . . I am wondering how you might respond to that.

Michael Schleifer: Epstein's book, that he calls *Envy*, has a chapter on political jealousy. He says the Holocaust, in great part, has to be understood in terms of envy. He then mentions in regard to the world now, that some of the understanding about the anti-American feeling, even 9/11, (we are getting into heated areas, it is not my view – I really haven't thought sufficiently about it) but Epstein does get into your question and thinks that there are repercussions for jealousy and envy, which are not just at, as you said, the level that I thought about, which is for me sufficiently complex – two or three people in a classroom or as parents or as educators, I am try to come to grips with that. But in the book, he goes so far as to say that he sees envy as the root of many of these things. That you have to understand terrorists in part, because of the fact they look at America and they are envious. And he says you have to understand what Germans did in part because they were envious of Jews.

Phil Guin: I am specifically aiming the question because of education. I mean you have whole societies where the children grow up to develop certain strong feelings, maybe jealousy, this will have a bearing on all of us. This is one of the things that Sam Harris says in his book, *The End of Faith*.

Paul Harris: Michael, could you say a bit more about the distinction between control and responsibility?

Michael Schleifer: What we say in our recent paper in Paideusis, like Sharon says in her paper, we are responsible for emotions. So if we take the emotion of gratitude, independently of whether or not I could have controlled it, I think about some event in the past where I think that I was not sufficiently grateful and the way I was at that time there was no way I could have done differently. That was the way I was and in any sense of control I can fathom, I could not have done otherwise. The classic philosophical question, I could not have done otherwise. I was going to be like that, I was not going to show gratitude to that friend in the way. But now in thinking about it, I can actually take responsibility in the same way as I take responsibility for my acts and consequences.

I may have done something, I hurt somebody in the past in an act and it may have been something that I could not have avoided at that time, given who I was and given the circumstances. Nevertheless, nobody else could be accountable for that act. And that is in a sense of moral responsibility that we defend. So if adults want children to be accountable for their actions, then they must be ready to say: "Yes, I did it! I feel badly and I apologize to you!" So we can work on regret that way, where we say "take responsibility for it," for example, not having had sufficient regret or having had too much regret.

We use both examples in the paper; regret or gratitude. I may not have felt enough gratitude. But I can actually, in thinking about it, get myself to feel the gratitude now, even years later. Therefore, I am taking responsibility directly for the emotion. And that is the best I can do, to sum up the view we have. Whether or not we can control something, whether or not we could have done otherwise in the past, we still must take responsibility; we argue that we want children to learn to take responsibility for their acts, for their consequences of their acts but also for their emotions. Examples being the basic ones like the anger, but also more complex ones like regret, like gratitude: they did not say sorry, perhaps the way they were they couldn't have said sorry, but they can now understand even in retrospect that they should have said sorry, perhaps felt the sorry. They may not have felt it. And we argue also, that is another issue, better not to say sorry if you don't understand the sorry or feel it. There are three parts of it.

So, if I could say that is the background, given that view, that we are responsible for our emotions, I want to argue that in regard to jealousy and envy, but I am just beginning to think about that, whether or not and in what sense they can be controlled, we're still responsible for them. I don't know if that helps.

Paul Harris: Yes. That helps. It seems to me you emphasize that there is the fact that, as agents of experience, we have a history, and, to some extent we talk the way in which we conceptualize what we have done and it may be much deeper than that.

If anything comes to my mind, you want to pursue the acknowledgment. There is a very interesting principle in, say, Alcoholics Anonymous (AA). The person, at a certain point in that program, will go to those that they have wronged, so to speak, and take responsibility in some sense and apologize. In a sense, for the very things you are saying, an activity which at the time might have been out of their control, I suppose you could say some other things about some of these institutionalized activities such as truth and reconciliation committees which in some sense say well these atrocities occurred, maybe these people didn't take responsibility at the time, but here is a new opportunity to reconsider.

Michael Schleifer: That example really hits directly, I think it is a good one, the Alcoholics Anonymous (AA) example. Because yes, I think there are times that we could not have done otherwise. If I am an alcoholic truly and I am addicted and so on, I might have done horrible things but I did not know that and you say sorry anyway. And that is the question.

There is a book that came out which helped us a lot, from Revizza and Fisher. They call it: *Responsibility without Control*. Now, they don't directly link to emotions. They are talking about beliefs, which is itself an interesting thing. Taking responsibility for beliefs is what they are getting into. And they are saying, basically the same thing, you must take responsibility for your beliefs. And they apply that to a whole group of things. They then say "our view applies to emotions as well." But nobody has worked it out. We have to work that out. But your example for me is perfect that way.

Jean-Claude Brief: You said: we are responsible for emotions, is that so? You said that. Can you explain more of that? Responsibility is an important word. What do you mean exactly? Can you explain more?

Michael Schleifer: Yes. First, I am going to say that online on internet, the article is on Paideusis, because it is 25 pages explaining just that. But in a few of words, I will try again. When I did my Oxford thesis for my B. Phil in Philosophy, that was my thesis: Responsibility, the one concept. And I have been thinking about this all my life. And I am still thinking about it. But if I have to sum it up, I will say: to be responsible is, the person, "qui va répondre", who has to respond, that is he is the author of what he has done or not done, or the consequences of what he's done or not done, in short, is to acknowledge that this act, which may be bad but could be good too. We often neglect that.

And that in short is it. It is etymology of 'repondare', to respond, I am the author of it, nobody else is. Traditionally, there is a consensus among philosophers that responsibility is complicated but we can sum it up that way, that if somebody is going to be punished, well it is that person. Now, it is complex there sometimes not the case. . . . and the question of whether to blame or to what degree and to praise and what degree, is very complex. But in short, if we have a situation and I am looking for the author who is going to respond for it, well I need somebody. Now it is complicated also, because with children it may sometimes be the parents. And we know that. And sometimes, they may be neglected.

So now what I am saying and this is relatively new, but I am still thinking it through, but I am convinced that emotions, like the simple ones, so called simple ones, basic ones: anger, fear and so on. The question is in what sense they can be controlled? What are we going to tell the children about control of the emotions? That is the theme of the Symposium. But independently of that, we also have the question of telling them about responsibility for their emotions. As of now my view, which I am hoping we will discuss over the next few days, is that in the same way that we are responsible for our acts, we are the author of them and we are the ones that must respond to them, and the consequences of our acts, and by acts I mean what we do and also what we don't do, that applies to emotions too. That is the thesis. Est-ce que cela t'aide?

Jean-Claude Brief: That is answering me pretty well. It is perfect.

Paul Harris: It seems to me, implicit in what you are saying, is that once you accept responsibility then that carries with it, I mean tangible responsibilities, things like reparation. So, it is not just the question of saying: "Oh yeah, I am the guy," so to speak. It impacts on one's relationship to people who, in some sense, have been the targets of those emotions.

Michael Schleifer: I agree.

Sharon Bailin: I think somewhere along that line that control, what makes one control when one couldn't do otherwise. But the notion of acknowledging responsibility seems to imply that which one can do it otherwise. With this new understanding from now on one can do otherwise. And there is a sense of agency there, implicit in taking responsibility. One could not in the past and now one can do otherwise.

William Arsenio: That actually ties to my question. There is one thing that I am not clear on. In what you are describing, is there always that temporal dimension? Is always: I did something in the past and now I realize that I can control it? Or, I don't think that is what you mean exactly. I am thinking about two basic examples of children's anger: getting angry in a particular situation and emotions have action potentials, they may move you into one direction or another. You can't help possibly to feel angry in a situation but you can help what that anger causes you to do behaviorally. Does there have to be a temporal dimension to the kind of thing we are talking about here? I don't see why there would be.

Michael Schleifer: I don't have the answer. That is another one that I like hopefully to come back to and talk about. But I should say, I did just recently reread the group of articles in Child Development, March-April 2004, I believe, a whole group of articles on emotions, regulation, and control. The final article is by Joseph Campos and the group from Berkley, who are philosophers and psychologists, and, among other things that strike me, is he said that the whole question is misplaced, we can't ask the question any longer, he was talking about regulation but I am not sure and I think it refers to your question too, because time is a problem. It is almost as though, the whole literature, and all these people, who are talking about the psychological dimension, we're saying: okay we have the emotion and then in a matter of time, we will have to work out about regulating the emotion and what we do about it. And his view was you can't even pry that apart, because emotions have built into them already, the questions of regulation and control and their very definition. So on the temporal aspect, it is though, at what point are we raising the questions. So that is one thing.

But I will say this, Catherine said earlier that emotions have many facets and one is the cognitive dimension, and then she talked about the expression, which could be facial or it could be other ways, how you will express the emotion and then perhaps the 'dégout' feeling aspect, but I was not, if I understood you correctly, trying to talk about responsibility for the emotions only in the sense of expressing it.

I know there is that view that we want to tell children: alright, anger, you are going to feel it and there is nothing to do about that and grateful: alright, you don't feel grateful but here's what you got to do, in terms of the behavior, if that's what you are saying then I am not there. I am saying that I am not making the point that there isn't anything they can do about the actual feeling of gratitude. I think we have to work on the feeling of gratitude or the feeling of regret. In other words, the child may very well not say sorry and or not say thank. I mean saying thank you is showing gratitude as saying sorry is showing regret. A child may be told, "no, whatever you feel, say it", because it is the right thing. My view is that it is much better to have them not say "thank you" or "sorry," if they don't understand why they should say thank you or sorry, and feel it. And that is a view we defend elsewhere. So I don't make that distinction which perhaps you did between the emotion and the expression of the emotion. And the time element, I am really still confused about it. Perhaps, we can get back to it.

Michael Schleifer: . . .there are things I can say about that still, and if one of the things I have to do is to stand up in a group of people at an AA meeting and say I am sorry, which is not easy I would imagine. I find it difficult to say sorry to anybody, because I would have to think I was wrong! (laughter) So it's a question that is future oriented, responsibility is not simply for the past, but it's right now, I am looking at the act, or the emotion, I think about someone that I hurt, I didn't show sufficient regret then and I don't perhaps even feel sufficient regret now, but I think I maybe I should feel regret, and I start to think about it, I think there is something missing. Why don't I feel regret when I think it might be appropriate to feel regret. Or somebody did something for me and I should have really felt much more gratitude. Felt more gratitude! The question of whether I expressed the gratitude is another question. I may not have said "thank you, " but that's okay I didn't even feel thank you.

This is a consciousness, and it can go so far as to taking action. So it is not simply "alright I am aware," but I can actually work on the feeling. I believe, I have done this, I have not felt gratitude or regret about certain things. But I now think *why don't I feel this*, and I can get myself to feel a certain bit more regret that I didn't previously feel. I am doing this now. So, yes, it is partly conscious and there are partly things I can do. But with the example of AA is much more concrete, if I understand Paul's example, they stand up and say "I am sorry for . . ."

Paul Harris: Just to clarify, they don't do this in those meetings, but at a certain point in their recovery the person makes a private appointment with those family members or friends, and in some sense talks through what physically was and takes responsibility for what was done. There is this very strong sense of reparation.

Michael Schleifer: This makes me think of the trial that just finished in the States. This trial with the terrorist, who may not have been a terrorist, who was caught when no one else was, and he just went up to trial and he won't have the death penalty. What they wanted for him is something like remorse, and he was not showing remorse, in fact quite the contrary: He was saying "ha ha, I'm glad."

Cynthia Martiny: On this point, when I think of the context of conjugal violence, very often, when I think of the emotion that the man felt in the moment had something more to do with his background than it had to do with his victim, his wife. When he does realize that he was acting out from his own personal ogres, then he has the desire to take responsibility, not for having felt that, because that was his real experience in the here and now, but for the consequence of his act and the pain, and he recognizes at that later moment that his wife suffered from his violence. So it is not unconscious awareness that I feel guilty about having felt my anger, but I realize the consequence of that felt emotion was negative on somebody else. I think in AA, the reason for the act of doing this is, in French we call it témoignage, you get up and witness in front of other people, is mainly to help repair the consequences of his act on those outside of him, even before he recognizes that he is responsible himself. It is a little bit premature often, because it is a step he comes to, he doesn't necessarily have to feel responsible before he talks about it, that may come after the fact.

Michael Schleifer: So you are saying that this act that I got so impressed with they may be doing, which is for the benefit of others, but they may not actually, genuinely be feeling it yet?

Cynthia Martiny: Maybe not, not necessarily, it's not something you can necessarily test out either.

Paul Harris: I think you were hinting that the AA meetings, which typically serve recovering alcoholics, it is a way in some sense, hearing what one has done by speaking out. As far as I understand, the step where one goes to speak to those they've harmed, it would be hard not to construe that as regret.

Cynthia Martiny: Yes

Wendy Turgeon: Just to build on that, it sounds more like Aristotle's argument. By saying I am sorry even though I am not feeling sorry, by learning how to do that, ultimately I might feel sorry. I am not so sure about your proposal that you shouldn't say something you don't feel isn't instanced in both of these cases where I do what I know I ought to do even though I am not feeling it yet, but by doing it, I then begin to feel it.

Michael Schleifer: On Aristotle, which I think he is misinterpreted here, but I won't get into that. Except briefly to say, when he says let's instill habits because those are important as part of moral education for young children. But if you look up the part where he talks about habits, the habits he says are much like the wise man would do. I interpret habit, not to be behavior, that is I think that he wanted it to be saying sorry with some understanding, even for a young child.

Wendy Turgeon: It may not start out that way.

Michael Schleifer:We can debate Aristotle at lunch. Whatever he said or not, my view is that simply getting children, as some parents and many educators think you want to get them to do, say sorry and eventually they will understand it more or at all, or feel it, at least they say it. I think it doesn't work, and it is wrong, it is not where you want to go. So yes, my view is, if that's what you picked up, I don't agree in any way that as part of education you should work on the saying it, and by the saying it at least they say it. And why it doesn't work is some psychological work that is done, and I can say this very quickly. You have a lady with two year olds take a drink, and you ask her " do you like this juice?" and she says "I love this juice, " but as she is doing it she makes a face of disgust, 98% of the two year olds will say she hates the juice, and they heard her say she likes the juice. This is very important because the non-verbal behavior is picked up very young. So when we socialize our children to say "sorry," or "thank you," and they don't understand or feel it, we think it's good because at least they have the habit, other kids won't be fooled. The unfelt sorry, the rude sorry, thank you, is worse in my view than no sorry at all. So perhaps we disagree on that.

Gérald Boutin: It is not a question of "politeness" sometimes, as we say in French. This is like conditioning sometimes, is that so. We begin when we they are very young and continue when they are adults etc. My question was more, when you talk about responsibility, I was thinking about Jean Paul Sartre. He recognized the "essensialism de humanism" recently, he recognized it is a great actuality to be responsible, it is a very bold question you see. It is linked to a very large discourse, I should say, large problem.

Michael Schleifer: I guess it is a very large problem for sure, but I think that overlapping all the concepts of responsibility, including Sartre's view of in what sense "je suis responsable" and so on, I think there is a basic idea that we can sum up, which comes down to: "You are the author of what you did or didn't do." Sartre has this view about what one could look at, but I think it fits into the umbrella notion.

William Arsenio: A piece that I think you are talking about is the notion of focusing on the consequences of what you did for others. So the thing we don't like about saying sorry to someone if there is no sense of being aware of what is wrong here, what I did is I caused harm to someone else, the consequences and that idea of reparation, then a key piece is missing. I am trying to get my head about what responsibility means. It is not just a sense that I could have done otherwise, so I think that is a part of it, but also an awareness of what this causes for other people. I think this is what we are bouncing around.

I wanted to do another thing that is not related to this while I am talking. I am wondering, this is getting back to the original jealousy and envy part. Sometimes I hear a little bit of almost a moral component in the sense that I am upset because someone else has something to which I think they are not entitled to. So why not me? But sometimes it doesn't have to be there. So I am wondering if in any way, that moral piece fits systematically, say more with envy or jealousy or if it's just a completely different orthogonal construct. Because I hear a little bit about that moral part, but I am not sure how it fits?

Michael Schleifer: They are sometimes called moral emotions, this group, the term has been used. Pride fits into that category and jealousy in its two senses. So yes, envy almost always involves the idea that that person who just went in for the research grant, if I use that, in so far as I didn't get it and he did. I don't think he deserves it because his application wasn't as good as mine and there is a bit of that. So it is partly "why him, and why not me," that capsulates I want what he got, but it is also that I don't really think he deserves what he got. This is something we are doing in a research program now, we are prying apart to see what is with the children that actually got the notion, it doesn't seem that they have it at two. Kieran Egan thinks they do, but we don't think so. At five they have it, at six they definitely have it, they are often using it much like an adult does. But still the following kind of paradigm, which Paul Harris has done when looking at the other emotions, in terms of its causes and consequences and so on. It's far from clear what exactly is getting cashed out here.

So part of this question is when they are willing to say that. For example, one of the variables that we have hypothesized, and we are looking at it, and I don't know if it is for a six year old or even an adult. And it is if I like a person as one of my friends, am I less likely, if the situation is identical, to not feel envy. In other words, I like Sharon a lot, she is one of my colleagues and she got the grant and I didn't,

I may still be envious, but a lot less than when it is someone I really can't stand and I perhaps don't think is smart or good or whatever and they get the grant, will I be even more envious? I mean it makes sense but I don't know if it's true, I don't know if anyone has done the research, we are trying to do it now. Another variable seems to be, do I care. If for example somebody says to me, "I just won a big swimming championship, " and even if the person is one I don't like, it doesn't matter because I can't get even get going with the envy because I don't swim. Now I gave my example, happen to play high level bridge, and when I see someone I don't like that much, but even if I do like them, I don't think they are as good a player as me, but they win, I have to confess that I do start to feel envy. These are activities that I care about, so then the question is, is that the point, do you have to care about it? I don't know, we are trying to see.

Sharon Bailin: Just to follow up on this point, I think there is another possible distinction here and that is the feeling one has when they think someone gets something they don't deserve but without us coveting. Seems to me to be more indignation than envy and it's not necessarily negative. That is if this person gets a job as dean and I don't want to be dean, but I don't think they deserve the job as dean, I might be feeling more indignation and I think that might be in the right circumstances a positive emotion.

Michael Schleifer: This is what I am convinced of, and it is very important, I am still working it out, and I tried to make the point, but I will try again. I think that there are a lot of emotions we feel of the positive sort like that. Some of them are: I look at someone, "well he shouldn't be dean, but I don't want to be dean, someone else should be, " so I don't think we should talk about envy at all, I don't think its envy. I think it's an emotion, and it's good, and so on and it may be something else, I agree with you. I think there was the other stuff. Other people say, "well I know what envy is, I'll look at someone else and see how well they do and I'll emulate them. " Emulation as Aristotle talks about. Or they speak of being inspired by someone, who is great, I will follow them. It seems to me that Epstein got it right and so did La Rochefoucauld and Schopenhauer. There seems to be something about envy something of that ugliness. But if that's true, then we are back to the other question. All these very smart people think that it's not part of human life, you could get rid of it, including Bertrand Russell and Daniel Goleman, he says let's work hard and get rid of it. The Dalai Lama thinks this is one of the things you have to get rid of. I am not sure you can get rid of jealousy, I am just not sure.

Gérald Boutin: You are talking about the difference between jealousy and envy.

Michael Schleifer: I was, but I have now come to the conclusion that you can't get rid of either. I'm not sure, I would like to hear what people think. I am convinced, that both envy, the bad one that gnaws me away and the classical jealousy that people think about, usually romantic or sexual. Bertrand Russell really thought that jealousy is a crazy emotion, it's irrational, I have to work on that, because here I am 95 years old and am still feeling jealousy with my fourth wife. (laughter) I used to think he was right. I have now come to the conclusion that even that kind of jealousy is always there.

Sharon Bailin: I just want to go back to this issue, the connection between the feeling and the behaviors. You were saying we want to encourage children to have a behavior fit and have the feeling afterward. I was wondering what you feel about the reverse. That is, you have the feeling, which is maybe an inappropriate feeling, therefore you ought to express the behavior. We should still be teaching children that when you have the feeling, you ought to nonetheless control the behavior. So you should work on your anger, but when you feel anger you should refrain from the behavior. It seems to me the latter is sometimes the best we could do, that we feel certain emotions and we know they are irrational but they are still in our grips, you know Sharon, this is irrational, but keep your mouth shut, I mean you are dying to say this, but don't say it. You know that in the social context it will make things worse, and you will introduce a negative element, so the best one can do is refrain from the behavior.

Michael Schleifer: I haven't said anything in this paper about anger, but I am hoping that in the next few days your question is for everybody. Anger is probably the best of the emotions in that way. And Aristotle again is great when he said feeling anger is easy. But feeling it at the right time, in the right way, in the right circumstances, to the right degree and intensity, and so on, that is not easy. In 2006, in a personal way and as an educator, anger is great, and there are all these components, and I work very hard on what I should or shouldn't do in regard to my emotion of anger as perhaps others do. What do I want to tell children about it? Well, that is one of the themes of our symposium, and I hope we get to it. So yes, I agree we have anger. I don't think anyone disputes that anger will always be with us, that has never been disputed, except that as you said, people have thought, if you take the philosophers on the other side, Plato, Emmanuel Kant, and others who have given us a view for a long time, if you are interested in doing the right thing or in the moral aspect, feelings are just the things that get in the way, what we want to do is squelch them. Partly because of the work that has been done in the last 30 years it is no longer the view. There is a consensus among psychologists and philosophers that emotions have a central part in the moral life. It is relatively new if we think about that for the past 2000 years that was not the going view.

Jealousy and envy, the so called moral emotions, because they are already thrown into the moral life, even when you talk about them, I mean that's the problem. I mean, anger on its own, as you say something to me and I feel angry, I don't do anything so the question doesn't come up, maybe inwardly I am feeling it, but nobody knows it if I am able to freeze it, as Cynthia has taught me. So the moral question probably doesn't come up because you don't know I feel angry. But with jealousy and envy, it's kind of built in, in a way, because I have already made an evaluation of some sort, or just the feeling that I don't like what you are doing because I want it. We see it with siblings, as a clinical psychologist probably the most common question I get from parents about their children: "My kids are wonderful kids and I taught them to love, but why is my three year old taking the one year old and hitting them and so on. I don't understand what should I do about it?"

Sharon Bailin: I agree that jealousy and envy have moral dimensions. Nonetheless I am not sure that the case is different. If I feel jealous I think I have to work on that obviously, that's my view that we have to get one's emotions to be more appropriate. Nonetheless, sometimes I am not doing very well at getting past the feeling, nonetheless, I recognize that this isn't rational, that the circumstances are not warranting this, this is maybe something in my history is making me feel this. The best I can do sometimes is to keep my mouth shut and to try and say this is not appropriate and freeze it.

Michael Schleifer: The stratagems, if we simply talk about that, there are stratagems, both to teach children and ourselves, so that the question of the emotion, could be anger or jealousy, there are stratagems: keep my mouth shut, walk away, talk to myself. These stratagems have been a part of common sense for a long time, count to 20, everybody knows that, it works with anger. I am not so sure that with jealousy that counting to 20 will work.

Wendy Turgeon: Not willing to abandon Aristotle just yet. When I read this whole thing there were some interesting issues raised here in terms of the possibility that jealousy and envy could be virtues. You made a point that if I don't feel jealousy it might be for a lack of creative imagination, which doesn't sound like a good thing, so that means I probably want some kind of jealousy, at least in some way. Even envy seems to have a positive side to it, as you say, because it could be a catalyst for me to pull myself up and write that paper or something. Which means, I am wondering if there is a kind of virtuous mean, or a way in which being jealous is a good thing, or even envy. Because you sort of suggest that and then you back off.

Jean Claude Brief: That is a direction I wanted to take. You mention in your paper that one cannot be proud of envy. So in some way it is shameful or unworthy. That makes it different from jealousy which can be worthy. So I wonder if envy is a discontinuous process, where jealousy seems to be on a continuum in the sense of love and hate. Love and hate is a qualitative continuum that doesn't work with envy, but works with jealousy. Love and hate nourish each other, polarity. Indifference as the polarity.

Paul Harris: I want to defend. Occasionally I do feel envious, but despite what you said I don't feel terribly. . . Say there is a person who seems to have more freedom to do research, more resources, and I think this person is absolutely deserving, there is no question in my mind that he is the person for the job. I do envy him that latitude. Should I somehow not feel that? Why?

Michael Schleifer: I promised not to say anything more, but I have to say . . . I believe, and I am borrowing this from Epstein again who I quoted at the beginning of the paper that envy is always ugly and makes you feel ugly. So I think that what you just expressed, by definition is not envy. That is to say that you don't begrudge this colleague, it is not eating you up, it seems to me. My test is the following: Are you able to tell this guy, with 100% honesty, "congratulations?" If so, I think you have some of the aspects of envy, but without the malice. You don't have the malice.

Ann Sharp: Resentment is interesting because it eats you from the inside, it seems that is the way you are describing envy, it eats you from the inside.

Part II

Victims and Violence

Chapter 3
Happy Victimizers and Moral Responsibility: Sociocultural and Developmental Considerations

William F. Arsenio, Ferkauf Graduate School of Psychology, Yeshiva University

Sociocultural and Developmental Considerations

Children's moral development, or what some call moral internalization, is one of the major tasks of childhood. How do children learn to distinguish "right" from "wrong?" How do they learn to balance their needs and desires with the needs and desires of others in a way that avoids intentional harm? And what role do adults play in children's moral development? In the present chapter I will begin to address some of these questions by describing some of the work my students, colleagues, and I have been conducting on the broad emotional and social-cognitive underpinnings of children's and adolescents' moral development.

More than 20 years ago, Gibbs and Schnell (1985) realized that there are vast differences in the two major theoretical approaches used to examine children's moral development. Moreover, depending on which approach you take, adults have a very different role in how they should talk to children about moral issues and moral feelings. Gibbs and Schnell described how one approach to moral development, the approach of Piaget, Kohlberg, and later Turiel (in a slightly different way), views morality as "construct-ed" by the individual child, with a strong emphasis on cognitive abilities (e.g., Turiel, 2006). In other words, the ways children attempt to understand and make sense of morality have a major influence on their behavior. From this perspective, adults' roles are deemphasized, peer-peer interactions are especially critical, and cognition is more important than affect.

By contrast, the socialization view emphasizes that adults play a more central role (e. g., Kochanska, 1993). In this approach, morality is initially seen as external to the child, and, by using highly affective processes (including empathy and attachment), adults impart moral behavior to children. For some, this socialization process primarily involves non-cognitive behaviorist principles, such as timing of punishments, but for others, children's cognition, although secondary, plays a meaningful role.

Despite the best efforts of Gibbs and Schnell, this split between cognitive-developmental and affective socialization approaches still exists, although perhaps in a slightly less extreme form. In what follows, I would like to present a preliminary attempt at a cognitive/affective integration. This account will begin with a very brief description of how and why children's beliefs or conceptions about the emotional consequences of moral events may play a key role in moral reasoning and behavior. This will be followed by sections which summarize: a) research on what these moral conceptions of moral emotions entail, both developmentally and, to some extent, cross-culturally; and, b) observational studies describing the actual emotions children display in the context of moral encounters and how these emotions relate to children's conceptions of moral emotions. Final sections focus on the relationships among attachment, empathy, and children's conceptions of moral emotions, and what these connections might mean for the development of children's moral responsibility and the role adults play in that emerging responsibility.

A Brief Theoretical Overview

> Affects, by being represented, last beyond the presence of the objects that excite them. The ability to conserve feeling makes interpersonal and moral feelings possible and allows the latter to be organized into normative scales of values.

– Jean Piaget

Many of our behavioral decisions are influenced by "an anticipation of the way we will feel in some future situation. A child's readiness to go to school, to brave the dentist, to seek out a new friend, or to run away from punishment is based on an appraisal of how he or she will feel when facing those situations" (Harris, 1985, p. 162).

Taken together, these two quotes suggest that children form conceptions of situational affect, that is, the links between specific situations and the likely emotional outcomes of those events. In other words emotions don't just happen to us and are then forgotten. Instead a critical part of human learning involves remembering aspects of the situations in which those emotions were elicited. Furthermore, these affect-event conceptions then provide us with an essential way of anticipating the probable emotional outcomes and personal meaning of a wide array of social and non-social behaviors.

The importance of these claims for adults is obvious. If an adult knows, for example, that a child is petrified of going to the dentist, the adult might use that knowledge to talk about how the upcoming visit is not likely to hurt because it's just for a fluoride treatment. Extrapolating a bit, similar types of affect-event knowledge will be important to children and adults during potential moral encounters. Inevitably, both children and adults will have strong emotional reactions to moral events that involve deliberate harm, hurting someone, cheating, or lying, and, furthermore these affectively- charged events will be hard to forget. Given the salience and importance of these moral affect-events links, adults' understanding of children's conceptions may help to promote effective parent-child moral discussions and, ultimately, what Kochanska (e. g., Kochanska & Murray, 2000) has called children's "committed compliance" to a common moral agenda. It is with these ideas in mind that my students and I first became interested in studying children's and adolescents' conceptions of the emotional correlates of various types of moral events.

Children's Conceptions of Moral Emotions

In our initial work (Arsenio, 1988), we presented children with a number of short vignettes depicting different types of sociomoral events involving, for example, deliberate harm to obtain a desirable object, helping pick up dropped objects, helping another child stop a bully, etc. Children in three age groups (5-, 8-, and 11 year olds) were asked them how different people in the story were likely to feel, and most of the results were not that surprising. One unexpected finding jumped out, however, when children were presented with acts involving victimization. Take, for example the following story: "Tom saw that another boy had a great candy bar in his lunch. When no one was looking Tom went over and took the other boys' candy. How does Tom feel now? How does the other boy feel when he finds his candy is missing?" We found that many children, especially kindergartners, expected that the victimizer would feel happy. At the same time, all of the children expected that the victim would feel quite negatively – a combination of sadness, anger, and fear.

This "happy victimizer" finding might have been easy to overlook, except that it had also emerged in two early studies by Masters and his colleagues. In their first study Barden, Zelko, Duncan, and Masters (1980) looked at children's conceptions of the emotional outcomes of various social events (8 categories), including one category they called undetected moral transgressions ("If you stole a ball, and no one saw you do it, how would you feel?"). Their overall results revealed substantial consensus in how the three age groups judged emotional outcomes with one notable exception:

> One interesting age change was that the youngest children expected a happy response to dishonesty (not caught), whereas older children moved to a consensus for fear reactions . . . Older children may have had more experience with being apprehended at a later time and also be more cognitively able to foresee such apprehension as a likely future event rather than dwelling on the success of a dishonest act for which one is not immediately caught. (p. 975)

In subsequent research (Zelko, Duncan, Barden, Garber, & Masters, 1986), they compared their findings for what 5, 8 and 11 year olds expected to feel following these 8 types of social events, with *adults'* predictions of what children in these different age groups would say (i. e., adults predicted the emotional outcomes they thought children would select, and whether these outcomes would vary for children of different ages). The resulting findings revealed that adults were, in general, quite good at predicting older children's emotion expectancies, but were much worse with younger children. One of the greatest discrepancies was for undetected dishonesty where adults expected 5 year olds to say they would mostly feel scared, rather than the "happy" outcome often selected by these young children.

This discrepancy between adults' expectancies for young children and young children's own expectancies for transgressions is a potential problem. If adults are going to help children discuss and understand their emotion expectancies effectively, then adults must have some idea of the emotional meaning that children ascribe to potential acts of victimization. Furthermore, moral socialization is an understandably major concern for adults – so young children's unexpected belief that successful victimization results in happiness is both practically and theoretically surprising.

Consequently, shortly following the Zelko et al. research, Nunner-Winkler and Sodian (1988) conducted the first study explicitly designed to address this puzzling "happy victimization" conception in more detail. Nunner-Winkler and Sodian began by arguing that:

> Moral events are likely to produce intense but conflicting emotions given that a person who violates a moral rule may, for instance, experience joy at the success of his or her forbidden behaviors and/or guilt, shame, or remorse at his or her immoral behavior. (p. 1323)

It seemed plausible, then, for these authors to expect that even young children would have mixed conceptions of the emotional consequences of deliberate victimization – including both positive and negative emotions. The findings from their three-part study, however, were quite different. Essentially, these researchers found that no matter how they manipulated the salience of the harm caused by victimization, young children (4 and 5 year olds) simply expected that moral victimizers would feel happy following successful acts of victimization.

Despite the clear sophistication of this study, my own experiences as a preschool teacher for almost ten years led me to question preschoolers' apparent "happy victimizer" conception. A few years later we (Arsenio & Kramer, 1992) did a follow-up study to examine Nunner-Winkler and Sodian's original idea that moral events are likely to elicit *mixed emotions* and would be remembered as such by children. We proposed that earlier failures to find mixed emotion conceptions in children probably resulted from some combination of methodological limitations and children's underlying cognitive difficulties with the task. So 4, 6, and 8 year olds were asked to judge the likely emotional consequences of acts of victimization and to provide rationales for those judgments for *both* victims and victimizers. In addition, all of story characters were described as good friends – making it less likely that children would think the victimizer was simply a bully. The first part of this two-part study revealed that nearly all of the 4 and 6 year olds expected victimizers to feel happy, as did about half of the 8 year olds (the story involved stealing candies from someone's locker). These results emerged even though children also judged that the victimizers would feel very negative emotions. In a second part of that study children were presented with different stories (e. g., pushing someone off a swing to get a quicker turn), and after providing their initial emotion judgments, children were probed about other possible emotional reactions that the victimizer might have. For example, an initial probe question simply asked children if the victimizer could be feeling anything different and what that might be. Two other probes became more specific up to a final probe where, for example, children were asked "You said your friend was happy when she got your swing. What if she saw you on the ground [where the friend had pushed her] and saw that you were very sad? Could she be feeling anything besides happy?"

Probe results indicated that nearly all 8 year olds and 75% of the 6 year olds responded to the least direct probe ("anything else?"), whereas 66% of the 4 year olds insisted that victimizers could only be feeling happy, even after being explicitly direct to the loss and suffering experienced by the victim on the final probe. Moreover, when a separate group of children were probed about *victims'* emotions, none of the children changed their initial evaluation (i. e., victim always felt negative), suggesting that the probe methodology, per se, did not produce changes in how children viewed *victimizer's* emotions. Overall, these findings supported what Nunner-Winkler and Sodian (1988) described as a moral attributional shift, that is, a developmental change from young children expecting victimizers to feel almost exclusively happy, to 6 and 8 year olds beginning to view moral transgressions in a more mixed light.

We argued that it is as though 4 year olds view victims and victimizers as having two non-interacting sets of emotional expectancies to this single victimization event. By contrast, it seems as though 6 and 8 year olds expect victimizers' emotions to be influenced by their victims' reactions. For example, even though nearly all 6 year olds and most 8 year olds initially expected victims to feel happy, they also provided negative emotion expectancies when asked the least directive probe question.

What does all this mean about young children's moral development and about the role adults can and should play in that development? Our sense is that this is a more complex question than we used to think. Essentially, we have argued (Arsenio & Lover, 1995; Arsenio, Gold, & Adams, 2006) that the age-related shift in children's emotion attributions highlights a basic developmental moral conflict; *victimizing* others can produce desirable gains and outcomes that can make you feel happy, but to be victimized is to lose what is yours and feel sad, angry, and other clearly negative emotions. Drawing on others' research and theories, we also proposed that a key aspect of moral development involves children's underlying *ability* and *spontaneous tendency* to integrate the 2 halves of this moral conflict – both to *understand* and *feel* that the victims' pain and loss will moderate one's own happiness regarding the gains produced by victimization. At the cognitive level, children need to be able to recognize and understand others' emotional states – they need to realize when they are responsible for producing the others' distress. At an affective level, children need certain empathic tendencies, "I feel your pain and it affects me. "

> Children's understanding of reciprocity, fairness, and justice may all depend on an early ability and tendency to co-ordinate the emotional reactions of victims and victimizers, both to understand and to feel that the victim's pain and loss will moderate one's own happiness regarding the gain produced by successful acts of victimization (Arsenio & Lover, 1995, p. 109).

But how do we know this is really how it works, that these are some of the relevant mechanisms at work? And where do adults fit into this transition to moral responsibility? Before addressing these questions, it is helpful to address another concern that was raised by these early studies on young children's conceptions of happy victimizer. In the simplest terms, do young children's "happy victimizer" conceptions really have any meaningful connections with their actual emotional behavior in these contexts?

Observational Studies

To date, our laboratory has conducted three observational studies related to this question (e. g., Arsenio & Killen, 1996; Arsenio & Lover, 1997), including one comprehensive project that will be described below. First, however, it is important to acknowledge that the focus of this observational work shifted somewhat from the earlier studies on children conception's of victimization. It is difficult to observe undetected moral transgressions and more covert forms of harm, so our observational studies focused more on aggressive encounters, both those that produced obvious material gains for children involved, as well as acts where the gains were less clear. Also, given some of the limitations in conducting observational studies of older children's transgressions, this work focused on preschoolers.

In our most extensive study, we (Arsenio, Cooperman, & Lover, 2000) observed an ethnically diverse group of 51 preschoolers (27 girls and 24 boys) between the ages of 4 and 5 ½ over a one-year period. After a 2 month warm-up period, observers coded 2 major aspects of children's behavior: their emotion expressions and aggressive encounters. Children's emotions were coded using Denham's (1986; Denham, McKinley, Couchoud, & Holt, 1990) live-action coding system (i. e., not from videotapes), which reliably codes the individual "happy," "sad," and "angry" emotion displays of young children as they occur in naturalistic settings. Separate assessments summarized the total number of children's emotion displays across the school day (baseline emotions), and children's peak emotions as victim or victimizer during any aggressive encounters (aggression-related emotions). Various aspects of preschoolers' aggression (defined as including either physical or verbal harm, but not simple disagreements or rough and tumble play) were also recorded. In addition to these observational data, children's emotion knowledge (emotion recognition, labeling, etc.) and sociometric status were assessed.

Overall, somewhat less than 200 aggressive interactions were observed, and nearly all children initiated at least one aggressive act ($M = 3. 29$) and were targeted at least once ($M = 3. 29$). Although, as is often found (Coie & Dodge, 1998), about 20% of the children initiated nearly half of all aggressive acts. The emotions children displayed differed strongly depending on the context. Outside of their aggressive conflicts (the overall "baseline" context) children were quite happy (91% of all displays), but during their aggressive interactions this dropped to just 25%. Furthermore, children's aggression-related emotions were very different depending on whether they were the initiator or target of the aggression. Not surprisingly, the targets of aggression were mostly angry, with some sad and neutral expressions. By contrast, aggressors' emotions were pretty evenly divided between anger and happiness (about 40% for each).

Other analyzes revealed that children's primary emotion displays (i. e., each child's anger and happiness as *percentage* of their total displays) were related to both their aggressive behavior and peer acceptance. Specifically, children who displayed more anger *outside* of aggression and more happiness *during aggression* were more aggressive and less accepted by their peers. Furthermore, the targets of aggression were more likely to be distressed (angry or sad rather than neutral) when aggressors were happy. Finally, children aggression-related happiness was somewhat directly related to their rejection by peers (other significant findings were mediated by children's aggression level). This last finding suggests that relatively non-aggressive children may view highly aggressive peers who are often happy during aggression as not taking these typically aversive acts seriously or, even worse, enjoying being mean.

Moreover, results from an unrelated study (Miller & Olson, 2000) provided some longitudinal support for these findings. Compared to their peers, preschoolers who exhibited more "gleeful taunting" during videotaped play sessions at the beginning of the school year were rated as being more disruptive by teachers and less liked by their classmates fully nine months later.

> gleeful taunting may function to instigate conflict among preschool children (e. g., by taking toys and laughing, or teasing and other forms of relational aggression), whereas anger and mild negative affect may appear primarily as emotional reactions to another child's actions (Miller & Olson, 2000, p. 348).

Overall, these studies reveal that preschoolers often express happiness – up to almost half of the time – when they commit aggressive acts. Although this figure is much lower than studies in which preschoolers' always expected victimizers to feel happy (e. g., Arsenio & Kramer, 1992; Lourenco, 1997; Nunner-Winkler & Sodian, 1988), it is quite consistent with most studies on how children expect that they *themselves* will feel after victimizing others and obtaining positive material outcomes (e. g., Barden et al., 1980; Keller, Lourenco, Malti, & Saalbach, 2003, but see also below). In addition to this normative pattern, however, there are major individual differences in how likely children are to be "happy victimizers." And those children who are more likely to be happy during aggression are both more aggressive and less liked by peers.

Happy Victimizer Conceptions – Individual Differences

Given these observational results revealing clear individual differences in young children's *actual tendencies* to be happy victimizers, the lack of variability in young children's *conceptions* of moral emotions (almost exclusively "happy victimization") seemed even more puzzling. Consequently, we (Ramos-Marcuse & Arsenio, 2001) decided to return to assessing young children's conceptions using a slightly different approach. For this study, we adapted a version of the Macarthur Story Stem Battery (Emde, Wolf, & Oppenheim, 2003), an approach that involves giving young children the beginning of some story or event and then allowing them to enact what follows by using interesting and age appropriate materials such as tiny figures and props.

Sixty-three mostly preschool age children were interviewed, including about half who had been referred to a clinic for early behavior problems, and about half from the same neighborhood but who were free of significant behavior problems. Children were presented with four story stems in which they were described as having victimized others (e. g., stealing someone's candy, taking their sled). Children were then asked how they would feel and why, and they were subsequently asked to use the play figures and props to show "what happened next?" Our analyzes of the resulting videotapes, revealed that, contrary to our expectations, the two groups did not differ in terms of their initial emotion attributions or rationales for those emotions. Nearly 80% of the time children said that *they* expected to feel happy following their acts of victimization (clinic $M = 3. 15$, comparison $M = 3. 21$ out of 4 stories), and children nearly always justified their emotions by referring to the concrete gains produced by victimization.

Revealing group differences did emerge, however, when we looked at the subsequent narratives that children provided for follow-up probes (e. g., "what happened next?"). Specifically, non-clinic children mentioned attempts to be positively responsive to their victims, including offering apologies, making reparations, or admitting blame (e. g., "but I would give him his bike back.") nearly twice as often clinic children (21%versus11% of all narrative responses). Another significant group difference involved a less common but revealing response. Nearly half of the clinic children versus17% of the non-clinic group mentioned death or killing at least once in their overall narratives (e. g., "I'd kill him if he tried to get his bike back"').

Once again, the lack of individual or group differences in "happy victimizer" expectancies was unexpected, although perhaps it should not have been. This same basic finding has now emerged for young children across a number of different cultures, including South Korea, China, Portugal, Germany, England, and various communities in the United States (see Arsenio, Gold, & Adams, 2006, for a review). In fact, young children's "happy victimizer" conception is considered so robust by some researchers, that there is a growing attempt to examine it in terms of underlying *cognitive* constraints affecting young children's ability to shift their focus from the salient gains produced by victimization to the losses experienced by victims (see, e. g., Lagattuta, 2005, for a recent Theory of Mind explanation).

Although these overall cognitive explanations are intriguing, it is important that once some young children got past their initial emotion attributions in the Ramos-Marcuse and Arsenio study, they tended to view their victimization in less favorable terms. We wondered whether this was the beginning of some important developmental shift in the moral emotion beliefs of children. Consequently, we decided to examine adolescents' conceptions of moral emotions, both because of the developmental significance of victimizing behavior in this age group and because basic cognitive constraints were unlikely to affect adolescents' abilities to conceptualize mixed emotions in various contexts.

As part of a larger study on affective social information processing in adolescents (Arsenio, Gold, & Adams, 2004; 2006), we asked adolescents' how they would feel following their victimization of others. For example, one story went as follows.

"Imagine one day that you were waiting in a line to see your favorite musical group. There was just one person ahead of you when you heard the ticket seller say there was only one ticket left. The ticket seller was in a small booth and couldn't see out very well. So when the ticket seller turned around to answer the phone, you knocked the guy ahead of you down to the ground with a push. Before that guy could get up, you bought the last ticket and walked into the concert. How do you think you'd feel at the end of that story?" We also asked adolescents to explain why they would feel that way, and we also asked them to predict what their victim would feel and why.

A total of 100 adolescents participants between the ages of 13 and 18 were included: 50 adolescents were behaviorally disruptive (i.e., diagnosed as having oppositional defiant disorder or conduct disorder) and 50 adolescents without behavior problems were recruited from the same public schools (66% of both groups were male, all were African American or Latino, and most adolescents were being raised by mothers with a high school education or less). In this study adolescents used ten "chips" to rate how they expected to feel by dividing up those chips in any way they wanted between 5 emotion categories (happy, sad, mad, scared, or just okay). So, hypothetically, a participant who was told she got a really good present for Christmas, might respond by putting 7 chips in the happy category and 3 in the okay category. In addition to adolescents' ratings, their classroom teachers completed a standardized assessment of adolescents' broad externalizing tendencies using the Check Behavior Checklist.

Results for adolescents' expectations of how they expected to feel following their victimization of others revealed a single group difference: behaviorally disruptive adolescents expected to feel happier than comparison adolescents (Ms = 3. 31 chips versus1. 67 chips, both out of 10 possible chips). By contrast, both groups primarily expected their victims to feel angry following that victimization (M = 7. 52) and there was no group difference for that anger attribution (i. e., neither group minimized the negative consequences for victims). Subsequent analyzes also revealed that adolescents' happy victimizer expectancies (i.e., the number of "happy" chips) predicted teachers' ratings of adolescents' externalizing tendencies for both groups even after controlling for verbal ability and other significant contributors.

Summary – Happy Victimization and Frustration-Anger Aggression Models

Much of the above can be summarized by saying that children's *normative* expectations that victimizers will feel happy following successful victimization decreases with age – from preschool through adolescence – while the *diagnostic significance* of the happy victimizer expectation (what it predicts behaviorally) seems to increases with age. When it comes to actual observed "happy victimization," almost nothing is known about developmental changes, but we do know that individual differences in preschoolers' happy victimization are pretty clearly linked with negative developmental outcomes. Questions remain, however, about what these findings mean for several theoretically and pragmatically important issues regarding children's moral development. For example, how should adults talk to children about happy victimization in a way that promotes moral internalization, and, in a related vein, when can children take responsibility for and potentially alter their emotionally positive views of victimization?

Along with my colleague Elizabeth Lemerise, we have begun to address some of these issues as part of a larger discussion (Arsenio, 2006; Arsenio & Lemerise, 2001; 2004) on the potential affective underpinnings of children's moral development and aggressive tendencies. We have proposed that happy victimization (and social cognitive biases and deficits associated with aggression) initially stem from failures or disruptions in children's underlying empathic tendencies. Happy victimization reflects a lack emotional responsiveness to others that runs counter to initially innate empathic tendencies (Hoffman, 2000). Moreover, along with others, we believe that these empathic difficulties are the product of shared adult-child interactional histories (e. g., attachment patterns) characterized by mutual emotional regulatory problems.

A schematic model of how empathy typically influences *nonaggressive* children's victimization (see, e. g., Hoffman, 2000) is shown in Figure 1. Young children may initially (developmentally) feel happy about the gains that result from victimization – the toy they want or the turn on the swing without waiting. As part of a gradual developmental transformation that includes both cognitive and socio-emotional changes, children are then subsequently more able and more likely to observe their victims' emotional responses (induced by victims as well as by other socializing agents).

Figure 1: Simplified view of victimizers' empathic responses to the pain and loss experienced by their victims (reprinted from W. Arsenio, 2006).

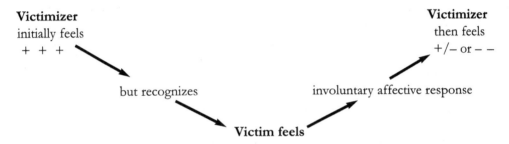

Once the victimizer becomes aware of the victim's negative emotions, underlying empathic mechanisms can then take effect and that victimizer will respond to and, to some extent, begin to share the negative emotions expressed by their victim. Accompanying this affective recognition and response is the victimizer's awareness that he or she caused the other child's (unnecessary) pain and suffering. Given repeated experiences in both the victim and victimizer role, most young children will develop mental schemas of victimizing acts characterized by strong mixed emotions. Finally, these schemas are likely be elicited even before children become directly involved in acts of victimization, serving a key anticipatory role as they contemplate such behaviors

For some children, however, this normative developmental integration of the cognitive and affective element empathy fails or become distorted. And a central contributor to these empathic disruptions is the problematic nature of some attachment relationships and their effects on parent-child and child-child emotional reciprocity.

Attachment, Empathy, and Behavior Problems

There is a growing literature on the connections between children's attachment patterns (i.e., parent-child affectional ties) and their emerging behavior problems and externalizing tendencies. It appears that when insecure early attachments combine with low socio-economic status and other socio-cultural stressors, affected children are at a greatly elevated risk for behavior problems (see, Greenberg, 1999, for a review). For example, in one longitudinal study (cited in Greenberg, 1999) the majority of children who had severely disrupted attachment relationships in infancy (i.e., disorganized attachments) and who also had a mother with psychosocial problems (e. g., depression) developed behavior problems in kindergarten, compared with only 5% of those children without either risk factor. Other studies also suggest that disorganized parent-child attachments play a unique role in the development of children's behavior problems, in part because these attachment relationships are often associated with parental abuse and neglect.

Although there is accumulating evidence regarding the connections among children's attachment, high-risk status, and externalizing tendencies, the mechanisms underlying these connections are still poorly understood (Dodge & Pettit, 2003). Furthermore, in terms of the present chapter, there is no research on why some children do not alter their initially positive emotional views of victimization. To address these issues, a brief explanatory model is offered; one that borrows freely from ideas elaborated in much greater detail by Hoffman (2000), Fonagy (2004), Cassidy (1994), and others (Arsenio, 2006). The basic elements of this model can be summarized as follows:

> a) Children's attachment status is, in large part, the product of a shared pattern of parent-child emotional reciprocity in which adults typically play a greater role; b) resulting patterns of emotional reciprocity affect children's empathic tendencies; and, c) in turn, differences in emotional reciprocity and attachment are connected with children's mental representations of victimization and aggression. In this view, patterns of parent-child emotional reciprocity provide the foundation for children's understanding of moral reciprocity (i. e., fair and equitable treatment) and influence subsequent aggressive tendencies (Arsenio, 2006, p. 111).

For securely attached children, this means they will have experienced a relatively consistent pattern of caregiver responsiveness to their biological and emotional needs, which will subsequently allow these children to freely share both their positive and negative emotionally-charged experiences with caregivers (Cassidy, 1994). Insecurely attached children, however, experience a very different pattern of parent-child emotional reciprocity than their securely attached peers. For many of these insecurely attached children, the implicit message from adults is that children must learn to filter or distort their emotional experiences before adults will respond. And those insecurely attached children who interact with fundamentally emotionally unresponsive adults (e. g., adults experiencing multiple risk factors such as mental disorders and extreme sociocultural stressors) are unlikely to receive even minimally psychologically adequate levels of contingent emotional responsiveness. These "emotionally abandoned" children are then likely to develop severely disrupted (e. g., disorganized) attachment patterns, and to develop internal working models of these relationships that reflect deep beliefs that "in this life you're on your own" and/or "others are out to get me."

The outlines of this speculative model are consistent with several studies (see, e. g., Troy and Sroufe, 1987, on connections among attachment, empathy, and aggression). The present approach is also related to a model outlined by Fonagy (e. g., 2004); a model in which he argues that insecure attachments undermine children's understanding of both their own and others' mental states in ways that increase the likelihood of peer aggression and victimization. The lack of contingent responsiveness between caregivers and infants, in particular, is seen as acting to weaken insecurely attached children's understanding of others' mental states. Given that less responsive adults inadvertently make their needs, beliefs, and desires somewhat more opaque to their children, these children will then go on to develop less elaborated Theories of Mind involving these mental states than securely attached children. Consequently, insecurely attached children are less likely to consider or understand the needs and feelings of others, and, as a result, they are more likely to victimize their peers.

Although Fonagy's accounts helps to understand the behavior of children who are aggressive because of a relative inability to recognize and/or understand victims' emotions, it is less useful for those aggressive children who do not appear to be suffering from deficits or biases failures in their social cognitive abilities (see, e. g., Sutton, Smith, & Swettenham, 1999). For this other group of children, the problem is more one of emotional responsiveness than of social understanding, per se (see also Arsenio & Lemerise, 2001; 2004).

Empathy and Reactive versus Proactive Aggression

The discussion above touches on the potentially important distinction between those children who victimize others because they are relatively *unaware* of emotional costs for victims versus those who victimize because they are *unconcerned* about the costs for victims. Fonagy's description of the empathically *unaware* is broadly consistent with models of children's victimizing aggression that involves anger-frustration links, or what Crick and Dodge (1994) call reactively aggressive children. Those children who have difficulties with understanding the needs, beliefs, and desires of others, are also likely to have difficulty understanding others' intentions, and consequently, exhibit "hostile attributional biases" (i. e., assume others are being deliberately provocative and aggressive when, in fact, they are not). Consequently, empathically unaware children are likely to respond with what they believe is legitimate (i. e., provoked) anger, frustration, and retaliatory aggression to ambiguous social situations. More proactively aggressive (i. e., those using aggression more instrumentally), however, may have fewer difficulties in recognizing or understanding the emotional reactions of others. Although these proactive aggressors may be less likely to engage in "misfired" (i. e., hostile reactive) aggression, their lack of emotional responsiveness to victims makes it easier for them to use aggression instrumentally, and to feel emotionally positive about resulting physical and psychological gains.

In summary, significant failures in parent-child emotional reciprocity (and resulting attachment disruptions) can distort children empathic tendencies and promote aggressive patterns in at least two ways. Some children may so self-focused they do not easily recognize their victims' pain and loss, whereas other children may learn to ignore victims' emotional reactions as irrelevant when those reactions conflict with the victimizers' own desires and goals. Furthermore, it has been argued that this second cause of empathic failures (i. e., a lack of empathic concern or responsiveness) may be especially predictive of higher levels of "happy victimization" and proactive/instrumental aggression. In terms of the origins of this pattern, these children may be temperamentally less responsive to parenting that utilizes power assertion and other fear-inducing techniques, especially when that parenting is built on an earlier base of insecure child attachment. Over time these parents may attempt to escalate their ineffective punitive socialization efforts, leading to even more disrupted parent-child emotional reciprocity, and a severing/truncation of children emotional responsiveness to others (including potential victims).

Implications for Children's Moral Responsibility

What does this discussion of "happy victimization" mean for children's responsibility for their moral emotions and parent-child discussions regarding those emotions? The simplest and least useful answer is that we still do not know. There has been very little research, to date, on parental contributors to children's conceptions of behaviors involving happy victimization (see Arsenio, 2006). Still, based on the research described above, several things are clear:

(1) Young children have a strong expectation that victimizers (including themselves) will feel happy following acts of victimization that produce gains. Adults are largely ignorant of this expectation.

(2) Children's *normative* happy victimizer expectations decreases with age – from preschool through adolescence – while at the same time the *diagnostic significance* of this expectation for predicting behavior problems seems to increases with age.

(3) Observational studies of preschoolers confirm that happy victimization is far from infrequent, and higher levels of actual happy victimization are linked with greater aggression, peer dislike, and teacher ratings of behavior problems.

Much of the previous literature on emotions and aggression (reviewed in Lemerise & Dodge, 2000) has focused exclusively on anger. In this view, children may get frustrated when a person, object, or event blocks their pursuit of a goal, which leads to anger and an increased probability of aggressive responding. Yet, psychologists have long known that aggression can also be used more instrumentally and not just as a hostile response (see Dodge, Coie, & Lynam, 2006, for an historical overview). What the happy victimization research suggests is that, contrary to adult socialization agents' beliefs, positive emotions also play a critical role in children's and adolescents' morally-relevant aggressive acts. It may be that happy victimization is part of younger children's more general expectation that they will feel happy about any act, moral or not, that achieves a desired outcome (Lagattuta, 2005). The frequency and diagnostic significance of individual differences in preschoolers' actual happy victimization, however, suggest than many children will not simply "outgrow" these early conceptions.

At a more speculative level, I have argued that individual differences in conceptions and behaviors involving happy victimization may be traced back to early-parent child relationships. Disrupted attachment relationships, in combination with other parent and child risk factors, are known to predict subsequent child behavior problems. One unexamined part of this connection involves how parent-child relationships influence children's views of emotional reciprocity. The claim here is that parent-child emotional reciprocity lays a foundation for the kind of emotionally reciprocity that is central to moral reasoning and behavior. Very young children who learn that their emotions are recognized and positively influence how caregivers respond to them are more likely to grow into preschoolers who extend that emotional reciprocity into their interactions with peers. In turn, these securely attached preschoolers will be more likely to recognize and care about the emotional consequences of their behaviors for others, a pattern that will eventually reduce levels of victimization and conceptions of happy victimization that, left unchanged, would promote continued aggression.

At one level this may sounds like an "emotivist" description of children's moral development in which cognitive processes and active parent-child discussions have no particular role (Turiel, 2006). Emotions and affective relationships, however, do not play an idiosyncratic or arational role in this account. In the attachment and functionalist emotion theories alluded to here, interpersonal emotional reciprocity become the basis of the give and take that makes subsequent conscious norms of fairness, caring, and concern for others' welfare psychologically meaningful (see Nussbaum, 2001). In his regard, Laible and Thompson (2000) found that when securely attached preschoolers discussed moral transgressions with their mothers, "they made more frequent references to feelings and moral evaluatives when discussing the child's past behavior than did insecure dyads" (p. 1436). Although there is a preconscious (for the child) and preverbal phase to early parent-infant interactions, those interactions subsequently provide a systematic foundation that influences both the content and quality of parents' moral discussions with their children, as well as how children understand and behave in affectively-charged moral interactions with peers and adults.

References

Arsenio, W. (2006). Happy victimization: Emotion dysregulation in the context of children's instrumental/proactive aggression. D. Snyder, J. Simpson, & J. Hughes (Eds.), *Emotion Regulation In Families: Pathways to Dysfunction and Health*. Washington DC; American Psychological Association.

---. (1988). Children's conceptions of the situational affective consequences of sociomoral events. *Child Development, 59*, 1611-1622.

---, Cooperman, S. & Lover, A., (2000). Affective predictors of preschoolers' aggression and peer acceptance: Direct and indirect effects. *Developmental Psychology, 36*, 438-448.

---, Gold, J. & Adam, E. (2006). Children's conceptions and displays of moral emotions. M. Killen & J. Smetana (Eds.), *Handbook of Moral Development*. NJ: Lawrence Erlbaum Associates.

---, Gold, J. & Adam, E. (2004). Self-attributed emotion knowledge regarding aggressive and nonaggressive events: Connections with adolescents' behavior problems. Manuscript submitted.

--- and Kramer, R. (1992). Victimizers and their victims: Children's conceptions of the mixed emotional consequences of victimization. *Child Development, 63*, 915-927.

--- and Lemerise, E. (2004). Aggression and moral development: Integrating the social information processing and moral domain models. *Child Development, 75*, 986-1002.

--- and Lemerise, E. (2001). Varieties of childhood bullying: Values, emotion processes, and social competence. *Social Development*, 10, 59-73.

--- and Lover, A. (1997). Emotions, conflicts, and aggression during preschoolers' freeplay. *British Journal of Developmental Psychology, 15*, 531-546.

--- and Lover, A. (1995). Children's conceptions of sociomoral affect: Happy victimizers, mixed emotions and other expectancies. M. Killen & D. Hart (Eds.) *Morality in Everyday Life: Developmental Perspectives* (pp. 87-128) Cambridge: Cambridge UP.

Barden, C., Zelko, F., Duncan. S. & Master, J. (1980). Children's consensual knowledge about the experiential determinants of emotion. *Journal of Personality and Social Psychology, 39*, 968-976.

Cassidy, J. (1994). Emotion regulation: Influences of attachment relationships. *Monographs of the Society for Research in Child Development, 59*(2-3), 228-283.

Coie, J., & Dodge, K. A. (1998). Aggression and antisocial behavior. In W. Damon (Series Ed.) & N. Eisenberg (Vol. Ed.), *Handbook of child psychology, Volume 3: Social, emotional, and personality development* (pp. 779-862). NY: Wiley.

Crick, N., & Dodge, K. (1994). Social information-processing mechanisms in reactive and proactive aggression. *Child Development, 67*, 993-1002.

Denham, S. (1986). Social cognition, prosocial behavior and emotion in preschoolers: Contextual validation. *Child Development, 61*, 1145-1152.

Denham, S., McKinley, M., Couchoud, E. & Holt, R. (1990). Emotional and behavioral predictors of preschool peer ratings. *Child Development, 61*, 1145-1152.

Dodge, K., Coie, J. & Lynam, D. (2006). Aggression and antisocial behavior in youth. In W. Damon & R. Lerner (Series Eds.) & N. Eisenberg (Vol. Ed.), *Handbook of child psychology, 6th ed., volume 3: Social, emotional, and personality development* (pp. 719-788). NY: Wiley.

Dodge, K. & Pettit, G. (2003). A biopsychosocial model of the development of chronic conduct disorders in adolescence, *Developmental Psychology, 39*, 349-371.

Emde, R., Wolf, D. & Oppenheim, D. (2003). *Revealing the inner worlds of young children; The MacArthur story stem battery and parent-child narratives.* New York: Oxford.

Fonagy, P. (2004). The developmental roots of violence in the failure of mentalization. In F. Gibbs, J., & Schnell, S. (1985). Moral development "versus" socialization: A critique. *American Psychologist, 40*, 1071-1080.

Greenberg, M. (1999). Attachment and psychopathology in childhood. In J. Cassidy & P. Shaver (Eds.), *Handbook of attachment: Theory, research, and clinical applications* (pp. 469-496) New York: Guilford.

Harris, P. (1985). What children know about the situations that provoke emotions. In M. Lewis & C. Saarni (Eds.), The socialization of emotion (pp. 161-186), New York: Plenum.

Hoffman, M. (2000). *Empathy and moral development: Implications for caring and justice.* New York: Cambridge UP.

Keller, M., Lourenco, O., Malti, T. & Saalbach, H. (2003). The multifaceted phenomenon of "happy victimizers": A cross-cultural comparison of moral emotions. *British Journal of Developmental Psychology, 21*, 1-18.

Kochanska, G. (1993). Toward a synthesis of parental socialization and child temperament in early development of conscience. *Child Development, 64*, 325-347.

Kochanska, G. Murray, K (2000). Mother-child mutually responsive orientation and conscience development: From toddler to early school age. *Child Development, 71*, 461-482.

Lagattuta, K. (2005). When you shouldn't do what you want to do: Young children's understanding of desires, rules, and emotions. *Child Development, 76*, 713-733.

Laible, D. & Thompson, R. (2000). Mother-child discourse, attachment security, shared positive affect, and early conscience development. *Child Development, 71*, 1424-1440.

Lemerise, E. & Dodge, K. (2000). The development of anger and hostile interactions. In M. Lewis and J. Haviland (Eds.), *Handbook of emotions* (2nd ed., pp. 594-606). NY: Guilford Press.

Lourenco, O. (1997). Children's attributions of moral emotions to victimizers: Some data, doubts, and suggestions. *British Journal of Developmental Psychology, 15*, 425-438.

Miller, A. & Olson, S. (2000). Emotional expressiveness during peer conflicts: A predictor of social maladjustment among high-risk preschoolers. *Journal of Abnormal Child Psychology, 28*, 339-352.

Nunner-Winkler, G. & Sodian, B. (1988). Children's understanding of moral emotions. *Child Development, 59*, 1323-1338.

Nussbaum, M. (2001). *Upheavals of thought: The intelligence of emotions.* New York: Cambridge UP.

Paiget, J. (1954/1981). *Intelligence and affectivity: Their relationship during child development.* Translated and edited by T. Brown & C. Kaegi. Palo Alto, CA: Annual Reviews Monograph.

Ramos-Marcuse, F. & Arsenio, W. (2001). Young children's emotionally-charged moral narratives: Relations with attachment and behavior problems and competencies. *Early Education & Development, 12*, 165-184.

Sutton, J., Smith, P. K. & Swettenham, J. (1999). Bullying and "theory of mind": A critique of the "social skills deficit" model of anti-social behavior. *Social Development, 8*, 117-127.

Troy, M., & Sroufe, A. (1987). Victimization among preschoolers: Role of attachment relationship history. *Journal of the American Academy of Child and Adolescent Psychiatry, 26*, 156-172.

Turiel, E. (2006). The development of morality. In W. Damon & R. Lerner (Series Eds.) & N. Eisenberg (Vol. Ed.), *Handbook of child psychology, 6th ed., volume 3: Social, emotional, and personality development* (789-857). NY: Wiley.

Zelko, F., Duncan S., Barden, R., Garber, J. & Masters, J. (1986), Adults' expectancies about children's emotional responsiveness: Implication for the development of implicit theories of affect. *Developmental Psychology, 22*, 109-114.

Discussion after William Arsenio's Presentation

Paul Harris: Bill and I talked during breakfast. I think its really fascinating stuff. I guess as Bill indicated, it's been going on for 20 years I guess. I get the sense that we're moving forward, but we still haven't figured out what exactly is going on. I'd kind of like to crystallize two different ways of thinking about it because I think Bill argued with the one and I think there is a different one. I think that Bill is emphasizing the fact that the child can focus on their gain from this misdemeanor and that's what the younger children believe. As they get older, they are increasingly inclined to incorporate into their assessment of the entire scenario, with victim's distress, the victim's loss. I think that's not what's happening.

In other words, I think the developmental change can be explained very differently. I think what's happening, and I agree with the first part, that young children are focusing on their gain, but I think that the developmental change is, that children increasingly think of themselves as moral agents who will, and should, feel bad if they don't live up to particular standards. Now, the reason why I think that very different view, is as follows: I can give a couple pieces of evidence which I think will support this second view. The view that I'm taking predicts that you get exactly the same pattern of children expecting a perpetrator transgressor to be happy. Even in situations where there's no victim. Say it's a game where you are supposed not to cheat, if you do cheat, ok, you don't abide by the standards, you don't abide by the rules but there's no obvious victim that you're hurting.

Well for instance, some results we have, we found even in those circumstances, you get the developmental age change. So in this case, it's wrong to construe that the child is gradually thinking to themselves, oh if I cheat, there's going to be somebody distressed. It's rather the child is saying to themselves, the cheating is not what the good person does, if I fail to live up to that standard, I'm going to feel bad. Now, the other piece of evidence, something I've spotted in the middle of your talk, now if I can get you to go back to it, it was particularly where you have the behaviorally disturbed kids.

If your analysis were correct, it seems to me you would expect these behaviorally disturbed kids to differ from the comparison group, precisely in their preoccupation with the feelings of the victim, those middle panels. But they don't, they differ with respect to the balance, with their concern for outcomes as opposed to moral considerations. I rest my case.

William Arsenio: As you were saying at that point, the whole empathic system is not hard wired in the sense it's not immune to social experience over time. That's it exactly, you're right. But at this point they're not going to have the same potential empathic response . . .

Paul Harris: But they are, they are showing respect.

William Arsenio: No, but that's not the same as empathy, knowing the consequence of the other person, I mean some of these kids are going to tell you, I don't care. I think that that's the important part, is that you can know about the consequences and at some level, essentially be able to turn to someone and say I don't care. But it doesn't do anything for me. I think for most of us, the fact that we feel kind of appalled and weird in that situation is because, for us, we have a deep sense that of course, you almost organically would feel an emotional response to the loss that you're causing. But these kids don't. I mean, there's a change that's happened in their empathic development over time. So, I think that empathy is not the same for some of these kids as it is for the way we're thinking about it.

Paul Harris: Well if empathy were the break, it ought to cut in so much earlier. I mean, all the data show that these happy victimizers recognize what the victim's distress is, and here they're focusing on it as much. So the issue is what is the break? And I'm saying its not concern for the victim, I'm saying it's the extent to what you feel ultimately in this situation where there is a victim. I ought to live up to a particular standard, and there's another situation where there's no victim equally, I should live up to a standard. So, I guess sometimes what I'm saying this phenomenon is not about happy victimization, it's about happy immoralists. In other words, the phenomenon is much more wide spread than you're suggesting.

Michael Schleifer: Well, can I just say something on this? Lying and cheating are things I've been studying for quite a long time, and again its a part of our book, we have two chapters, and we've been talking about card games, and when cheating and lying with my colleagues. I think, I don't know if this is going to help, but everyone lies and cheats sometimes. And in card games we all know what it's like to peek and so on. And with my grandchildren as one of the issues, everybody does it. Okay, I'm just going to make the general statement, even if people disagree with me. In a panel show earlier, I just realized one psychiatrist, and one student, and one psychologist and I were saying we're going to react to lying. And the psychiatrist was talking about the psychopathology of lying and the psychologist was talking about at what age, stage, whatever, and the student said, everybody lies sometimes. Sometimes lying is right and sometimes lying is wrong and they asked me, and I said, well I agree with the student, and they kicked me off the show.

But my point is the general notion about cheating or lying is everybody does it. I think there is something important here if this data is true, if I'm understanding it, that not everybody, at least older ones are happy victimizers. Not even four year olds are happy victimizers, that was my little question. It wasn't unanimous, you had what 28, I don't know the percentage or numbers but you had about six of them, even at age 4, who didn't say they were happy. So I know this is important because the two general explanations, yours . . .

Paul Harris: I mean, the data I briefly mentioned did involve looking at whether kids were prepared to cheat. And it's wrong to say that everybody cheats, there are individual differences in cheating too.

Michael Schleifer: Everybody cheats sometimes. Everybody lies sometimes

Paul Harris: Yeah, but everyone will be aggressive sometimes. What we're talking about is some overall disposition to be more or less aggressive, more or less prone to cheating. So, I'm trying to say that the same considerations apply to cheating, and in so far as the same considerations apply to cheating, it's hard to construe it as the recognition of victim distress.

William Arsenio: What is the mechanism here? Why essentially is it that you shouldn't cheat or do things when there's no obvious, immediate victim. I mean, I guess in part I'm trying to understand is whether you're saying that there are standards. I guess my argument is that there are standards and part of the way kids understand these standards is kind of like classical construction, a Piagetian notion, you've got to experience it at both ends, you know what it feels like, so therefore you put that together, and from that, that causes you . . .

Paul Harris: If anything, I'm driven back to an almost a Freudian account.

Michael Schleifer: Super ego I was hearing, guilt.

Paul Harris: Well, it's a little more pedestrian than Freud. I think what is going on and here I pretty much emphasize on the parental input. I think what's going is that, as I was saying this morning, I think some parents treat children as moral agents, in whom they will be disappointed, if those children don't live up to certain standards. Gradually children internalize those standards, and gradually they feel disappointed in themselves if they don't live up to those standards. Other children have less invested parents, who don't treat those children as moral agents and so the child never acquires this sense of feeling good and proud of themselves when they maintain the standards, which to some extent at an intellectual level, they subscribe to, but it takes all the centralization for them to feel good about the sense of being a good person.

So I think it's almost as if the young child, the young child looks at these situations says yes, that's the right think to do. What should I do? Let's do something else. Whereas the older child says under what circumstances would I feel good. I will feel good in so far as I do the right thing. In fact, conjunction, the parent I think is responsible for bringing about.

William Arsenio: I agree, but I think an interesting thing that parents do in those situations is what is the nature of those standards? It's because we talk about going back a long time ago, the idea of induction that you as a parent, what are you saying in the situation. You're not saying, don't steal because if you do, I'm going to spank you, or I'm going to stop loving you. Don't steal because how would you feel if someone did it to you. So there's this long old history of what is it that you are conveying in a parental induction to a child, and what you are trying to get them to do is to see that there's a "semi-rational" consequence of their behavior for another person, and it's a negative one, that they have some control over.

Paul Harris: The child knows the consequences when you steal. You don't need to explain that to the child. The child knows the consequences when you hit someone you don't need to explain that. The trick is to get the child to see that, in some sense give them enough propaganda to convince them that they'll feel better if they don't do it.

Sharon Bailin: I was thinking about, of the case amongst adults well, happy victimization or happy immorality, which ever way this plays out, because I think, it could play out either direction. You think about the adults who are unhappy victimizers of people outside a certain circle. So they wouldn't and would consider it wrong to victimize members of a family, or friends, or members of the in-group but past that might be but it would be very, in fact happy to get a gain in business against someone else or that kind of thing.

And I can think of two ways in which that might be explained. One would be that they haven't in a kind of way, which I think is related to, to your perspective that the circles of affect haven't gone out far enough. But also, I think one could explain in terms of they're only looking at the level of harm and anguish, they can see close up but haven't internalized more general, moral principles, that this is the wrong thing to do even if its not to folks who are harmed and we can see that close up. So I think one could go probably either way, in looking at that kind of a case.

Paul Harris: Vegetarianism would be a good case, where you can think of it in each of the ways we've discussed. In what way is the principle vegetarian, not the diet vegetarian, different from meat eaters? It could be, and I think this would be Bill's intonation, it could be that the principle vegetarian in some sense, integrates the terrible life that the factory chicken has into that conception of the gains to be acquired from eating meat. But it could also be that the principle vegetarian in some sense expands the circle of meat eating as falling into the category of bad things to do and tries to live up to that standard in a way that I myself deviate more times than I care to acknowledge.

Wendy Turgeon: I'm going with what Sharon asked, and wondering to what extent the children voiced the sense that they didn't know that not only did the victim feel bad. But they would feel bad because the other children wouldn't like them anymore, or that they would be excluded from the group which is sort of what you were getting at when you're thinking in terms of "I feel badly now that I've pushed him off the swing, because now the other children don't want to play with me." Or "Mom and Dad are upset with me." What point then did anyone volunteer that as an explanation rather than simply, I realize the victim feels lousy crying there, therefore I feel badly.

William Arsenio: I think it's fair to say there were surprisingly few mentions in a lot of the studies that were done, of parents and this is a different question. There were fewer punishments, you know, they don't talk about how I might get caught later, that's why I feel sad now. The other thing about talking about other peers will regard them also doesn't come up that much. We've never really phrased that, or put that out as a possibility.

Ann Sharp: But don't you say it with the preschoolers that if I was a happy victimizer, nine chances out of ten, I would not be liked very much? Doesn't that moment leave you?

William Arsenio: Yes, that's true. You're actually right. So there's a link between if you're a happy victimizer and your peers are less, observationally a happy victimizer, your peers are less likely to like you.

We have no good evidence yet of direct connection. I think you're right it would be between that judgment of happy victimization and peer regard. But you're saying that they should be mentioning peers as kind of bringing in, kind of extending the circle.

Wendy Turgeon: It seems like it's a step in the empathetic growth, I can imagine the other children of the class won't like me. Therefore it's not a good thing to feel happy about this before I have to leave to a principle position where it's wrong because it goes against some law of parents, or God, or whatever.

Paul Harris: And it's not as if the evidence supports you. The older children don't talk about it, popularity, a fear reaction, they don't.

Wendy Turgeon: But they care deeply about, children do ultimately. They behave anyway.

Paul Harris: If you're looking at what the children are saying in support for that line of thinking, the children as they get older talk increasingly about, not in terms of punishment but in terms of being conscience stricken.

Phil Guin: I'm trying to think of how to form the question. What you get with the studies that you've done, you get the conclusion. What is the case, that your preschoolers, moving up the stages to the adolescents. And low and behold, at some point, kids discover empathy or fairness.

William Arsenio: I think that happens, but much, much earlier, the roots are between age one and two.

Phil Guin: Yeah, I guess I'm thinking in terms of education, how we facilitate getting kids to form empathic relationships with their peers and how do we get them to have a sense of fairness.

William Arsenio: You know, it's funny because this kind of goes back to the discussion were having this morning too. I have a student who does anger management programs in prisons – it's a daunting kind of work. He describes the issue; clearly some of the prisoners, he's dealing with anger management kind of issues. He says when it comes to anger management, we have ideas, we have their whole curriculum, we know what to do when dealing with anger management. Essentially you're loosing control and all these techniques. But, there are another group of prisoners he sees, who are much more into the manipulation active views of aggression, and they are very conscious to alter their behavior . . . will say the right things. We are really talking about psychopathy.

What we were talking about earlier this morning the idea that if you want to change this happy victimization, that one key piece is that if you're not going to talk them out of it, like when he's dealing with these older prisoners, he says, this is prison, and its not really working for you. You have to see that what you're doing with your life isn't a good thing. And their response is really interesting. So if they're rational enough to make that kind of response, what they say to him is next time, I'm gonna do it better. I've learned how to do this whole thing, I know what I want out of life. I know life is a question of power, not fairness. So, next time I'm going to clean up the mistakes that I've made and do it right. So for him, it's really frustrating, we know what to do with the anger part but when you're dealing with someone like that, it's an important question. You can't talk someone out of this. But I think for young kids, I think one of the important things you can do is you create a climate where they feel emotionally attached to other adults. That in this case, the logic you'll be able to talk them out of it. Hopefully earlier on, you're going to alter the emotional relationships so, and from that, they will be able to hear things that they couldn't possibly hear about later. I do think in that discussion, that to make certain kinds of changes, it has to start, I mean there is cognition involved. There has to be an affective base, something that you do, as a preschool teacher or elementary school teacher, or a professor, you have to form an emotional bond before you find a way to talk about things.

Chapter 4
When Adults Lose it, Do Children Catch it?
What to say to Children who Witness Interadult Violence
Cynthia Martiny

Children Witness Interadult Violence

Disclosure hesitance masks the real number of children exposed to domestic violence, however in view of the current levels of divorce, spousal abuse, child maltreatment, domestic violence, and the dependent nature of a child's relationship with their caretakers for nurturance and protection, it is safe to estimate that the number of children finding themselves present during a violent dispute is in the millions every year. In Canada alone, at least a half a million children are estimated as witnessing conjugal violence each year (Statistics Canada, 2002). These innocent bystanders are exposed to physical and verbal abuse ranging from hearing insults, watching a parent receive a slap on the face to observing fatal assaults with guns and knives. Some children are nonconsensual participants in domestic violence as they are used as human shields to protect one parent from another, taken hostage as leverage for possessions or injured from the crossfire. Clearly, despite the lack of accurate prevalence data, large numbers of children that are exposed to domestic violence, and it is more than likely that this exposure occurs more than once over the course of their development (Edleson, 1999), need help. The question addressed in this paper is what is happening and what would be helpful to say to them.

Consequences for children

Research on children's exposure to violence has underlined a wide range of detrimental developmental outcomes including social (aggressiveness to inhibition), emotional (fearfulness to hostility), behavioral (antisocial to clinging), cognitive functioning and attitudes (lower functioning and approval of violence) and general health (alcohol abuse, depression, low self esteem) in the short and long term (Edleson, 1999; Wolfe, Crooks, Lee, McIntyre-Smith, & Jaffe, 2003). In 1990, Jaffe found similarities between the effects of being exposed to family violence with the effects of war on children, of being a child with parents with psychiatric disorders and they show symptoms similar to those children suffering from post traumatic stress syndrome. Societal reactions to these negative outcomes have given rise to the criminalizing of violence and other laws to protect children. This compounds the emotions felt by children ranging from fear to terror, who have witnessed violence with, for example, the experience of the police preventing their parent from returning home or by having to move into sheltered care to include guilt, sadness, anxiety, anger and even happiness when the episode is over.

Without minimizing the fact that exposure to adult domestic violence is devastating for children, some studies have shown that large numbers of children who have witnessed violence demonstrate no negative developmental problems and even some children displayed strong coping abilities (Jaffe, 1990; Edleson, 1999; Wolfe, Crooks, Lee, McIntyre-Smith, & Jaffe, 2003). Children's resilience suggest that protective factors, such as dispositional attributes and family or outside support, play a role that questions the assumed causal relationship between violence exposure and negative effects. It is assumed in this paper that these protective factors, as well as information about intervention and emotions, could be empowering for children to know about because they feel powerless, their physical and psychological safety could be at risk and their future intimate relationships could be affected by the intergenerational cycle of violence. Research does indicate that children do seem to catch the anger they watched their parents lose.

Correlations have consistently been found between the elevated risks of individuals who were maltreated or exposed to violence as children and of child abuse perpetration as adults (Merril, Thomsen, Crouch, May, Gold & Milner, 2005). These findings support the social learning theory (Bandura, 1973) and the cycle-of-violence hypothesis as well as suggesting that children learn that violence resolves conflicts, that violence is part of family relationships, and that violence is a way to control other people. According to Osofsky (2003).

> Thus, the context of domestic violence for children is an aversive one that goes beyond just exposure to violence. Children learn from what they observe. They learn from being exposed to domestic violence that this behavior is permissible and acceptable. They also, unfortunately learn the confusing message that the very people who are supposed to protect and nurture them may be placing them in harm's way. What is often underestimated is the potential effect of violence exposure on later relationship difficulties, violence, deviant behavior, and psychopathology. These problems highlight the need for effective intervention strategies for violence-exposed children. (p. 64)

Current intervention strategies include criminalizing abuse, obliging citizens to report any situation that compromises the safety and the development of children and offering alternative shelter homes or foster care to those in need. Consequently, children oftentimes are left without a parent, in a new home, confused and grieving, yet for parents in need of support, there are hotlines, therapy, legal aide, and support from either professional or nonprofessional (volunteers, friends and relatives) help. The aim of this text, however, is to inform those who want to help children who have witnessed conjugal violence about what to say about the control and the regulation of the anger they observed and experienced between their adult caretakers so they can make sense of their experience and to decide for themselves what to do, how they want to be and how they want to express their feelings within their own relationships.

Anger

Theoretically anger is neither a positive or negative emotion, but it gets bad press. Rarely are people attracted to anger expression and, when someone is angry, it evokes less sympathy than sadness. Demonstrative displays of anger are looked down upon in most social arenas when the other basic emotions (Ekman & Friesen, 1975) including sadness, joy, fear, disgust and surprise are tolerated and even encouraged. Actually, it is not so much the repression of anger that is expected from others but an acceptable form of anger expression that is desired. Aristotle summed it up when he wrote that one must know how to be angry "at the right things and towards the right people, and also in the right way, at the right time and for the right length of time" (Nicomachean Ethics).

Anger serves a function. Without anger problems would go unrecognized and corrective actions would not be identified. Since anger is experienced both subjectively and physiologically, the absence of anger expression is known to be physically and psychologically unhealthy. It can lead to a variety of negative psychological states such as burn-out, depression, and suicide and it has been linked to poor physical health including cancer (Pennebaker, 1997). Anger expression therefore is necessary in maintaining emotional and physical fitness.

The problem is that anger is often considered the most dangerous emotion because part of the experience of anger is losing control. LeDoux (1996) explains that when the amygdala gets activated by the senses, it arouses the neocortex and keeps it engaged so that there is cognitive interference and controlled decision making processes by maintaining the focus on the emotionally arousing situation. All other inputs on the working memory are blocked out. The amygdala, thus, has greater control over the cortex than the cortex has on it, which serves to explain how emotional arousal does, at times, dominate and control thinking.

Damasio (1994) provided the hypothesis, illustrated by describing the case of Phineas Gage, that there is a link between the body and the mind via the ability to learn and express emotions *in context* dependent on the decision-making process. Mr. Gage was a railroad worker who received a steel rod in his left cheek and out of the top of his head. Still able to walk and talk, this man was said to have changed from being a dutiful, gentle and polite employee to a rude, irresponsible man who couldn't make decisions anymore. According to Damasio, patients with brain lesions in this area of the brain tended to lack empathy. He provided the hypothesis that there is a link between the body and the mind via the ability to learn and express emotions *in context* dependent on the decision-making process. This indicates that perceiving feelings is integral to the thinking process (instead of being responsible for the distortion of it).

An encounter with interference, for example, can result in frustration and arouse anger. The feeling colors the behavior depending on the reading of the context. Anger can also be provoked as a result of a perceived physical or psychological threat. Another source of anger is watching someone violate a personal moral value. The perception of threat may or not be evaluated before the reaction is acted out. Anger erupts because of a failed personal expectation or triggered in response to another's anger. The debate continues over what comes first, the behavior (facial expressions, for example) or the emotion, but "in terms of understanding the relationship between expression and well-being, the interplay between affect and cognition is far more important than which component is primary" (Kennedy-Moore and Watson, 1999, p. 21).

Ekman and Friesen (1975) describe the physiological characteristics of anger. It can gradually accumulate or it can occur abruptly and full-blown. It varies in intensity. Blood pressure increases, so the face sometimes reddens and the veins stand out in the neck or on the forehead. Breathing changes and the body appears to become more erect as muscles tense. These authors map the face into three areas including the upper forehead region including the brows and the eyes, the nose and cheek area and then the mouth and chin area. They claim that there is ambiguity unless anger is registered in all three facial areas. For them, thus, anger is manifested as:

The brows are lowered and drawn together. Vertical lines appear between the brows. The lower lid is tensed and may not be raised. The upper lid is tense and may or may not be lowered by the action of the brow. The eyes have a hard stare and may have a bulging appearance. The lips are in either of two basic positions: pressed firmly together with the corners straight or down; or open, tensed in a squarish shape as if shouting. The nostrils may be dilated, but this is not essential to the anger facial expression and may also occur in sadness. (Ekman & Friesen, 1975, p. 95)

This bodily expression displayed communicates anger. The demonstration of the presence of anger itself doesn't warrant any more a reaction from the perceiver than does the display of the physical manifestations of happiness or sadness. Experience and the display of these particular bodily expressions warn, however, that if the stimulus, rightly or wrongly associated with the onset of this emotion isn't discontinued, harm can follow. Thus, children need to know that anger, their own and in others, is acceptable. Feeling it, showing it, and expressing it are human processes that serve a purpose. It is aggression and violence that are unacceptable.

Conjugal violence

Some theorists distinguish healthy anger from disturbed functioning by examining the motivation triggering it (Tangney, Hill-Barlow, Wagner, Marschall, Bornenstein, Sanftner, Mohr & Gramzow, 1996). Malevolent goals such as revenge, hurting the anger instigator, getting someone else to comply with one's own personal wishes, or being violent with someone in order to feel better, are different from the constructive goals of maintaining a relationship, asserting authority, or resolving a problem. Those with disturbed functioning are characterized by avoiding active confrontation and ruminating hostile thoughts (Mikulincer, 1998). If this describes the parent of a child seeking help, it may be helpful for them to know that these people rarely seek help for their violence as they would not feel a need to change (Addis & Mahalik, 2003). Since people target most of their anger on people they know well, like, and love (Kassinove, Sukhodolsky, Tsytsarev, & Solovyova, 1997), children with parents that demonstrating violent behaviors and do not seek to change are children at risk of harm.

Conjugal violence concerns adults having difficulty with close interpersonal relationships. One way to receive help is through therapy. It implies the necessity of creating an alliance with a therapist and agreeing on the goal of therapy which would omit it as the type of treatment suggested for the above-mentioned types of disturbances. For those who seek therapy venture towards an understanding of intimate violence of which Scalia (2002) says "*it is of utmost importance to underline that when an individual batters, it is to regulate his overwhelming affect, he is not intending to victimize anyone, at least not consciously, at least not as a primary action. The motive to batter is always secondary to the primary motive of protecting the inner self*" (p. 22). In other words, violence may be voluntary but not premeditated. This author claims that the first and most common motivational factor of intimate violence is the experience, during childhood, of a helplessness and vulnerability that seemed to have threatened their survival. Striving to prevent being overwhelmed by a reactivated early trauma, the batterer attacks the threat. The hurtful action was thus motivated to regulate internal affect and to maintain or restore personal narcissistic equilibrium. This sadness or fear underlying the angry response may not be conscious to the aggressor.

An example of this would be a spouse complaining that his wife picked up the phone when they were on the verge of stepping out for a walk together. For him, the significance of her responding to the phone call meant that he was unimportant and any caller could replace his company. It never occurred to him that she was expecting a call from her father who was in urgent need of advice about his health and that she loved going for walks with him. Another priority needed her attention in the moment which activated an intolerable sense of rejection belonging in the past such as not being the favored child. He uses verbal violence with insults and intimidation. While in action, the unwanted feelings of inadequacy disappear.

A second motivational factor is impairment in the capacity to experience the other empathically. Empathic disorders can happen, like autism, from a faulty intersubjective differentiation (Braten, 1998). Egocentric, self-absorbed, and narcissistic personalities also lack empathy. Aside from pathological dis-orders, projection is a process that impairs empathy. Projection is the experience of unacceptable aspects of ones' experience transferred onto the other person who acts in accordance to them. The other ceases to exist while the batterer experiences only an imagined other in the moment. At that precise moment, the aggressor was unable to recognize the projective processes taking place within and reacts to 'someone else.'

A third motivation concerns identification with past aggressors. They attribute justifications for the abusers who abused them or those around them and feel compelled to do what they rationalize as just. When belief systems (for example patriarchal attitudes, male dominance, sexism, etc.) are challenged and ruled false, the injustice becomes intolerable and guilt grows. The violent behaviors were uncovered to be mere imitative behaviors that were modeled to them by their own caretakers that they themselves copied without questioning the rational or the justifications.

An examination of these motivations for violence, brings to light its pathology. Some of this pathology can be cured by therapy, but not all, and the before-mentioned intent to inflict harm necessitates the withdrawal from society. In addition to above mentioned motivational triggers are compounding contributing factors to violent behaviors. Damaged interpersonal relationships (meaning that both members of the partnership are struggling with alcohol abuse, mental health, sickness, and so on), enmeshment in a like-minded peer groups who share in the acceptance of anger, patriarchal ideologies, cognitive distortions, low self-esteem, grieving, stress from job loss, financial difficulties, and having the responsibility of multiple children under five, are just a few of the stressors contributing to some of the disputes precluding conjugal violence.

The factors linked to conjugal violence are multidimensional, multilayered, and intertwined. There are also different types of aggressors. The topic is complex. However, for the purposes of what to tell those children about the control and the regulation of the anger they observed and experienced between their adult caretakers, it is important to emphasize that conjugal violence does not necessarily mean parental violence. Although there often is a spill-over effect, some men are violent towards their wives but never towards their children. The motivations that trigger conjugal violence are not necessarily present while parenting. The two relationships can be differentiated. For those parents that take responsibility, feel guilt and shame for their transgressions, there is hope for a positive outcome with treatment (Chamberland, 2003).

Psychotherapy

After reviewing the anger-research literature, DiGiuseppe and Tafrate (2001) recommended six core intervention strategies to be included in a comprehensive anger-treatment program. The first is to create a therapeutic alliance with the client. This is true with all clients entering into a therapeutic relationship engaging in the process of change. The difficulty that therapists encounter with angry clients is the development of their empathy towards the person who provokes their own feelings of anger or disapproval. Knowing that the lack of therapist empathy is highly correlated with the failure of treatment, the therapist probes into the storytelling of the incident to cultivate it by perspective taking until there is some intersubjective commonality shared between them. Once this has been accomplished, the therapist is less dismissive about the clients' means of expressing anger and a more effective facilitator towards change.

The second core component is to address the motive for change. It is difficult for clients to desire change because violence works. Exploration focused on their experience and the consequences of their violence, however, increases angry clients' desire for improved relationships and less complicated lifestyles. It becomes exhausting to sleep elsewhere, repair the consequences of an argument, and to feel the guilt and shame from hurting loved ones.

Another core component is to manage physiological arousal. Anger, as already mentioned, has distinct physiological characteristics. These communicate the presence of anger to the other. They also indicate the presence of anger to the angry client. Awareness of them can be used to signal the need to take distance before reacting. Increasing awareness of the signals preceding an outburst can indicate to the couple that there is a need for a 'time out' so that bodily tension can lower before continuing any further interactions.

The fourth component to change is to foster cognitive change. "Angry clients are prone to distortion and exaggeration concerning aversive life events. Cognitions concerning blame, unfairness, demandingness, and suspiciousness are also common in anger experience. Helping clients foster realistic and accurate perceptions, as well as a more flexible cognitive philosophy, leads to emotional and behavioral change" (DiGiuseppe & Tafrate, 2001, p. 268).

Another important recommendation for therapy with angry clients is to use role-playing or process interventions to implement behavior change during therapy sessions so the clients can practice and rehearse interactions. They learn perspective- taking by hearing the therapist during a nonthreatening session review the interaction played out. In this way new and more appropriate responses are learned. The most effective treatment, however, is for angry clients to express negative emotions live while in therapy. This works to experience the previously uncorrected perceived injustice in a different way that allows the angry client to access a new understanding about why it worked out as it did. Without reliving the raw emotion, this unfinished event continues to erupt again and again. In this way, the client can legitimize the anger and condemn the behavior in a safe environment. To be able to do this in therapy allows the client to experience real change. This goal is more durable and reliable concerning repeat behaviors than the mere control of emotions.

Lastly, DiGiuseppe and Tafrate (2001) advised to teach relapse prevention because it is likely that the home environment will continue to confront the client with anger-triggering events. Maintaining change is not easy when the context remains stable. Very often, clients need to cultivate support within their environment as well as outside.

Optimism is justified if these therapeutic components and recommendations are respected, according to DiGiuseppe and Tafrate (2001), as improvement has been demonstrated to be consistently moderate to large and that treatment effects has appeared to be durable. These authors also found that not only do angry clients report improvement, but their spouses do too. Although contingent on many factors, effective intervention strategies do exist and can play an important role in mending some families.

What to Say to Children who Witness Conjugal Violence

Maughan & Cicchetti (2002) "underscore the deleterious effect that maltreatment has on emergent emotion organization in children, the development of subsequent psychopathology" (p. 1539) and the difficulties a child experiences as "inter-adult violence is part of the ecology of a maltreating home environment" (p. 1540). Children need to know that violence and aggression are unacceptable. When it happens, and it does to many children, it negatively affects their development and emotional adjustment. It is associated with sadness, anger, fear, worry, guilt, shame, behavioral problems, and danger when they are concerned. Children exposed to conjugal violence are known to internalize problems and either become withdrawn or act out their distress. They need to know that they are not responsible for conjgal violence, and that bearing witness to inter-parental violence may cause to post traumatic stress (expressed through, for example, denial, repression, disassociation, desensitization or identifying with the aggressor). It is also possible that children learn their parents' scripts that later turn into violent behaviors when they get older. By hearing some of the symptoms children frequently display who, like them, have seen their parents acting violently, may help them identify and talk about their own fears and reactions.

Children may feel relieved to hear that the same author also found in previous studies that about one-fifth of the maltreated children were able to develop healthy emotion regulation abilities despite their adverse childhood experiences. Since conflict is inherent in all relationships, coping skills and learning independence could be regarded as positive outcomes. To understand how others succeeded could be of help to others. Lee (2001) suggests that children may regulate sensory intake by ignoring the emotionally arousing environment around them. They may leave the anger area, watch television, play with toys, avoid being around, or seek nurturance from trusted adults. They use distraction techniques and limit information gathering. They also cognitively change their interpretation of what is going on by telling themselves stories. Some of these coping skills may resemble some forms of psychopathology. The difference is in the conscious awareness and intentionality of the behaviors.

Since it is known that children who talk about conjugal violence tend to have had the experience more than once, it is therefore important to talk about the next time. It is important to acknowledge that when parents fight, their anger can turn to aggressive behaviors. When this happens, children have four choices about what to do. They can get involved and try to stop the fighting, avoid it, observe, or call for help. Children experience powerlessness when they try to stop the fighting and getting near a fight can be very dangerous. They could get hurt. Observing and avoiding a dispute between their own caretakers make children feel guilty, sad and anxious about not doing anything, but at least they remain safe. One way to avoid is to leave. The last option, calling a relative, a friend, a neighbor or the police to inform them of the problem or to be rescued is available if the children have a means of contact (telephone available, knows the number, and knows who can be trusted).

Traumatic events such as domestic violence can affect a child's self esteem, their perception of the world as a good place and the belief that life has meaning and purpose (Condly, 2006). Restoring their confidence in themselves and others through emotional expression means breaking the 'conspiracy of silence' about the abuse that in some cases was kept secret for years (Humphreys, Mullender, Thiara and Skamballis, 2006). Often children are referred to counselling when they can't or won't talk about their problems with the caretakers around them. The first task a counselor undertakes is to establish a therapeutic relationship with the child so the child can think, feel and talk spontaneously about problems experienced in the company of an adult without worrying about negative consequences stemming from their disclosures. This is something friends and neighbors can also do. The ultimate goal of therapy with victims of conjugal violence is for children to gain communication skills, personal security, self-worth, affect regulation skills and to minimally understand their past family experiences so that they can build healthy relationships. Viewed from a developmental perspective, these are the very relational competencies that develop across the life cycles in preparation for later satisfying roles as partners and parents (Carroll, Badger & Yang, 2006). Children can learn that reasoning and discussion rather than fighting can be strategies to adopt and practice so as to ensure positive relationships later on based on fairness and justice. Through the experience of interactions of this sort, meaningful relationships can blossom and children can imitate something other than the aggressive and violent behaviors that one or both their parents modeled. While parents work on improving their interpersonal issues and behaviors, children could be learning through healthy interactions with counsellors, teachers, friends, neighbors, and their parents in the process of change.

References

Aristotle (1934). *Nicomachean Ethics*, Cambridge, M. A. : Harvard UP.

Addis, M. E. & Mahalik, J. R. (2003). Men, masculinity, and the contexts of helping seeking, *American Psychologist*, 5-14.

Bandura, A. (1973). *Aggression: A social learning analysis*. Englewod Cliffs, N. J. : Prentice-Hall.

Braten, S. (1998). *Intersubjective communication and emotion in early ontogeny*. Cambridge: Cambridge UP.

Carroll, J. S., Badger, S. & Yang, C. (2006). The ability to negotiate or the ability to Love? Evaluating the developmental domains of marital competence. *Journal of Family Issues, 27*, 1001-1032.

Chamberland, C. (2003). Violence Parentale et Violence Conjugale. Des Réalités Plurielles, Multidimensionelles et Interreliées. Sainte. Foy, Québec: PUQ.

Condly, S. J. (2006). Resilience in children. A review of literature with implications for education. *Urban Education, 41*, 211-236.

Damaiso, A. R. (1994). *Descartes' error: Emotion, reason and the human brain*. New York: Avon Books.

DiGiuseppe, R., Tafrate, R. C. (2001). A comprehensive treatment model for anger disorders. *Psychotherapy, 38*, 262-271.

Edleson, J. L. (1999). Children's Witnessing of Adult Domestic Violence. *Journal of Interpersonal Violence*, vol. 14, 839-870.

Ekman, P. & Friesen, W. V. (1975). *Unmasking the face. Englewood Cliffs*, NJ: Prentice-Hall, Inc.

Jaffe, P., Wolfe, D. & Wilson, S. (1990). *Children of battered women.* Newbury Park, CA: Sage.

Humphreys, C., Mullender, A., Thiara, R., & Skamballis, A. (2006). 'Talking to my Mum' Developing Communication Between Mothers and Children in the Aftermath of Domestic Violence. *Journal of Social Work, 6*, 53-63.

Kassinove, H., Sukhodolsky, D., Tsytsarev, S. & Solovyova, S. (1997). Self-reported anger episodes in Russia and America. *Journal of Social Behavior and Personality, 12*, 301-324.

Kennedy-Moore, E. & Watson, J. C. (1999). *Expressing Emotion. Myths, Realities and Therapeutic Strategies*, New York: Guilford Press.

Lee, M. -Y. (2001). Marital Violence: Impact on Children's Emotional Experiences, Emotional Regulation and Behaviors in a Post-Divorce/Separation Situation, *Child and Adolescent Social Work Journal, 18*, 137-162.

Maughan, A, Cicchetti, D. (2002). Impact of Child Maltreatment and Interadult Violence on Children's Emotion Regulation Abilities and Socioemotional Adjustment, *Child Development, 73*, 1525-1542.

Merril, L. L., Thomsen, C. J., Crouch, J. L., May, P., Gold, S. R. & Milner, J. S. (2005). Predicating Adult Risk of Child Physical Abuse From Childhood Exposure to Violence: Can Interpersonal Schemata Explain the Association? *Journal of Social and Clinical Psychology, 24*, 981-1002.

Mikulincer, M. (1998). Adult attachment style and individual differences in functional versus dysfunctional anger. *Journal of Personality and Social Psychology, 74*, 215-524.

Osofsky, J. D. (2003). Prevalence of Children's exposure to Domestic Violence and Child Maltreatment: Implications for Prevention and Intervention. *Clinical Child and Family Psychology* Review, *6*, 161-170.

Pennebaker, J. W. (1990). *Opening Up. The healing power of expressing emotions.* New York: Guilford Press.

Scalia, J. (2002). *Intimate Violence.* New York, N. Y. : Columbia UP.

Statistics Canada. (2002). *Family Violence in Canada: A Statistical Profile 2002* (85-224-XIE). Ottawa: Statistics Canada and Canadian Centre for Justice Studies. www.statscan.ca

Tangney, J. P., Hill-Barlow, D., Wagner, P. E., Marschall, D. E., Bornenstein, J. K., Sanftner, J, Mohr, T. & Gramzow, R. (1996). Assessing the individual differences in constructive versus destructive responses to anger across the life span. *Journal of Personality and Social Psychology, 70*, 780-796.

Wolfe, D. A., Crooks, C. V., Vivien, Lee, McIntyre-Smith, & Jaffe, P. G., 2003). The Effects of Children's exposure to Domestic Violence: A Meta-Analysis and Critique. *Clinical Child and Family Psychology Review*, vol. 6, 171-187.

Discussion after Cynthia Martiny's Presentation

Michael Schleifer: Let's take a few questions now. Okay! Let's start with the AA because I didn't understand the answer. Paul had said that what you were saying in your group sounded a little bit like the AA example but you said it's not the same.

Cynthia Martiny: I'll explain it. In AA the idea is that there are specifics steps to follow and there is what we call a witnessing moment where they talk about how they feel. However, there is no follow up on that. So many of the AA survivors come into therapy to deepen and to change. Whereas AA can be a way to ventilate and to explore but without the specific work on exactly what it is to unlink or to discover. So it's the first level where they can learn to control emotions. Whereas I'm in favor of changing the distortions and the triggers that provoke the anger and the violent behavior. It's a little more: that's how I see it, restructuring.

Catherine Meyor: Is it true that 50% of therapies succeed?

Cynthia Martiny: Yes, about 50% of the men who engaged in therapy persevered, and we're talking about conjugal violence, yes, they finish therapy.

Catherine Meyor: okay so what happens to the other 50%?

Cynthia Martiny: The other 50% drop out, they repeat behaviors, they try other techniques (medicine, marijuana, leaving their wives, etc.) but they don't finish the process to go through change.

Catherine Meyor: What I understand is that for those who fail, they fail, and sometimes they succeed and the succeeding moments have to do with the underlying emotion of anger, sometimes doing with the past. There's a change which will allow them to get to this basic element of their past. My question is: is there necessarily underlying anger, something like sadness or abuse. Can we just cure anger of a murdering sort? Is there pure anger that makes it difficult for us to control? Is it possible that there is anger that is not related to childhood past experiences?

Cynthia Martiny: Yes, of course! Pure anger. It would probably have a different intensity in the way that it is reacted upon. For example, somebody can come into therapy because his wife wants to divorce him, and the only thing that makes him angry is that she wants 90% of his salary. And so, we don't have to go far into his childhood to help him become less violent, he needs financial help. And so the answer is yes, and it's a much faster therapy process.

Catherine Meyor: Okay you have underlying reasons and underlying emotions but is there pure anger, no causes? There are mean and angry people? Is it possible that maybe you keep looking for reasons but there are no causes, it's just pure meanness?

Wendy Turgeon: Physiological, like Gage here?

Cynthia Martiny: Well they probably wouldn't come in for therapy. Because the motivation for going into therapy is that they want to change, so the purely angry person wouldn't come into a therapeutic situation.

Pierre Laurendeau: You talk about the necessity in psychotherapy to revisiting and actually re-feeling the emotion as a part of the therapy. I work in Philosophy for Children, with discussions and we work on re-understanding anger or any emotion, but not reliving the emotion. Is it possible for you?

Cynthia Martiny: It's possible for me and it happens. There is, for example, there is a man (in Yalom) whose wife is dying and she is very difficult to live with, so there's a moral dilemma: leave her and she's alone, stay and be an absolutely difficult person to live with. Which is better for her? He's caught, it can be thought rationally and it will take a long time, it takes a long time, and at some point he's just going to exhaust himself and just find a solution. Or he can start to feel the pain that the situation makes him emotionally disturbed and he evacuates that and then realizes what is important: more important the relationship or more important himself to survive? And very often the emotion is the guide because he is able to ask what's making him cry? Where is the sadness? That helps him identify the decision and which way he goes. So for what I've experienced up to now, and it's been 7 years, my experience is we can talk about it, and he'll rationalize it and come up with millions of answers and reasons, when he actually feels it, that's where he is guided by the emotion. It could be wrong, but it goes faster.

Paul Harris: He might be guided by the emotion but that doesn't confirm ultimate authenticity at all. It could be that he would have been better off not re-feeling this sense of frustration, recrimination, anger which this appalling situation is upon him, and explore it in a more intellectualized fashion. I know, it seems to look like a terrible dilemma.

Cynthia Martiny: Yes, I hear what you're saying. It could be, but if he doesn't go there, because nobody will cry on purpose, so they will not cry and leave therapy and they're going to keep thinking about it. See that's where there is no choice on my part: if a man doesn't want to feel, he won't.

Pierre Laurendeau: I think that in a Community of Inquiry, which is where in Philosophy for Children we have discussions, it is not purely rational. There has to be a feeling component.

Pierre Lebuis: But there is a crisis moment. I'm not sure.

Pierre Laurendeau: I'm not sure! When the men are in therapy with you, they are not necessarily in the crisis stage at the moment?

Cynthia Martiny: It's very rare for a man to be in therapy if he is not in a crisis state. Actually men are really resistant to getting help, they are not help seekers. And literature recognizes that therapy is really good for women. But men are not the biggest *clientèle* out there. They only go when they've lost their job, they're probably threatened to lose their wives, and their children and they are practically suicidal and the court has forced them.

Michael Schleifer: In some of the groups, they have no choice, the crisis is such that they're stay to prison or they're going to be in Cynthia's group. Is that possible?

Cynthia Martiny: Yes! I'm not doing that alone, there are two therapists, and there's always a man next to me.

Pierre Laurendeau: But I have two senses of a crisis: one sense is a situation right now which is a crisis and the other is a situation but I don't leave and can't talk about it. For me it's two different things.

Gérard Boutin: Is there only a positive aspect when you express your anger? Because you said: "anger expression therefore is necessary in maintaining emotional and physical fitness." There's also a dark side of expressing anger. Could you say a word about that?

Cynthia Martiny: Yes, well if there is repression and anger is not expressed, then there's a correlation between mental health issues and also physiological health issues, and that's been shown by many studies recently. We know about psychosomatic tendencies and also we know that people who don't express their emotions get sick.

Gérald Boutin: I have another question also. When you talk about education, it is not so easy to teach a child to express his emotions, anger, etc. We have a master's student here at l'UQAM, Francine Veilleux, who is working on verbal violence, in her school study. I remember you said that we need to pay attention to that problem, that to avoid violence is not so good either; to ignore violence is the same as pretending it didn't happen. This is the same line of thinking.

Cynthia Martiny: Yes, I think I'm coherent, predictable. In that sense I said that to totally say it's the wrong behavior makes it so that you don't take the opportunity for the educational situation to discuss it and start to choose the values that are . . .

Michael Schleifer: To put it into context, I have a student who is looking at verbal violence in classroom, which has become prevalent; 68% of teachers in Quebec are saying that children are verbally violent, this is the problem. And in this context, Cynthia as the evaluator of her thesis said "well you have a prejudice, don't you?" She is a teacher that thinks that verbal violence, including swearing and all the rest, is bad! And she said "Yes! All teachers think that" and Cynthia said "well you've got to have an open mind!" So as today, she is reminding us that anger can be good, it's not the anger that's bad, it could be good or bad, you also told us that verbal violence could be . . .

Cynthia Martiny: It creates an opportunity for discussion. If we just say it's not acceptable; then you have told the person who has been verbally violent – who is showing themselves, and disclosing a part of themselves – that the behavior is not tolerated, I am not interested, whereas it can become an educational situation for the child and the teacher and the others in the group. They can learn about it: "how does it affect me? What do I think? How do I feel? Where does that come from? What is the consensus in this room about that?"

Michael Schleifer: On the general question of anger as an emotion, that you defended today, being neither *en soi* negative or positive, but making the distinction there is perhaps more of a consensus, perhaps . . . On the other issue, which you wanted to defend, I believe that even verbal violence of a sort, of somebody calling their teacher horrible names, using racist remarks, and not that you think it's a good thing, but you want us to remember that: "where is that coming from? Where did they learn it? There is positive aspects. . . you have more or less of a consensus. The teachers that are all there didn't buy it, they said: "We want that out!" Barbara Colorossa who works on bullying (her work is well known) says it's unacceptable. She was a nun then a philosopher, then a teacher and one of her main things is that when she is in a classroom and she hears that a child says to a other child: "you bitch" or "fuck you" or whatever, she stops the classroom and screams at that child in a dramatic way. But then she will take the child aside and talk to them. So for her it's negative.

Gérald Boutin: I think that there's a moral aspect also.

Cynthia Martiny: Yes! Which can be discovered or it can be imposed. And I'm going for the discovery!

Ann Sharp: I would like to come back to this idea of pure anger, pure happiness. I think that if we agree to that, then the education of the emotion is going to go down. My view is that something underlies every emotion; I might not be conscious of why I'm anxious, I might not be conscious of why I'm angry. Sharon said sometimes you're in the midst to be really angry and you don't know why you're angry. But I would assume that if you would want to work on it you might not be right with the reason you come up with, you might talk to your friends, you might talk to your spouse, you say "why can't you be happy today?" But sometimes, you can bring to consciousness the underlying belief that you hold, and it's only then that you have a chance to evaluate it. In other words: "is it appropriate anger? Is it a good guide to me? Should I be feeling angry?" Because I would be thinking with the Community of Inquiry one of the questions we can ask each other, not so much with the violence, I tend to agree with the nun, if it's there then it's there. But I think we should ask ourselves why. But with the emotions I don't see anything wrong with saying: "Pierre you seem very assertive today, you're cutting people left and right, what's with you?" He might not know. I don't see anything wrong with that because he might not know! I'm just saying I'm not sure there is such a thing as pure anger, pure happiness, or pure anything.

Leonie Richler: I just wanted to comment on the men when they're expressing their raw emotions and making them so vulnerable. I just wanted you to address the fact that they're in a group and what impact that has on the shift. I don't think it's just the fact that they're expressing their emotions and being vulnerable to two leaders but it's also to their peers and that has a tremendous impact. And when you're working with children in a group, you also see the shift take place a lot faster when it's in a group setting. It's not the same as just one-on-one with the therapist. As a matter of fact, from my understanding from the literature on men with conjugal violence that there's not much head way on one-to-one psychotherapy, it's really has to do with that impact within the group. With children there's verbal abuse and conflicts that may not get to the point where they feel violent. When I'm able to get two, three and four kids together that's when I find the shift takes place and they're able to move. If it's just with myself and the child, it's work and energy forever. But when I get the group together, I can still do the same work, that shift, it just moves a lot faster. But I find too, I have to get a little bit more to that raw emotion in order to make that shift. It seems to be that it is the vulnerability that makes it. I just wanted you to comment on that.

Cynthia Martiny: To express the emotion in its raw state publicly makes it real. It's difficult to say that it didn't happen. Because when they hear themselves, when all of us feel an emotion and recognize that other people have witnessed it and have been with us, it intensifies the recognition that this is a valid moment. And that must be authentic. And that's what your question was because I wouldn't put myself through that spontaneously, that's just not something I would do to myself. So I think that the group does have that effect.

Leonie Richler: Just one more little thing: the skill and let's say the problem within a group to deepen the understanding is the real skill because otherwise you get a group of people who feel sorry for themselves. That's the danger of a group. You don't want a whole group of people kind of feeling sorry. So the skill really is to get them to be moving from that raw emotion to a deeper understanding to move on.

Wendy Turgeon: I'm still interested is this 50/50 success story thing and a little while ago it was suggested that the difference was between those who choose to participate in the group and those who don't. No? Okay! But in any case, obviously not everyone chooses, maybe many of them are mandated to do this, they are required to. Now I hear another suggestion that maybe it's the actual efficacy of the group itself, one group might be working well, another might not work well. I'm curious if there's any way to study that? Which groups or which situations effective? Why do some of them make it? Why do some of them don't?

Cynthia Martiny: There's been lot of research on perseverance and there's somebody called Prochaska . . . he talks about the change process and there are stages of the motivation for change which has to be examined. Some of the reasons for coming into the group may just be to make their lives simpler, and that doesn't seem like having a holding effect on anyone. This may be because life can go on in spite of the fact that nothing has changed, but the fact that the man has gone to therapy often means his wife puts less pressure on him because she thinks that it's secure; so, he goes home, it's fine, they don't talk about it anymore, then he just drops out. But the realisation that change could have a positive effect on many aspects of his life, and he sees that, the motivation deepens to have had some positive effect on his relationships, including either his wife, his children or maybe his future relationships, because there's been a lot of reasons for it to be complicated. Then the motivation will change, it's going to be a little bit higher. So I think the more abstract it becomes, the less concrete, the more effective the therapy process will be. Does that make sense? So it's like the difference: if the motivation is to stay out of jail and they've been out of jail for four or five weeks then the reason for being in therapy has been taken care of.

Wendy Turgeon: Is there something you can do that will help us get better as opposed to recidivism or dropping out?

Cynthia Martiny: If the therapeutic relationship can become intense, the trust is there, then yes. But that has to do with the man and the therapist of course. Because there is a desire for closeness and understanding and so that becomes in itself a reason for going into therapy and the reciprocal relationships within the group, there's a large cohesiveness, when a man goes in a group, it's somehow restructuring his family life that sometimes never was as close as these men can be. The real intimacy that can be created within the group is sometimes a draw and keeps men in group for a long time. Sometimes for years!

Phil Guin: I just wonder if Moby Dick would profit from the analysis?

Cynthia Martiny: I don't think so. I don't think he would even come.

Michael Schleifer: (laughing) Is that a joke?

Phil Guin: No it's not a joke! We're talking about angry people. Their whole lives are caught up in a sort of animosity towards everything! And I'm just asking if you have a more specific kind of person that is having trouble with their wife or their children or whatever and these people may or may not profit. But I think that there are people out there, some of them are pretty dangerous.

Cynthia Martiny: Yes. I'd rather not have them in my group, but I can choose. The truth is they are resistant to change because it's really effective to be violent: they get what they want. I think you were a little bit alluding to that way too. It's "I got the swing and I'm violent and people have given me what I want! So why would I change?" There's no reason, the motivation for change is just not there.

Michael Schleifer: I'm wondering if we can make the link also with what Bill said, temperament was mentioned as a factor in the end. Now, temperament as far as I followed it, in this regard you mentioned a generally angry person. But Aristotle was brilliant in this way, I mean, he said anger is really complicated and he gave us four words for it one of them was the irascible person. And the irascible person sounds like somebody who is just generally by temperament, angry, that is he tends to get angry more quickly than others and his anger lasts longer than others and he's just that kind of person. And it goes back to early infancy because temperament, as you were saying is hard wired. If we take temperament seriously then is that what you meant, I mean it's almost from early infancy, long before we're conscious and the child knows how to use the word anger and any other word with that matter, some things are happening in his little baby life and some of them by temperament are going to be what you name as angry people. And so maybe Catherine's question is right after all, she says, but well, there are just angry people. Daniel Goleman who always reminds us temperament is very important, there are just timid children and nontimid children, and there are angry people and non-angry people. But then he also says, in his book *Emotional Intelligence*, temperament is not destiny; it's his famous slogan. So you can take very timid children, and work very hard on them, and make them less timid. I suppose also that we can take someone who by temperament is the angry person, and work very hard on them, then they can become less angry.

Catherine Meyor: The idea is that I make a difference between good and bad. But can't we just accept that the bad exist? And then work with that?

Michael Schleifer: If we take that the starting point was if we take violence, and certainly the violence that Cynthia works with is bad, we seem to have a consensus about that. Somebody who takes their wife and batters her with a hammer or their children is bad; we agree on that. But then Catherine is saying: "look, we all agree it's bad, why don't we stop there and say it's bad – purely bad– and we have to work with that badness." And before you said no, you don't think pure, well you were talking about pure anger, and now we're back to pure badness.

Ann Sharp: Oh! But violence is an action and anger an emotion.

Michael Schleifer: So pure anger in your view does not exist.

Ann Sharp: I hope that if I work on it with my friends long enough I could come up with a reason of why I'm this angry.

Paul Harris: Can I just come back to the 50% who do succeed? Something more positive! So I'd like to relate it to the discussion we had with Bill about the developmental change he observed. Again it seems to me that these men are moving in two different directions, maybe both at once, but maybe it's important to talk of the distinction. So on the one hand, it could be that in the context of these group therapeutic experiences they are alerted to the suffering they cause. And they in some sense integrate that more effectively in their conception of what it is they're doing when they engage in these violent tasks. I think that's the expectation Bill might have of what was the therapeutic change that you are bringing about.

Cynthia Martiny: Because you only get that after they express their feelings about their own suffering, when they themselves have been recognized. . . . The availability to the other is not immediate.

Paul Harris: So, taken to a point that they have to get some validation of their own feelings of anger before they can begin to empathize . . . I'm blocking at that empathic possibility, it's the critical moment. But it's also possible, I think it begets at the alternative of what you were saying also. It's that in some sense you give them a moral perspective, in other words they lived in a world where it was acceptable in their own eyes for them to be a violent man.

Cynthia Martiny: See, that's what I was afraid of.

Paul Harris: Whereas it's possible in the context strictly in this group, where, in various degrees, all the men are trying to move away from violence as a way of life. The group ends up encouraging them to think of themselves as possibly capable to bring this violence under control, and to live a different way and to be in some sense critical of themselves, disappointed in themselves when they engage in those acts.

Cynthia Martiny: That comes to your point earlier about socialized standards . . .

Paul Harris: Yes! I guess I'm inviting you to hold those two possibilities in mind and to ask yourself which is the more plausible. What are the changes? Because in some sense you are seeing a developmental change.

Cynthia Martiny: Of course. I've had this discussion with Michael. And when I hear you talking about the children and I do find similarities often. But why not both at the same time? I don't think that we have to make a choice. I think that both processes are going on at the same time, simultaneously and probably more than just those two.

Michael Schleifer: That's what I was going to say earlier when you raised the two interpretations of Bill's research parallel and you've done it again now with this. Let me try the following: On the one hand you have a possible interpretation of what goes on in happy victimization, and also people working with conjugal violence also in terms of something like empathy, and an increased empathy. And the other possibility, which Paul's been throwing out, perhaps in favor, is what is going on is in fact a development of morality, if I can sum that up. This might be different from Bill's perspective and you are throwing it out to Cynthia. So I think the following: like Cynthia, I also believe that the two come together. Now let me try the following thing, it depends a lot on what we mean by empathy (this seems to be the key). The question is: Can one be empathic and be bad? That is, can one have true empathy and all of its manifestations (seeing the point of view of other, verbally and non-verbally, the affective components), but do it for his own needs, do it to manipulate others.

Now we saw a play recently, in which you have a person who is defined, by the playwrite, it's described as a person who is at the highest level of empathy. Which means that she feels it and it's terrific and understands everything and she's actually a therapist and all the rest of it; but we find out that – I'm going to give away the end of the play – what she does is for her own ends. She takes a person who she pretends to fall in love with and he believes it, but she actually puts him up as part of her doctoral thesis showing that she can change him and then she manipulates him, purely and thoroughly. We all are seeing this person as being a bad person in terms of morality, or are aghast to what she did! She really took this guy, pretended to love him, had sex with him and then took photos of it and it was her doctoral thesis which she got really high marks! But we all understand she had to be technically at the highest level of empathy, she'd followed all the courses, she could read other people's manifestations, she was a terrific therapist but she did it not for the ends of the others but for her own ends. And my view about this is that you cannot be truly empathic, I don't believe a person can be truly empathic and not also be moral. So for me empathy has a moral dimension.

Ann Sharp: But isn't that why Nussbaum makes a distinction between empathy and compassion? She gives the example of not a psychiatrist but a torturer. A good torturer is empathic, a good torturer is somebody who even senses that . . . What she says is in that sense is the more empathic you are the better manipulator you can be.

Michael Schleifer: Well I confronted her at the American Philosophical Association on this point and I confronted her because I think that she misuses the term empathy.

Ann Sharp: Not compassion though! She says compassion forces you to be moral. . . but what does empathy mean? It means that I can put myself; I can see the world from your perspective. It's an imaginative jump.

Gérald Boutin: This comment is about empathy, it seems to me that we are just thinking about humanistic psychology with Carl Rogers. And I think there are many definitions of empathy. It's complex.

Cynthia Martiny: Yes, I agree! It took me three years to define it in my doctoral thesis.

Lee Londei: I just want to say two things, first of all I think the play Michael referred to is called "The Shape of Things" and it's also a movie that you can rent easily. Secondly, I would just like to say that I think it's important, at least it's important for me to highlight, that empathy is for me an exchange between two people and in the play and as you're describing it, it matters who the recipient is, simply.

Cynthia Martiny: If you define empathy as a process, then the recipient will give some reciprocity to the way it's been received, and so it will continue. But in the way you're using it it's unidirectional and not bi-directional.

Michael Schleifer: Which is one of our reasons for not accepting empathy as being manipulation. Because we see empathy, in addition to all its complexity: verbal, non-verbal, affective, cognitive, etc. There is a dimension of intersubjectivity is a process. And in manipulation, one clear thing is that the person who is empathic may have all those dimensions but one clear thing is not going on, that the recipient is not involved in this. . .

Ann Sharp: Did you see *Cold Blood*? Do you remember in the end, when the character starts crying in front of the prisoner and says "I'm sorry." I think he recognized that he used his empathy for his ends.

Michael Schleifer: Compassion, just that. Empathy can be many things as we know. It's multicomplex, we know. In the way we are using it, we're using it not only as multicomplex such that it will have a moral component.

Compassion is linked in English to pity and in French it's the same thing, pitié. We have pity when someone is suffering, which is very important, no doubt that compassion is important too, but you don't ever use the word pity or compassion when you're trying to tune in to the other person's successes or joys or pride. But empathy however, does have that general understanding.

William Arsenio: Just saying the same things that we've talked about. The correlation between the affective and cognitive component of empathy. It's been 30-35 years in psychology since people were arguing about that kind of issue and I think it's really important. When I understand empathy, I think Fesbach and other people later, they focused on the idea that you have to have both a cognitive understanding, an accurate reading: What is this other person feeling? That's one piece, but then the other piece is that you need to have an emotional reaction that is more or less consistent with this other person's experiences. It doesn't have to be the exact same emotion but broadly consistent. And so, for me, some people were studying psychopathy, like Paul Frigg, he distinguishes that there are people that are very good at reading other people's emotional cues, so they got that part of it, they are very accurate and veridical and so on. But they are using that information to manipulate and control other folks. In that psychopathy skill it makes a clear distinction between the cognitive awareness and the emotional resonance. And so for me there's empathy automata and my definition includes the emotion resonance and maybe that's part of what is going on. Maybe they're not quite tied together as tightly as I think. But when I think about it, I can't think about it without the moral dimension. There are people who talk about the empathic and get aroused, Nancy Eisenberg talks about that and you can essentially get over aroused and just tune out the other person because you can't cope with it yourself. So there are different routes by which empathy can become not useful for addressing other people's problems.

Michael Schleifer: But it could get mixed up with, we know, contagion, and projection and other false states but there is that too, the psychological dimension. For example, the person in "The Shape of Things" who was completely empathic but manipulated somebody using her huge power of empathy, is not truly empathic. She had everything except that moral component, yet maybe that moral component is crucial.

Paul Harris: I think, Michael, you are proposing that empathy has this moral component almost by definition. And I sense that Bill is beginning to agree with you. (laughter) You were tempted to agree with Michael and it seems to me to conflate too many things and to make it very difficult to tell an interesting developmental story. Here's the reason: if you take non-human primates, chimpanzees for example, you will see some embryonic empathy even in those species. For example, there will be a fight between two of the members and a third will come over and help them and will offer empathy gestures to the one who's been victimized not to the one who was the aggressor. If you watch the comforting person, it's not necessarily that they themselves are feeling distress, so in some sense in putting themselves in the shoes of this other person, because they don't feel the exact emotion themselves, they're reading what the other member of the group feels. You see very much the same thing in 18 months to 2 year olds, they also go over when they see somebody who's hurt themselves or in distress or crying. They put their arm around them like, they go to fetch comforting objects, they try many tricks to try to make this person feel better.

Now, Michael, it seems to me that you're faced with a choice, either you say this is not genuine empathy, or you allow the fact that there is genuine empathy at this stage without a moral component. And that's my point, that would be the way I would go. I would say also even as a process 4 and 5 years olds that Bill is talking about, they understand what it is in some circumstances to be empathic and may display empathy. But in these circumstances, where they've been free agents they're pursuing their own aims but they're not seeing it in some sense to be obligatory upon them to be empathic such that it would short circuit their free agency. So it's in that sense that it seems to me important to distinguish between empathy, which is in some sense a primate characteristic and human empathy, which I agree eventually has a moral component.

Cynthia Martiny: So you're saying that the moral component developmentally kicks in?

Michael Schleifer: We don't disagree with that. We see empathy in stages and we see rudimentary empathy or the roots of empathy at very early ages, and in our book we have pictures of these roots of empathy which exist. The question is kids are generally kind, they drag their mother along when they see somebody else is in pain . . . They'll drag their own mother along to come and help. So I agree that the primate showing this rudimentary empathy are more like young infants who show it too perhaps, I think human infants show it in certain ways that other animals don't, but that's another question. But I do think they're the same. But full blown empathy, as we like to say, will have a moral component.

Cynthia Martiny: I like what you say, Paul, it makes me think of Bateson when he was trying to discover pure altruism and was having a very difficult time. Because he was finding empathic responses, that actually the motivation was to alleviate an emotional distress. So people were jumping in the river and saving people and dying, and the reason was perhaps to have a free ticket to go to heaven. That's the example he used, and I thought it shocking at first, but then it made sense. So as the developmental moral component develops, that's what we are hoping to find and we would love you to tell us what age. But it doesn't seem to be age related because I see men as still developmentally looking for that moral component sometimes. So I'm wondering if we couldn't find a universal type of test to find out what triggers that, the development of the moral component.

Sharon Bailin: I just want to say that it seems to me in your examples that the rudiments of the moral component are there, so it's not just in the case of young children case that there's some reading of the emotion of the other but in order to manipulate them but there is some reading and there's some attempt to alleviate the distress, it's not a full blown moral component but there's a beginning of the moral dimension in there. It's quite different from the case of "The Shape of Things" where someone is reading to do something really immoral.

Paul Harris: Well by saying that, it brings us back to the fact of a 2 year olds where it's not obligatory!

Cynthia Martiny: But my fear is that it's not even obligatory for counsellors when they finish their Master's. I wonder how can we, as educators, create this climate and this situation that we can be assured that we educated it in before they finish their diploma and they're out there treating other people. That's an issue that I don't have an answer for.

Michael Schleifer: Because, just to tune in and make it specific, in forming our therapists and counsellors, which we do, some of whom are excellent, they're at the highest level and one of the ingredients being, them being empathic, they fulfill every definition of it but we're never completely convinced that they actually have the moral component to it. And that's the problem. Can you be truly empathic but nevertheless just have the technique? Or is it true empathy? But I see your challenge, the one you gave to Bill, I can see that for us too. 'Cause you're saying the true story is not going to be told because we're confounding perhaps too many things and we have to separate them out and that is a challenge. I'm hoping we can get help with this little symposium in a little way to make the story better, if we're confusing it by conflating two things and I got perhaps an ally now, a new ally. (laughter)

William Arsenio: What's missing in the 3 year old's sense of empathy that makes it non moral? 'Cause for me the part of empathy is that another person has this reaction, I recognize that reaction and I have an emotional response. You're crying, I see you're crying, I understand what's going on, it makes me feel sad, I want to go over and alleviate. So I'm a bystander and I understand what to do. Now on the other hand, I'm a 4 years old, I just wanted your swing, I pushed you off the swing, I got the swing and now I look down on the ground and I go: Oh! Wait a second. You're crying, I understand your emotion I feel this response inside of me and go to the one who fell and that I think Oh my God! I'm the one who did that, I'm the one who's responsible for creating this other person's pain. And that to me are the rudiments of moral development. So having that kind of emotional response, and realizing that you were the free agent, you were the active agent in this interaction who caused the pain for the other person. And when you put that piece on top of that, you're aware of that, then how is that non-moral?

Paul Harris: It's not enough, because this child could say "I'm the author of your distress," which brings us back to the discussions we were having about verbalizing authorship. But we could also say that circumstances are such that I needed this swing and therefore in the context of my selfish action, I was the author of your distress. You only get to be moral when you're saying to yourself "In and so far as I'm the author of your distress, and in pursuit of my own ends, I should not have done that."

Michael Schleifer: Perhaps feel badly about it, then perhaps, want to do something about it.

Wendy Turgeon: It's the prescriptive claim you are looking for: I ought not to have done that.

Part III

Development

Chapter 5
Understanding the Flow of Thoughts and Feelings
Paul L. Harris and Suzanne Duke, Harvard University

Understanding the Flow of Thoughts and Feelings

In this chapter, we discuss children's developing appreciation of the flow of thoughts and feelings that constitutes our inner life. First, we describe some early experimental work that focused on children's understanding of the time course of emotion. The main conclusion from that work is that 6 year olds and even 4 year olds realize that an initially intense emotion persists beyond the precipitating situation but gradually wanes over time. Next, we discuss whether children understand that thoughts about an earlier emotionally charged situation could moderate that waning process. Specifically, we ask if children understand that external reminders of an emotional event are likely to trigger thoughts about the earlier event and thereby reactivate the emotion associated with the event. We conclude that preschoolers have a surprisingly clear insight into the impact of such cues. Next, we discuss why young children are so insightful about this link between thinking about the past and the re-activation of feelings. We speculate that children are often invited to explain themselves when their emotional state is not consistent with their current circumstances. Finally, we ask about children's wider understanding of the stream-of-consciousness. In particular, we focus on their comprehension of the fact that thoughts – including those thoughts that reactivate emotion – are not always under voluntary control. We conclude that although 5 and 6 year olds clearly appreciate the impact that thoughts about the past can have on one's current emotional state, they do not fully appreciate the extent to which such thoughts may be involuntary. By the age of 8, children have a more comprehensive insight into the way that such involuntary thoughts can disrupt the gradual waning of emotion that normally succeeds an emotionally charged encounter. By implication, 8 year olds are well placed to identify and report on such intrusive thoughts – and even to adopt strategies for their suppression.

Understanding the Time-course of Emotion

A considerable body of work shows that young children – even 3 and 4 year olds – are good at grasping and remembering the emotional implications of various situations. They realize that a loss is likely to make you sad, that obstacles are likely to make you angry, that threatening situations and creatures will make you afraid, and so forth. Thus, if we tell preschoolers about the situation facing a story protagonist, they are good at predicting how the protagonist will feel (Borke, 1971). Conversely, if we tell them how a protagonist feels, preschoolers are good at proposing a situation that might have provoked such feelings (Trabasso, Stein & Johnson, 1981).

This knowledge of situation-emotion links is obviously foundational for navigating the social world and for making personal decisions. It allows children to anticipate both how they and other people will feel if they encounter or create a given situation. At the same time, knowledge of such links does not guarantee that children fully understand the sequelae of an emotionally charged experience. Consider one key aspect of such an experience. Even after we leave the precipitating situation – whether it is a quarrel, an accident, or a sporting event – the emotion triggered by the situation is likely to persist and gradually wane over time. Of course, episodes sometimes leave permanent scars but generally speaking our emotions grow less intense as we distance ourselves from the precipitating event.

Given the ubiquity of this waning process, children might recognize and anticipate it. On the other hand, if children are strict 'situation' theorists with respect to emotion, they might not acknowledge its time-course. They might assume that our emotions are aroused by the precipitating situation but dissipate more or less instantaneously thereafter when we move on to a different situation. Alternatively, they might assume that an emotion once triggered has a more or less indefinite life that long outlasts the event that triggered it.

To explore these possibilities, we told children stories about a child who woke up in the morning and learned about either a very negative or very positive event (e. g., a bicycle being stolen; receiving a dog) or a mildly negative or mildly positive event (e. g., a bicycle being scratched; a dog recovering from an illness). Children were then asked to say how happy or sad the protagonist would feel that morning and at various later points in the day. Figure 1 illustrates 6 year olds' judgment as a function of Time of Day and Type of Event (Harris, Guz, Lipian & Man-Shu, 1985, Experiment 1). As can be seen, 6 year olds judged that both negative and positive emotion would persist for some time beyond the initial encounter but eventually revert to some intermediate baseline.

Figure 1. Mean judged intensity of negative emotion (where 5 = very sad and 1 = very happy) as a function of Time of Day and Type of Event

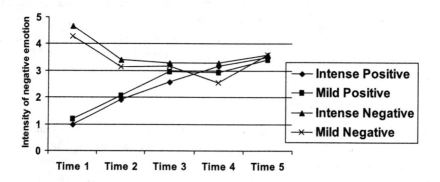

In two follow-up studies with both English and Chinese 6 year olds, this pattern of findings re-emerged. The children judged that a story character's emotion gradually wanes in intensity over time. However, when we asked children to explain the waning pattern that they expected only about half the children explicitly attributed the change to purely mental factors (e. g., "Because he got used to the puppy"

or "Because he forgot"). The rest referred instead to external circumstances (e. g., "Because his bike came back home" or "because he would able to play with friends"). Nevertheless, more explicit probing showed that these 6 year olds did understand the way in which emotion can be modulated by thought. We asked children how the story protagonist would feel the next day if he or she either thought back to a positive or negative event, or forgot about it. Figure 2 shows English and Chinese children's judgment as a function of Type of Event and Mental Act (Harris et al, 1985; Experiments 2 & 3).

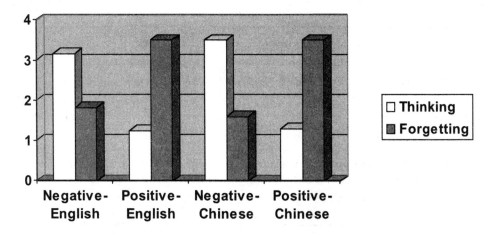

Figure 2. Mean judged intensity of negative emotion (where 4 = very sad and 1 = very happy) as a function of Type of Event (Negative versus Positive) and Mental Act (Thinking versus Forgetting)

The pattern was remarkably similar in England and China: Children judged that the protagonist would feel worse when thinking about a negative event – as opposed to forgetting it. Conversely, they judged that the protagonist would feel better when thinking about a positive event – as opposed to forgetting it. These findings clearly show that children understand that emotion can be reactivated or attenuated depending on one's pattern of thought.

In Experiments 1 and 2, we had also interviewed 4 year olds but their judgments were more difficult to interpret because they appeared to have some difficulty in using the emotion scale that we had devised. In Experiment 4, we re-assessed 4 year olds, having given them some pre-training in the use of the emotion scale. We asked them how a story character would feel immediately, later on that morning, and later on that afternoon. Inspection of Figure 3 shows that 4 year olds also expected the emotion to be intense at first but to wane in strength in the course of the day.

Figure 3. Mean judged intensity of negative emotion (where 5 = very sad and 1 = very happy) as a function of Time of Day and Type of Event

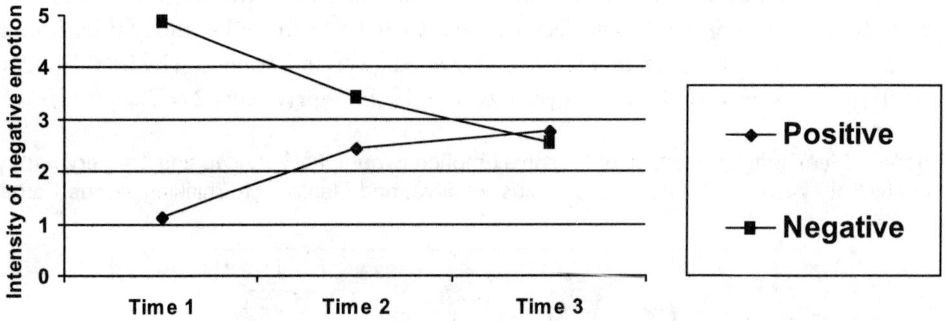

As in the earlier experiments, we also probed children's understanding of the links between thought and emotion. We found that some 4 year olds offered mentalistic explanations for the waning pattern that they expected. Moreover, as Figure 4 reveals, they showed some ability to differentiate between the impact of thinking about versus forgetting the earlier event.

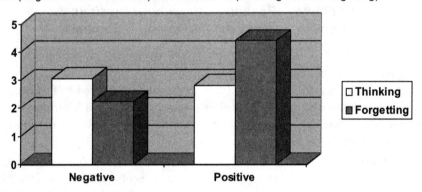

Figure 4. Mean intensity of negative emotion (where 5 = very sad and 1 = very happy) as a function of Type of Event (Negative versus Positive) and Mental Act (Thinking versus Forgetting)

Summing up the results from this series of experiments, it is evident that preschool children have a relatively firm understanding of the fact that emotion wanes over time. In addition, 6 year olds – and, to some extent, even 4 year olds – display an appreciation of the psychological process that underpins that waning process: asked to explain it, they sometimes refer to mentalistic factors such as forgetting or habituation. They also show some understanding of the fact that thinking about the original episode – as opposed to forgetting about it – is likely to re-activate the original emotion.

Reminders of the Past

In the experiments just described, children were asked about the impact of thinking about versus forgetting the earlier, emotionally charged event. The nature of the potentially arousing thought was explicitly mentioned when children were probed – for example: "What would happen the next morning of David started to think about his bicycle? How would he feel?" Lagattuta, Wellman and Flavell (1997) broadened this issue by asking whether preschool children understand that external cues can also be potent re-activators of prior emotion.

In an initial study, they gave 4, 5, and 6 year olds stories in which the protagonist experienced a sad event – for example – the death of a pet fish. Later, the protagonist encountered a reminder of that sad event – for example, the protagonist saw the empty fishbowl and started to feel sad. Children were invited to explain this sad reaction. Lagattuta et al. (1997) found that children often produced what the researchers called *cognitive cuing* explanations. These were responses in which children mentioned three connected parts: (1) the eliciting cue; (2) the thinking it provokes; (3) and the event that is thought about, for example, "He sees the fishbowl and it makes him remember his dead fish. " These were very widespread among 5 and 6 year olds – with almost all children producing at least one *cognitive cuing* explanation but less frequent among 4 year olds – with less than half producing at least one such explanation. Two follow-up studies carried out by Lagattuta et al. (1997) reinforced these conclusions. In these studies, which involved less elaborate stories, even 4 year olds managed to produce cognitive cuing responses, particularly if the cue in question was an object or animal that had actually been involved in the original emotionally charged episode and not just meaningfully associated with it in some way.

Akin to the thinking-forgetting probe used by Harris et al. (1985), children in the initial study were also asked a more explicit pair of questions about the link between thinking and emotion. Specifically, children were asked to say what would happen if the story character either thought about the past loss or thought about a distracting alternative instead. Most 5 and 6 year olds were able to provide at least one mentalistic account of what would happen, for example: "He feels okay because playing the piano is pretty fun and it might take his mind off the fish" By contrast, only one 4 year olds formulated such a response.

Taken together the results from this study consolidate and extend the earlier findings of Harris et al. (1985). They show that 5 and 6 year olds readily understand how a past emotion can be re-activated. They understand that an external object can bring about this re-activation by serving as a visible reminder of the past event and they can put this causal sequence into words. Thus, they frequently offer cognitive cuing explanations that refer to the external cue, the thinking or remembering process triggered by that cue, and the event that is recalled. Second, they understand that thoughts of that past event – even in the absence of any specific external reminder – can re-activate past emotion. Finally, they understand that not thinking about the past event – either via a process of forgetting or by thinking about some distracter – helps to de-activate the emotion.

Why are Young Children so Insightful about the Link between Thinking and Feeling?

The above studies demonstrate quite forcibly that preschool children realize that a person's emotional life and his or her immediate, external circumstances are not inextricably locked together. There may be a disjunction between one's current circumstances and the way one feels. This introduces a major qualification into the general claim that young children think of one's emotional state as being brought about by the situation that one is in. Children clearly recognize that the way we feel at any given moment is closely connected to the flow of thoughts and ideas that occupy our consciousness.

How do children come to this important insight? One possibility is that children figure it out for themselves. More specifically, they notice that there is mismatch between the way they currently feel and the circumstances that they are in. For example, they are at a birthday party but they feel sad. However, a plausible objection to this line of interpretation is that it offers no explanation of why children should do anything more than simply register the mismatch. Simply noticing that one's feelings do not match current reality is not obviously sufficient to trigger an analysis of those feelings in terms of the ongoing flow of thoughts and memories. Thus, it is reasonable to look for alternative explanations.

One plausible alternative is that attentive members of children's social circle alert them to mismatches. Seeing the child express an emotion that is not consonant with his or her current circumstance, adults are likely to probe the reasons: "What's the matter – what's bothering you?" On this hypothesis, children do not spontaneously seek to analyze why their feelings do not match current reality. Instead, they are lead to do so by other people. If this hypothesis is correct, it is reasonable to expect children to be particularly sensitive to the part played by thinking about a prior negative event, as opposed to a prior positive event, in eliciting emotion. After all, caregivers are likely to be especially concerned about children who look distressed in otherwise positive circumstances whereas children who remain cheerful in the face of negative circumstances are likely to appear unproblematic. So, children are likely to find themselves being questioned by parents – and indeed by other children – about why they feel sad or angry when there is no obvious explanation to be found in the immediate situation. For their part, children may be puzzled by friends and siblings who appear to be upset for no apparent reason, seek some clarification, and receive an explanation couched in terms of some earlier episode that continues to evoke negative feelings. Certainly, the analysis of spontaneous conversation confirms that when children and adults pose open-ended questions about emotion, the majority of those questions focus on negative as opposed to positive emotions (Lagattuta & Wellman, 2002).

Taking these considerations into account, it is plausible to expect that children will be likely to offer *cognitive cuing* explanations with respect to negative emotions that do not fit the current (positive) situation. These are the circumstances in which children are especially likely to be quizzed about what is bothering them. They will be less likely to offer cognitive cuing explanations with respect to positive emotions that do not fit the current (negative) situation because they will rarely be asked for an explanation. Lagattuta and Wellman (Experiment 1; 2001) obtained strong support for this prediction. Children were invited to explain negative and positive emotions that either did or did not fit the current situation. Figure 5 shows the number of cognitive cuing explanations that 3, 4, and 5 year olds supplied in each of the four possible combinations.

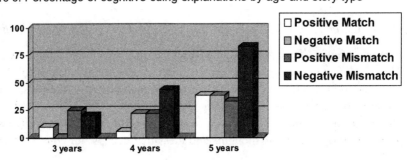

Figure 5. Percentage of cognitive cuing explanations by age and story type

Inspection of Figure 5 shows that cognitive cuing explanations were rare among 3 year olds, but increasingly frequent among 4 and 5 year olds. This increment was especially marked for negative emotions mismatching the story character's current situation. A follow-up study using similar methods and a wider age range produced similar results: 4 and 5 year olds again produced more cognitive cuing explanations for negative emotions that mismatched the situation. Among 7 year olds and adults, the production of such explanations was more wide-ranging. They frequently provided such explanations across the board.

Thus, negative situations that mismatch the current situation appear to offer children an early foothold in their understanding of cognitive cuing. Having secured that foothold, their understanding eventually extends to positive emotions and to emotions that are congruent with the current situation. More generally, these suggestive findings are consistent with a broader set of results showing that children's understanding of mental states, including emotion is guided and facilitated by the extent to which caregivers, notably the mother, engage in conversation with their children about psychological matters (Harris, de Rosnay & Pons, 2005).

Children's Understanding of Intrusive Thoughts and the Nature of Consciousness

In a famous statement about the source of poetry, Wordsworth (1800) spoke of: "emotion recollected in tranquility." He went on to suggest that: "the emotion is contemplated till, by a species of reaction, the tranquility gradually disappears, and an emotion, kindred to that which was the subject of contemplation, is gradually produced, and does itself actually exist in the mind." Wordsworth's emphasis on the tranquil contemplation of past emotion suggests a semi-voluntary and deliberate process of reactivation. Yet it is often the case that we think back to past episodes in an involuntary fashion, thereby triggering unwanted emotions. When do young children start to conceptualize such intrusions into the ordinary flow of consciousness?

To explore this question, Duke and Harris (2006) presented 5 and 8 year old children with stories about a protagonist who was either engaged in a cognitively demanding task (e. g., thinking about math homework) or sitting quietly, not engaged in any particular task. In all stories, irrespective of the protagonist's current activity, children were told that the protagonist began to think about an emotionally charged episode that had occurred on the previous day, for example either a pleasant bicycle ride or alternatively a nasty bicycle accident. To help children conceptualize the sudden thought intruding into consciousness, they were shown a sequence of pictures in each of which the protagonist was portrayed with a thought bubble. The first three pictures showed the protagonist thinking about the math problem, for example, whereas the fourth picture showed the protagonist thinking about the bicycle that had been ridden the previous day.

Having set the scene in this fashion, the experimenter posed various questions about the mental processes of the protagonist. Specifically, children were quizzed about whether the protagonist would: 1) feel the emotion consonant with the prior event (e. g., positive emotion in the case of the pleasant bicycle ride and negative emotion in the case of the bicycle accident); 2) have meant to start thinking about the event; 3) be able to think about both the current and intrusive thought at the same time; and 4) want to stop thinking about the event especially if engaged in a task (such as math homework) and/or if the event in question was negative.

Children could receive a score from 0-4, depending on the number of questions that they answered correctly. The main finding was that 8 year olds showed a more systematic conception of such intrusive thoughts than did 5 year olds. Figure 6 displays the mean number of questions answered by younger and older children as a function of whether the story protagonist was engaged in another cognitive activity or sitting quietly doing nothing.

Figure 6. Mean number of questions answered correctly as a function of age and type of activity.

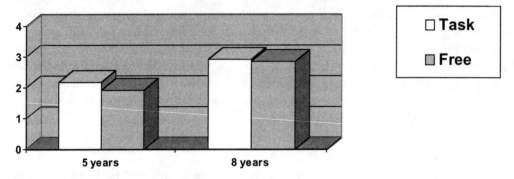

As shown in Figure 6, 8 year olds answered three out of four questions correctly, on average. Children had roughly a 1 in 10 chance of being correct on three or four questions. Just over three-quarters (75.8%) of the 8 year olds reached this target whereas just over one third (37.5%) of the 5 year olds did so.

The flavor of the findings can be conveyed by taking a closer look at children's answers to two of the four questions. One question concerned the protagonist's cognitive intention. In the case of the bicycle story, for example, children were asked: "Does David mean to start thinking about the bicycle ride?" Five year olds were invariably at chance in answering this question. By contrast, 8 year olds were likely to claim that the protagonist did not mean to start thinking about the bicycle ride. This denial was especially frequent when children were asked about the bicycle ride that had resulted in an accident. However, even when the bicycle ride had been pleasant, most 8 year olds appropriately denied that the protagonist wanted to think about it if he or she was engaged in another cognitive task, such as math homework. Only when the protagonist was sitting quietly, not engaged in any task and the past episode had been positive did 8 year olds allow that the protagonist might intend to think it. Overall, then, 8 year olds, but not 5 year olds displayed considerable awareness of the intrusive and involuntary nature of certain thoughts about the past.

In a second question, children were asked whether the protagonist could both think about the past event and also think about something else, such as math homework. Five year olds were again unsystematic in answering this question. The majority of 8 year olds, by contrast, denied that such divided thinking was possible. Only when the protagonist was sitting quietly, not engaged in any task, and thought back to a positive event, did 8 year olds say that the protagonist might manage such divided thinking.

Eight year olds' answers to these two questions – one about the involuntary nature of thought and one about the possibility of two concurrent thoughts, suggest that 8 year olds have some definite conception of what, in common parlance, we would refer to as concentration. They regard thoughts that intrude upon some specific cognitive focus as unintended and they regard such intrusive thoughts as potentially incompatible with, or disruptive of, that focus. Only when the mind is idling – not engaged in any particular cognitive task or activity – do they acknowledge that someone might intend to retrieve and keep in mind another thought – particularly concerning something positive.

How should we conceptualize this emerging insight? One possible interpretation is that children are gradually coming to appreciate the limited and directed nature of consciousness. More specifically, they increasingly appreciate that when one's mental focus is on a particular task or topic, that absorption serves as a constraining factor on other mental activities: one does not, or cannot, deliberately activate unrelated thoughts and if such unrelated thoughts occur involuntarily, they compete for restricted cognitive resources.

Earlier research with 8 year old boys at an English boarding school lends some support to this interpretation (Harris, 1989). When questioned about how to stop themselves from feeling homesick, the boys often mentioned keeping oneself occupied. One 8 year olds put it this way: "If there was a film on that night, you could go and watch it and distract yourself, or you could go swimming or play a game of marbles or something. " When pressed further to explain how such activities might be helpful, the boys typically explained that they could prevent you from thinking about your home or your homesickness. The assumption that consciousness has a limited capacity was implicit in several of their replies. For example, one 8 year old explained how taking part in school activities helped in the following way: "Well, once you get started and you're really doing it, then you forget about being homesick and don't really think of it." Another explained that thinking about other things than home helps: because" it takes your mind off feeling sad. It occupies your mind. I don't think you can think two things at once."

The replies clearly suggest that 8 year olds understand a good deal about the limited nature of consciousness – and even put that understanding to use in regulating their emotional life. However, the developmental course of that understanding is less clear. The research with boys in boarding school was conducted with 8 and 13 year olds. Younger children were not interviewed and so we do not know how far they would have articulated similar coping strategies. As noted above, the study conducted by Duke and Harris did include 5 year olds and, unlike the 8 year olds, they showed little appreciation of either the involuntary nature of intrusive thoughts or the difficulty of thinking concurrently about two separate topics. Their unsystematic reply to the latter question implies a failure to grasp the limited nature of consciousness. However, it is appropriate to be cautious. Initial probes of young children's grasp of a given concept often underestimate their capacity. For example, 5 year olds may not have fully registered the fact that the interviewer wanted them to evaluate the possibility of *concurrent* thoughts, as opposed to oscillating or alternating thoughts. After all, it is clearly possible to think about one's math homework while intermittently recalling some past experience.

More generally, there has been surprisingly little systematic research on this core notion, namely that consciousness has a limited capacity that restricts the number of items that can be concurrently processed. Pioneering research by John Flavell and his colleagues has shown that children increasingly recognize the incessant nature of the flow of consciousness – the fact that we cannot voluntarily suspend the flow of thoughts and images (Flavell, Green & Flavell, 1993; 1995). However, young children might understand that unstoppable flow without appreciating its constraints. For example, they might conceive of the flow of consciousness as a more or less boundless river – a veritable Mississippi – able to entrain any number of vessels. On this conception, children would assume that it is possible to do one's math homework, think about dinner, and ruminate about a squabble with a best friend, all at the same time.

In order to probe this question more thoroughly, Duke and Harris (2006) asked 5 and 8 year olds to think about two different protagonists – one engaged in an absorbing activity such as listening to the latest Harry Potter story and the other engaged in something less absorbing – for example listening to a familiar and somewhat dull story. Children were then invited to think about three different types of psychological intrusion – perceptual intrusions (e.g., being called to dinner), somatic intrusions (e.g., feeling thirsty) and cognitive intrusions (e.g., a memory of a prior event). Children were asked to make two kinds of judgment – to indicate which protagonist would be more or less likely to notice the intrusion and which protagonist would be more or less likely to stop concentrating on their current activity following the intrusion. The results of the study were highly systematic and surprising. Both 5 and 8 year olds performed well above chance across all types of intrusion. Thus, whether they were asked about perceptual, somatic, or cognitive intrusions, children were systematic in their choice of which protagonist would be more or less affected. Thus, in contrast to the implications of the earlier studies, even 5 year olds showed some emerging grasp of the limited nature of consciousness. Further research is needed to discover whether 5 year olds also understand the way in which that limited capacity can be put to use in the context of emotional regulation. As noted, our interviews with the boarding school boys suggest that 8 year olds have taken that additional meta-cognitive step. Realizing that the fully absorbed mind serves as a kind of protection or fortress against incursion, from ruminations on unrelated but sometimes painful topics, they explicitly advocate the anesthetic function of mental absorption. Whether 5 year olds understand that type of emotion regulation remains to be seen.

Conclusions

We have identified various key findings in children's understanding of the flow of thoughts and feelings. It is too early to tell a complete and detailed developmental story but various landmarks are evident. First, even 4 year olds understand that intense emotion wanes over time. By the age of 6 years that realization is stable and systematic. Second, 5 and 6 year olds do not simply conceive of this process as a simple, temporal distancing from the initial, precipitating event. Instead, they grasp that the process is modulated by cognitive factors. More specifically, they understand that thinking about the past event is likely to reactivate the original emotion whereas not thinking about it may weaken it.

Third, there are indications – which further research may consolidate – that children situate their understanding of the intertwining of thoughts and feelings into a larger conception of the mind. More specifically, they come to understand that consciousness is limited. Therefore, thoughts about the past and the feelings that are thereby reactivated can disrupt concentration on a cognitive task. At the same time, concentration – or absorption as we have called it – may serve to keep painful thoughts at bay. In this respect, we assume that children gradually come to the realization that even if many thoughts and feelings arise involuntarily, it is possible to take some control over the flow of consciousness. Its limited capacity can sometimes help to banish, at least for a while, painful feelings.

References

Borke, H. (1971). Interpersonal perception of young children: Egocentrism or empathy? *Developmental Psychology*, 5, 263-269.

Duke, S. & Harris, P. L. (2006). Children's understanding of intrusive thoughts. Paper in preparation.

Flavell, J. H., Green, F. L. & Flavell, E. R. (1993). Children's understanding of the stream of consciousness. *Child Development, 64*, 387-398.

Flavell, J. H., Green, F. L. & Flavell, E. R. (1995). Young children's knowledge about thinking. *Monographs of the Society for Research in Child Development, 60* (1, Serial no. 243).

Harris, P. L. (1989). *Children and emotion.* Oxford: Blackwell.

Harris, P. L., de Rosnay, M. & Pons, F. (2005). Language and children's understanding of mental states. *Current Directions in Psychological Science, 14*, 69-73.

Harris, P. L., Guz, G. R., Lipian, M. S. and Man Shu, Z. (1985). Insight into the time course of emotion among Western and Chinese children. *Child Development, 56*, 972 988.

Lagattuta, K. H. & Wellman, H. M. (2001). Thinking about the past: Early knowledge about links between prior experience, thinking, and emotion. *Child Development, 72*, 82-102.

Lagattuta, K. H. & Wellman, H. M. (2002). Differences in early parent-child conversations about negative versus positive emotions: Implications for the development of psychological understanding. *Developmental Psychology, 38*, 564-580.

Lagattuta, K. H. & Wellman, H. M. & Flavell, J. H. (1997). Preschoolers' understanding of the link between thinking and feeling: Cognitive cuing and emotional change. *Child Development, 68*, 1081-1104.

Trabasso, T., Stein, N. L. & Johnson, L. R. (1981). Children's knowledge of events: A causal analysis of story structure. In G. Bower (Ed.), *Learning and motivation* (Vol. 15, pp. 237-282). New York: Academic Press.

Wordsworth, W. (1800/2003). *Lyrical ballads and other selected poems.* Ware, Herts, UK: Wordworth Editions Limited.

Discussion after Paul Harris's Presentation

Phil Guin: Is it possible that children when they are asked to forget that they might treat the act of forgetting negatively even though the content might be negative or positive?

Paul Harris: That is doubtful because, if you remember, when the children were asked what would happen if you forgot about a negative event, they generally judged that they would feel cheerful. If they were inclined to think that forgetting have painful effects irrespective, they shouldn't draw that conclusion. I think that they're alert to whether you're forgetting something positive or negative, or thinking about something positive or negative, I don't think it's the act itself, the mental act itself which they deem to be negative or positive, I think they're focusing on the content judging by our results.

William Arsenio: This is more an extension than a question: it seems that a lot of what you presented is a normative developmental picture of what goes on in these processes and I'm wondering if you or anybody else is focusing on individual differences in various ways? One simple thing, just off the top of my head, I have these students who are interested in ADHD because of studies looking at emotion recognition, emotion abilities in kids with ADHD. And I'm wondering what their understanding of this process would look like, is their understanding of their attentional process somehow different? When do they start to recognize that their attention mobility and consciousness control may be different for themselves then it is for other people?

Paul Harris: You're absolutely right! So far this is mostly looking at normative development but we do hope to be able to apply it to these clinical groups, and children with ADHD would be a very intriguing target group. In principle you could imagine two really different outcomes. You could imagine that in so far as ADHD children are besieged by all sorts of intrusive thoughts, they might show a more precocious understanding than a normal child. But I suppose that you could also speculate that in some sense the flow of their consciousness is less dirigible for them, it's more chaotic. Maybe their insight is hampered to that extent. So a fairly open question is to what the outcome will be, but that is one of the extensions that we have in the back of our mind.

The other thing that I didn't mention in my talk is that we (Suzanne and myself are in collaboration with Manuel Sprung, who teaches in Louisiana) are currently looking at a campus called LongBeach which was more or less devastated by Katerina. Sprung's life, and well as the lives of many of his colleagues, was turned upside down. But he's been fairly courageous in trying to turn it into good by trying to get funds from National Science Foundation (NSF) to study the effects of Katerina on the local children. One of the likely effects of Katerina is an increased vulnerability to intrusive thoughts about the storm. When he came to visit us in Boston, he brought with him a home video of the storm and I don't know whether any of you have ever seen this kind of thing. First of all, the storm itself, even though he was 60 miles back when he was making this film, the storm itself is just horrible to watch and to hear. But he also showed us some clips of what it's now like in LongBeach and the landscape is very grim to behold. You see uprooted trees, upturned cars, devastated houses; it's apocalyptic when you see this landscape. And when you talk about the really benign example of this child who lost his pet fish and sees this reminder of the fishbowl. Well these children and of course their parents and families are surrounded by daily reminders of this storm, so it wouldn't be terribly surprising if these children are having various forms of intrusive thoughts about Katerina. So Manuel Sprung's got a whole battery of questions, some of which have included our probes about intrusive thoughts. He's also been testing children in the Boston area, as a control group, so far as they were exposed to the storm, and in a few months we should begin to get some results from that. So we've been exploring that, sometimes it's a non-normative sample, it comes with this pretty awful experience.

Wendy Turgeon: Building on that, were there any studies done after in New York city after 9/11? And, with respect to that, I remember an anecdote: my niece was ten or nine and she went to school in the city and at one point she said to me "I'm just so tired of talking about 9/11, I just want to go to school!" But they spent a lot of time in school trying to talk about how they felt and what they had seen . . .

Paul Harris: I don't know of any work targeting the extent to which the children, either close to the twin towers or further from the twin towers, for example, suffer to varying degrees of intrusive thoughts. I do know that a colleague of mine at Harvard, Richard McNally, in collaboration with one or two others, has done some analysis of various interventions that followed 9/11, and has indeed raised some questions about the extent to which bombarding people with questions and conversations about what happened is a good thing. There's been naturally inclination to assume that it is a good thing. But he raises various questions about that. I think that raises a more general question, which we were talking about a moment ago, there is a lot of work suggesting that when people try to put into words a very distressing experience, and render it coherent for themselves, it has beneficial effects; both on their physical well-being and their emotional well-being. On the other hand, there are these questions marks, that people like McNally have raised, about interventions which are in some sense designed to do that. So under what circumstances those kinds of conversations and narratives help? Under what circumstances they fail is an important question as well.

Michael Schleifer: This is related in a way. To make the connection between the developmental picture and precisely what can be done in regard to conversations: We are actually taking up Ann's point about preschool whereas we're talking about parents, but let's talk about 5 years olds who don't quite get it in the developmental picture and not necessarily with specific groups, but just simply, what would you expect might be the role in having discussions about these questions say with four or five year olds that might not have it yet? Make the link between the developmental work and the work that we do about having discussions about these things.

Paul Harris: I think it's important to distinguish between two possible gains: one gain might be that the child's psychological insight is increased, in broad terms (and I will say a little more about this in a second). The other possible gain is that the child's acceptance, assimilation, digestion of an emotionally charged negative experience is improved. Now, if we take the first, the broad brushstroke understanding, I find that in the past 5 to 10 years there's been a convincing stream of research showing that, particularly mothers who use a lot of psychological words in their conversations with children end-up having children who are more advanced on many of these milestones that we think of as the child having a so called theory of mind or showing an understanding of emotions or a folk theory of the mind. Whether we're talking about, one of the classic litmus tests as I'm sure some of you know is the appreciation that people may have a mistaken belief but may act, nevertheless, on that mistaken belief. Children who have mothers who engage in a good deal of psychological talk do better on those kinds of tasks then children who don't. If we push that a little bit further, children gradually understand that not only do mistaken beliefs dictate the way that you will act but they can also dictate what you feel. You may misunderstand a situation, but your misunderstanding is critical for your emotional reaction to that situation. So if you mistakenly think X as opposed to Y then you feel an emotion appropriate to X and not Y. Again, evidence is pretty clear that mothers who engage in this king of psychological talk are promoting that kind of understanding well. There's even evidence, which is fairly dramatic: if you interview mothers who are pregnant, you give them an interview about their relationship with their own mother, and there is ways of coding this from attachment theory, mothers who give a relatively coherent psychologically well balanced representation in their narrative about their relationship with their mother, end-up having children, when you come back to them 5-6 years after, who do better, for example, in understanding that certain situations elicit not negative feelings and not positive feelings but a mix of both, which is a developmental challenging task for children.

Summing up, there are a variety of landmarks that developmental psychologists would agree, I think, that children pass through as they move upwards from to 2-3 years of age to 8-9 years of age, and I could say more about those landmarks. The general result is that children who are growing up in homes where there's a good deal of psychological talk pass through those landmarks more quickly than children who grow up in homes where there's less such talk. Now exactly how the talk facilitates the understanding is an open question. Some are focusing on the actual semantics, just having the mental state terms at your disposal. Some people talk about the complicated syntax which mental state discussion presupposes because when you say "I think that" you have those imbedded clauses. You could even imbed them further: I think that she knows that he wants and so forth. So with that kind of complicated syntax, perhaps emanating from the mother perhaps helps the child to arrange in some sort of hierarchical fashion of their understanding of the tieredness of mental states. It's also possible that there's a more pragmatic component, because when you have conversations of a sustained nature with your parent, you're constantly been reminded of the fact that you may know something that your mother doesn't, you tell her what happens in preschool, she may introduce something into that conversation that you didn't know. So sustained conversation is a constant tutorial in the fact that different interlocutors bring different knowledge to bear, and good conversation constantly requires you to take into account that difference in knowledge. And a lot of the psychological task that we're talking about invites children to thing about different perspectives. So we could make a very general claim that, sustained conversation which is coherent is a constant tutorial in sensitivity to one another's view point. Syntactic, pragmatic, semantic, who knows, maybe a mix of all three. Even though the interpretation of what's going on is unclear, the evidence that you can promote child's psychological understanding is very convincing, in my eyes. And they're even training studies, as well as the longitudinal correlational studies and that convergence is especially convincing.

When we turn now to the more specific question of "What if you talk to a child about a particular emotionally charged episode? Is that a benefit to the child?" Then I think we know less. One could suppose that the mother who does engage in conversation with the child, reminisces about the past, including past negative episodes, is going to help the child construct, so to speak, a coherent narrative in their own mind about this emotionally charged event, and to some extent to come to terms with it. But I actually know of no studies, even though all our intuition would suggest that this probably is going to be effective, I don't know of any studies showing that. We know of lots of studies with adults, but we don't know of studies with parents. So the measures that have been taken have been looking at the child's landmark progress rather then the child's negotiation of stressors. And that would be perhaps just as important if we could explore it. Do you have the same intuition Bill?

William Arsenio: At first, I didn't understand what you mean but you're talking specifically about stressors and that makes sense to me. Because I know that there's tons of people in the attachment literature, as you just describe, who we're talking about the fact that coming out of secure attachment, part of what goes on is that the parent and child are talking about desires, needs, emotions, that kind of exchange, is essentially just probabilistic. Insecure attachment, you are just probabilistically less likely to have those kind of conversations with your child over time. Cumulatively, that's gonna have a effect. But we're talking specifically about a stressful or negative event . . . I don't know.

Michael Schleifer: Let's take the two general possible ways that conversations or dialogues could be beneficial. Leaving aside the second which is more problematic and we don't know. The first, which is in general for the solid understanding of emotions, about that dimension. And in that first, I want to be more specific now, to relate it as we said to Ann's intervention "what about preschools?" and you pointed out that first of all the evidence is murky. But you gave two good explanations as to why in general it might be murky, because we know we aren't dealing with one on one, even if we have a great educatrice and also we can't possibly have enough information because we aren't their parent.

But you again in answering the question we're talking about, you're talking about parents. They are educators, parents are educators, primary educators. But we have for example, we talk about 5 years old and 6 years old, which is the target group for most of the work we're doing here in Quebec but also with Ann and other collaborators. What would you say about, because some of the problems that you mention about both the ratio and the lack of knowledge that an educator would have about a 3 or 4 years old are compounded because in any school situation we are dealing with in the classroom (we do philosophy in the classroom). So in the maternelle with 5 and 6 year olds, may have 20 children and there typically the teacher may get to know them quite well or the people doing Philosophy for children. Could you say anything about that? Would you expect that there would be the same problems in regard to the general helping of children to comprehend these questions about control of emotions but more specifically with this aspect of intrusive thoughts or any other aspect?

Paul Harris: Well presumably you could take some precautions against some of the obstacles that you face in the classroom. First of all, I suppose you can try to circumvent your lack of knowledge in the individual child's biography, by so to speak, finessing it perhaps by everybody reading or hearing about a particular story character, so that everybody is on the same page with respect to the dilemma or emotionally charged event facing this particular story protagonist. And I suppose after a point you could also try to minimize the ratio problem by hopefully having a collective discussion that's relatively sustained and coherent about this episode or story character. I don't know enough about your methods but that would seem to me like an optimistic way forward. I guess the trick is going to be a every skilled educator who could in some sense orchestrate this conversation such that it speaks to all the individual children in roughly the same way. Children are going to bring their own take to the story . . .

Ann Sharp: And I think that's probably why, in philosophy for children at least, teacher formation is just so important. If anything goes wrong on that level, 9 chances out 10 there is very little educational significance into the class.

Cynthia Martiny: I'm just fascinated by the link that I make with what you do and with what group counsellors do. Because it seems to me that both issues could be resolved in some way in using group counselling skills. Because you can make it personal and link personal experiences by using some of our techniques. I think that there's maybe some discussions to have between what we each do.

Michael Schleifer: I'm raising a general question, and perhaps after the talk today and going back tomorrow, we can try to make some of these links because they are more general and not specifically about your paper. But I guess I will try it in a different way. There is evidence of the effect of discussions or dialogues, of which you call one on many or many on one, the group. In my case, the one I'm the most excited about is, on elements, for example, of judgement and with a content of violence specifically. We worked on the design of asking children, some of these materials I think you've seen in our book, we used judgement tests based simply on children being able to pick out what is not like the others. They became increasingly complicated and some of our scenarios were with a content of violence. So we did this targeting with 5 years old, and you had some people do karate and some other people do violent sports but then you had scenarios where you have somebody beating up on somebody. The question was to see if five years old could pick out that scenario and give an explanation as to why it's not the same. And to our great surprise 5 years old could not do it, no better than chance.

Paul Harris: I did not quite understand . . . they're supposed to pick the one that's not like the other?

Michael Schleifer: Yes. And we also gave them to adults, not all, but most adults would say something like "that's the one because unequal or dominance, submission. " And with 5 years old we expected they could, and some of them did, but maybe not more than 5% would pick out and come up with a reliable explanation in their own words; something like "That's not fair!"

Paul Harris: Was it a question of fairness or was it a question of sport versus non sport?

Michael Schleifer: The few that we got would say something like "it's not fair", we got that. And we may have some who say sport. At the end of the year, we did a design in which there were interventions, philosophical conversations using some of the materials that have been created where children talked about among other things of what was acceptable and non acceptable violence. There were dramatic improvements in the experimental group at the end of the year as opposed to our control group. My research assistant said "you won't believe this. " So that kind of result, and there are others that people have been involved in, gives me hope that the interventions can make some actual . . . So it's with that in mind that I was wondering, in regard to some of these other dimensions whether we would think this would be useful?

Paul Harris: It's a great pity that Francisco is not here, because he's thought a bit more about these classroom interventions. Just briefly to say that, we were asked at some point, Francisco and 1 that is, to evaluate a curriculum that was been used in Oxford. Which was deliberately aimed at promoting children's understanding of emotion. We used a test that Francisco developed on the strength of earlier research on the mind, the test was called the Test on Emotion Comprehension (TEC). So it probes the child about 9 components of emotion roughly ordered in terms of difficulty. Basically what we did was to pretest 2 groups of children, one of them went on and had the curriculum and we post-tested them. And we did find a modest gain following the curriculum. Having said that, we were not responsible for the curriculum, that was just something that we were invited to test, it did have some of the elements that you were talking about: stories, conversation, dialogue and so forth. It was quite a melange of elements, and what exactly the effective element is requires investigation.

Michael Schleifer: I don't think I've heard of that study, but as in our study, what we know is that there is an impact on certain dimensions and they seem to have to do with comprehension: even in the case of my so called Judgement Test, they seem to understand some things better and can also articulate better. But in regard to some of these other aspects, which is simply their comprehension of these factors they're able to articulate it but are they able to. . . in regard to the question of the seminar: What might be your guess if one would be to intervene as we do in discussions of the ongoing sort of philosophical character, over the course of about a year with people who are well trained? Wouldn't we expect that your 5 years old, in regard to some dimensions that they don't have, would at the end of the year begin to do better than some in the control group?

Paul Harris: Do better in regards of the things that they typically can not get? Judging by the results of this intervention we did, the answer would be a tentative yes. But I also hear you raising another important issue which is to what extend is this, so to speak, cognitive understanding insight translating into better regulation, better social interactions. Is that right? I think the answer to that is just unknown. What we do know is that if you measure children's understanding of emotion or theory of mind, there's encouraging evidence that children who do better on those kinds of tasks have better peer relationships, are perceived as more likable and are more popular children with their peers. Now, that's a correlational result so it could be interpreted in various ways. Maybe children who spend lots of time playing with other kids just have more opportunities to learn about how the mind works, for all we know. But the nice thing about what you're proposing, it seems to me, that it provides ultimately a lever to explore these causal links. So here's the thought experiment: we looked at the beginning of the year at children's social relationships and we measured the extent to which this child does have good friendships, doesn't get involved in many quarrels. So we assess the child's social relationships.

We then introduce the curriculum that you have in mind and of course presumably there could be various foci to that curriculum, you've emphasized the topic of violence, but there could be other foci. At the end of the year, we then come back, and it seems to me that you actually want to measure 2 different aspects: you want to measure the child's cognitive progress, with respect to the concepts that you targeted in with the curriculum, but you also want presumably to measure any spin off that may have accrued for the child's social interactions. If you did find gains there that would be very encouraging evidence, for we cautious psychologists, in assuming that there are these gains to be made by virtue of cognitive progress. And the correlation that I mentioned a moment ago between social cognitions on one hand and peer interaction on the other, is indeed due to the fact that social recognition facilitates peer interaction. So I thing you would be doing a tremendous service to the psychologists if you could design such an intervention with various motive assessments both at the beginning and at the end. You have the intervention group you get ABCDEFGH, you have the control group you get nothing.

Cynthia Martiny: I have a couple of specific comments and maybe a question. The part where you talked about asking children in the mismatch moment: "How come you're feeling when there's an expectation?"

You said it was because . . . I sort of assumed that the reason why they're so good at it is because they've been practicing. So it isn't because maybe the questioning from the parents is sort of giving them the answer? Because we use that situation really often as parents, you know "Wait a minute, I'm giving you a favorite meal and you're grumpy, why aren't you happy?" Just by the stimuli of asking that question the children know that there has to be a response that will please the parents. And so is it because they understand it or is it because they can second guess their parents and are empathic to the need of the parent at the moment? See what I mean?

Paul Harris: I mean my guess is, what happens is this question sets off a train of thought in the child which is roughly the following: So what is it I'm feeling at the moment, indeed I'm not feeling anything consonant with what's going on? I'm feeling upset: why am I feeling upset? Well if I think about it a moment, it's because I had a quarrel with my best friend as we walked home from school. So I'm assuming that the parents serve the role of not dictating what the child answers but setting off some kind of introspective inquiry by the child to "why they feel as they do?" And presumably the child, after many experiences of this nature, comes to the broader conclusion that the way you feel is very much a function of what it is that's on your mind at the moment which often times is not connected to what you're doing at the moment. Because it's rumination about something that has distressed you.

Cynthia Martiny: Well we've done some research here. The reason we are coming from . . . is that I've taken two people in a dialogue and I've filmed them face to face so that we can look at it and when we ask one person "what were you feeling now?" Our confusion is that they're not always going down on thinking "how do I feel?" but because of the situation they're really often thinking what the other person is feeling and then it's a little bit close to the question you asked yesterday: "is it not meeting the standard of what is expected that I'm empathic or that I'm thinking of the parent to diminish the stress of the moment?" So it's really difficult to know whether you're going into themselves or you're meeting the standard expected at the moment. And we've tried to screen this out for a while and I would say they are being empathic to the parent because a child is dependent on their satisfaction and they want their parent not to yell at them because they're not meeting their standards and so I'm not sure they are necessarily understanding. My research is with adults but I've been thinking of my children, you know my research at home . . .

Paul Harris: The thrust of your comment is that this question by the parent is not always going to be effective. It's not always going to trigger the kind of relatively objective self scrutiny of what we'd like. But the brutal point still stands that presumptively, as I was trying to insist, even though it does not always work, chances are this request for that kind of introspective work is most likely to occur in the circumstances that I described, where it's a positive event but the child is for whatever reason showing signs of distress.

Cynthia Martiny: So you're giving them the opportunity . . .

Paul Harris: Yes! Even though the child does know he is taking it . . .

Lee Londei: Sort of following up with this mismatch . . . What happens when there's a negative event that has an incongruent positive, well say a child manifests a positive reaction? Well like the dog died and the child is laughing hysterically. We understand that we don't necessarily call the child on this display of emotion because we rationalize and we say "well they can't deal with the intensity of the negative emotion so there's this outburst" but we don't have that cue, we don't ask them those cues in that particular instance. So I would imagine in that mismatch the child doesn't develop that questioning, that cognitive cue because . . .

Ann Sharp: There was a story after 9/11 about this classroom; they were showing the planes hitting the buildings. The second one hits the building and one boy in the class smiled, so they expelled him just on the basis of his facial expression.

Lee Londei: The point is that it's not normal, the actions are not what we are used to see, there's not much of a dialogue there, there's reactions and . . .

Paul Harris: To be honest I don't know how to answer your question partly because what we're all presuming and second guessing is what parents and to some extent educators do when they are confronted with these so called mismatches. I mean you're putting your finger on a mismatch which is different from the mismatches I was talking about. You know what we need I suppose are much more naturalistic data about what's going on in the home or what's going on in their classroom.

Wendy Turgeon: One answer might be simply that we analogize. I learned that when I have one kind of mismatch I start learning to introspect. I then when I have a different kind of mismatch I continue to introspect. But I think that parents do call on their children on that, if you were at a funeral and you're acting silly your parents will say this is not the time for that, you know be quiet, we're not asking you to cry but. . . Maybe not at the doctor's office, we're not going to ask you why are you so happy? But I think that a lot of times, we do try to teach appropriate emotions, even negative emotions in some way.

Paul Harris: But teaching the child the appropriate emotion would necessarily . . .

Wendy Turgeon: But calling them on is what I meant to say. Calling them on "why are you so happy this is a sad occasion? Why are you laughing?"

Paul Harris: But what I was about to say was that you were typically encouraging the child to display the appropriate emotion but I don't know whether you probe them very much whether they were feeling the inappropriate emotion.

Lee Londei: When you're talking about ADHD children in the idea of even if you probe an ADHD child as to a mismatch in behavior, whatever it may be, I don't know if their cognitive cue . . . If they're going to develop that sense because it's not something that they can make sense of because a physiological influence is causing them to react a certain way. So cognitive process in terms of emotion comprehension isn't unfolding with those ADHD children for example.

Michael Schleifer: We don't know, the research has yet to be done.

Paul Harris: But, we have strong intuitions about it!

Michael Schleifer: Well there's a research project there for you!

Cynthia Martiny: Absolutely! I think there's a research project for you to try because it does happen in clinical sense with sexually abused women in the hospital where they give inappropriate responses like hysterical laughing when discussing a very traumatic event, we know that.

I want to ask questions about the conclusions (unless we want to continue on this topic). When I read "wanes over time," in the first conclusion that you have, I feel like adding "but doesn't disappear," but I'm not sure about that. And then I look at the next one and I hear not thinking attenuates the emotion. It's almost as if all the conclusions could say to us that 5 and 6 year olds realize that if they think about their past it reactivates the emotion so the conclusion could be "well then don't think about it!" When I heard you talking about the gains, the parental talk, and the inquiry about how the emotion helps the child introspect in order to digest and possibly repair it, and that's interesting. Yet I don't know how far we can go with that. And then I come to the last one and I was thinking that you're helping me understand a little bit of how therapy works in this age group. You say that they realize that intrusive thoughts disrupt concentration and then you say concentration may keep intrusive painful thoughts at bay. Although this can sometimes be pathological, when it's done in a conscious way it is intentionally keeping an emotion at bay. I'm aware that I'm doing that, and that's healthy! So that shows something about the control of emotion, is that I can consciously not think about it with intention.

Michael Schleifer: Is that what you call freezing emotion?

Cynthia Martiny: Yes, of course. Because when it's an intrusive thought, and you cannot keep it at bay; that's talking about another kind of problem, as I understand. So with those comments I'm thinking that isn't that interesting because I could use those same results and apply them to adults . . .

Paul Harris: Sure!

Cynthia Martiny: Maybe you don't have the answer but is it possible that we can fix violence early on? I can play with that idea that we can teach this and then later on a painful event won't become one that reactivates the anger and the violence. I mean, isn't it something that is interesting to think about? It's just because, here, I look at those conclusions and I think "Well Geez! All we have to do is teach a 5 and a 6 year old how to control their emotions by freezing them, by putting them aside and also by helping parents introspect so they digest and it doesn't become a reactivator later on, it's sort of a finished business instead of an unfinished business, so that these do not become later on violent people. That's the links I'm making, but I don't know if I'm just pretending that I can find solutions.

Paul Harris: I think we were talking about that context yesterday worrying about children who are resilient to conjugal violence or parental altercations, then I suppose that it's conceivable. There's two things that are conceivable in the line we're discussing: on one hand it's possible that children have another confidant outside of the family to whom they can turn, with whom they can rehearse and make coherent these family problems; but, it's equally possible that these more robust children have islands of activity and security – where they are sufficiently absorbed, sufficiently at ease – that provide some kind of mental fortress against the intrusion of that chaotic family life. Maybe they get on well with their school ,or maybe they play soccer on the street, etc. But these seem to be two very different ways of thinking about resilience. The standard clinical thought is "let it out, discuss it, and reorganize it" but if you look at some of the psychological literature, especially on handling illness and surgery and so forth, the capacity to cease rumination and to set to one side is also important. And it may be that's also a skill that children have to master and that's a skill that ADHD children often would lack. Bill you wanted to add something?

William Arsenio: Just for what you were saying, the question is can you teach these things, at a kind of cognitive, verbal level later. Can this kind of relation between thought and emotion, stuff that we talked about yesterday, I mean can you cover this with the cognitive piece later and is this enough or realizing that a lot of the individual differences that we see early on are the result of a kind of affective ground in the kind of relationship that existed to begin with. I mean these things come out of an affective context and sometimes you get this kind of cognitive products at the end. Then the question is: are you trying to do remediation, is it enough to get to their cognitive products? You say "here, I'm going to teach you how to do these things and now you're going to change." The reason I bring it up is that there's a lot of work on trying to deal with remediation with aggressive kids and there was a lot of focus on the idea "oh they're missing this or that kind of cognitive piece," and if we get them to focus on intentions better and to understand how that works, they'll be fine. And I think that a lot of that literature is been less impressive that people thought initially. The intervention that you could just target the cognitive deficit is being questioned; I think people are starting to rethink how their cognitive deficit merging function.

Paul Harris: As a cautionary point, by the time the kid is 6 or 7, and you're seeing the cognitive sequeli of the earlier disturbances, anything as rational as dialogue and reeducation may not do it.

William Arsenio: I am slightly more optimistic; maybe it's naïve. I would say that for the kinds of things that you're hoping to do in the classroom that a part of the context, and it probably happens automatically, is that there has to be a kind of a level of emotional inclusion and trust and that you build from there. Part of what goes on is that you are laying that foundation and there is a lot of work by [Piante] and others dealing with the affective nature of the teacher/student relationship, and how that plays a unique role in cognitive outcomes throughout the time. So, especially as teachers, you still have to deal with that affective piece, kind of straight on it. Most teachers and daycare teachers kind of intuitively know that's where they have to start, you have to build trust and connection for kids to be able to evolve.

Ann Sharp: Just to comment on that: in Philosophy for Children we had a sense of practice before we had a theory. The theory, the first time we tried to express it, did not include this affective component. In other words there was a lot of emphasis on critical thinking, a lot of emphasis on dialogue, there was a lot of emphasis on modelling, dialogue in the stories, creativity, etc. But it did not include – it did not systematically pay attention to – the training (the consciousness, if you want) about the importance of caring thinking. After realizing that emotions themselves are judgements and exploring emotions, and exploring emotions in the community and realizing that there's a link between caring thinking and the kind of moral perceptions that we have, and the moral behavior that we engage in, how all this plays out in individual communities. People like Rorty for example, talk about slow kids, I'm thinking particularly children who don't come from homes where their parents are talking to them, many of them are absent, many of these kids are key chain kids. And so, with that in mind, the transformation of a classroom into a Community of Inquiry must be a slow building of a feeling of safeness, a feeling of trust, a feeling that we can explore these topics and that the world is not going to collapse. And the slow feeling of a building of solidarity means a child can say: "this is the one place that I can kind of count on to be halfway reasonable, because when I go home all hell lets loose." That's important for children who don't have that security and dialogue and trust and welcoming.

Paul Harris: It seems to me as you talk you mentioned two different components which I'd be tempted to separate in my mind but maybe in the end they are inseparable. On the one hand you started talking about the extent to which you change the curriculum . . .

Ann Sharp: No. We didn't change it, it was there . . . we added to it. We were unconscious of the importance of the affective in the preparation of the teachers in our consciousness of what constitutes our functioning group community.

Paul Harris: Okay, your conceptualization of the curriculum was enlarged to include these more affective and moral dimensions. That was one thing that you emphasized. So, in some sense, that is an expansion of the range in scope of the curriculum but the other thing that you emphasized, which it seems to me is possibly related but in the end one could conceptualize it as distinct, is the emotional atmosphere in the course of the discussion, and the emotional atmosphere in the course of the discussion could be one of, on one hand, trust and cooperation, collaboration or it could be one of you know more combative, competitive debate. And that second component where you have the variation in the atmosphere could equally apply to the discussion of the foundations of mathematics, as it could apply to violence in the home. . .

Sharon Bailin: This is a big, general issue that I'll throw out; it's probably for tomorrow, but it's coming both from Bill's question about the connection between the conceptual understanding and behavior and Michael's earlier question about the same issue in terms of the classroom and the students at the end and is the relationship between their improved conceptual understanding and the actual relationship with peers and so on. That's sort of the bigger issue, the relationship between the conceptualization under-standing and the actual behavior in terms of regulation of emotion, I mean it's kind of basic question for us I guess. So I wonder whether there have been different studies with adults in terms of adults that are good at psychological talk and their actual behavior. I think there is – I won't say counter example – an example that's interesting to look at: are there therapists who are good at psychological talk better in their interpersonal relationship and of anecdotal evidence at least make something that we can (laughs) . . .

Cynthia Martiny: The thing is that, judged from the outside, perhaps no, because they talk about it, they make it explicit all the wrong things that they do because they're comfortable with it, whereas maybe it doesn't mean that they're better but at least they make it exposed so that everybody have a lot of fun with it. It's a good question.

Paul Harris: Look at all the squabbles among psychoanalytic circles, I mean there are some pretty good examples of dysfunctional behavior among clinicians. (laughter)

Part IV

Classroom Discussions

Introduction to Wendy's Paper Presentation

I teach philosophy, so I approach our subject from a slightly different perspective than the developmental psychologists. I hope I am not drummed out of the room for lack of experimental data. I spent some time this morning reflecting on what's been happening here; I am going to try to situate my paper, to what's been happening here. The issue that comes to mind, really since we started, is the Meno question. Plato wrote a dialogue called the *Meno*, named for a character featured in the dialogue, which opens up by saying "alright, Socrates how do you make kids to be good? Do you teach them? Is it something they practice, or are they born lucky? How does goodness happen?" Socrates response is: "first we need to figure out what being good or what virtue is." For virtue, I think we substitute emotion and then we have basically what we've been working through the last day and a half.

In trying to reflect on what we have accomplished, these ideas have come to my mind, and, although they are certainly not comprehensive, I want to highlight some of them so I can situate my paper and my work within this larger, context.

First, I've noticed this theme of the emotions and reason as being interconnected, and I am going to say some things in along similar pattern. I think there are questions as to how far they are culturally shaped. By cultural I mean both within the family context, but also within the larger societal culture. Also in terms of the genetic component, if there is a genetic component, how would one measure that or tease that out? I think even in the articulation of what an emotion is, is a fairly daunting project, as we saw when we looked at the concepts of jealousy and envy. When are they desirable? When are they undesirable? When is it jealousy? When is it envy? The complexity of that issue was brought home to my mind.

We also looked at the interplay between emotion and action. When we looked at victimizers, we looked at child bullies, but also adult abusers of various ilk. How does my emotion affect my behavior? If I control my behavior is that controlling the emotion? If I control my emotion will that control the behavior? All of those clusters of questions come to my mind. All of this leads me to the direction that I want to take us in, and that is: how do we educate emotions? Is it an issue of community engagement in rational dialogue, or is it an element of self reflection? Maybe through community dialogue I can internalize the conversation within myself. Is educating emotions a form of nurturing empathy – an empathy that allows me to link my emotional experiences with those of others and co-feel? Perhaps it is a form of internalizing moral standards and principles? If so, then I self regulate my behavior because of the rules that I care about and feel I ought to follow and obey. I also am still puzzling over distinguishing between moral responsibility and control. Can I be morally responsible for something I have no control over? How does that work itself out? Focusing on early childcare giving patterns of attachment seems like a very important concept as well. To what extent do my early experiences shape the kinds of emotions I have and how I act on those emotions?

Therapeutic talk, accompanied by reliving, or maybe emotional relearning within a community is also an idea that has been put on the table. Finally, I see intimate parental conversations that encourage children to reflect on their own experiences of consciousness and of emotions and the situatedness of emotions, the internal and external as a way of educating the emotions. All of these seem to be ways in which we might pursue a form of moral or emotional education. Questions remains at the end of this paper (I do not address them all), but I am thinking about them more clearly. I am still puzzling to what extent emotions are learned, to what extent are they innate, to what extent are they culturally dependent, and to what extent are there natural human emotions? What role does culture play – both culture within the family, family patterns of attachment, and family patterns of learning and interaction? And also the larger culture, my societal patterns of learning, anger is a meaningful concept in my culture, and might not be in someone else's. And of course just personal experiences, things that have happened to me.

When I was very young, my family and I were sailing back from Australia, and my parents parked me in a highly recommended nursery in England for a period of about six weeks. And I just stopped eating, so my mother and father (I am sure they were not happy about this), had to rush back and cut their tour of the continent early. Years after that, whenever I was acting surly, especially as an adolescent, my mother always blamed it on the fact that they had abandoned me and this was me acting this out. Certainly we have seen the issue that young personal experience, even as infancy in young children has an effect on what emotions we experience, and how we experience them and how we act on them. Are emotions educable? Are they controllable, or is it the behavior through which we show our emotions that is controllable in some way? Or perhaps some combination thereof.

Much like Meno, I am going to have to ask your indulgence, and allow me to wildly and non experimentally speculate on this question of educating the emotions. I am going to assume, for the purposes of my paper, that there is some degree in which they are educable and explore at least one way of approaching that challenge. My essay builds on a comment of Sharon's yesterday where she mentioned that the arts give us access to feelings beyond our range of our personal experience. When she made that comment yesterday I thought well here is a point of connection and I am not in complete outer space with what I am writing. The paper, introduces this concept of the arts, how they factor into our emotional lives and might we be able to find a key to our moral/emotional education, they are not quite the same thing but I am going to link them for the purposes of how I was thinking here. My paper gave a rather quick and necessarily cursory look at how western philosophers have viewed the role of one art, specifically music, in the education process. I am going to touch on a couple of themes here, realizing I am not doing them justice.

Chapter 6
Emotion Recollected in Tranquility? Learning the Emotions Through Art: Aesthetics and Philosophy for Children

Wendy C. Turgeon

In Donizetti's *L'Elsirir d'Amore*, one of the characters – a charlatan doctor named Dulcamara – convinces some naïve locals to buy his cure-all remedy. One peasant is desperate to have a young lady return his love so he buys what turns out to be ordinary Bordeaux, hoping to entrance and win over the saucy young minx. It works, or rather, events conspire to make it appear to work. As with true opera buffo, all ends happily. But any listener knows that the real power to entrance the emotions is this luscious music that Donizetti uses to captivate us. Since ancient times our artistic impulses have produced works that have aroused, appealed to and educated our emotional lives. The arts evoke deep feelings, affirm beliefs and appear perhaps to influence magically the nature of reality as they shape human experience. Early humans realized this and often accompanied the strategies of battle with music: luring and soothing songs for the battle of love and rigorous, invigorating ones for the battles of war. From trumpets to bagpipes, from flutes to lutes – music can inspire deep emotions in the hearers. This power of the arts, certainly prominent in music but also in the arts of sculpture, visual imagery, poetry, story-telling and all, has always been recognized as a two-edged sword. Because of this enormous power over our hearts, souls and minds, we must be cautious how we use this tool from the gods. No one is more aware and cautious about this than Plato; Aristotle, while more amenable to the arts in society, also cautions on how to use the arts in ways conducive to virtue. But how do the arts achieve this deep generative connection to our hearts? Therein lies our question for consideration. Some Greeks described the artists as divinely inspired or possessed, an incomprehensible gift that, like the box of Pandora, must be opened and appreciated, carefully and with awe of its expectedness. Others saw the influence of music over our souls as viscerally predictable, once the compositional strategies were carefully studied.

In this essay, we will explore the Greek concept of artistic expression, centred on the musical arts, its connection to human emotions and its potential role within the process of educating the individual within society. For focus value, we will be looking at music alone[1] although much of what we hope to discover will be applicable for the arts in general. After a review of the foundational Greek viewpoint, we will skip forward, lightly touching upon later views of music and emotions as we moved into the very contemporary debate about our topic. Using a recent exchange of ideas in the journal, *Philosophy of Music Education*, we will explore the question of how music represents/models/evokes emotions in the listener and how this might factor into the larger vision of educating the human person. Finally, we will introduce some aspects of the curricular idea of "philosophy for children" that might function congenially to allow us to revisit the Greek question of how music can assist in the education of good character through its appeal to the emotions.

123

Plato: Art as Deception

The Greeks do not problematize the question of music as emotive; they assume it and then explore the consequences. One of the most famous philosophical statements on music is that of Plato in the third book of the Republic. Music is considered to be so powerful a force that it must be carefully regulated so that the inexperienced are not improperly influenced by it. As Plato says, "rhythm and harmony find their way to the inmost soul and take the strongest hold upon it, bring with them and imparting grace . . . if one is rightly trained."[2] Plato goes on to examine the types of musical modes.[3] He claims that some modes,[4] the Mixolydian and Lydian, have sorrowful qualities and are appropriate for such sad occasions as funerals. However, the Ionian mode sounds soothingly and softly. He qualifies that the Lydian can also elicit such responses as well. The Dorian and Phrygian modes are likewise tailored to certain types of occasions or situation. A warrior needs to hear quite different music than a peace-maker.[5] Music is discussed not simply as a soundtrack to life but as a critical aid in helping us form the correct feelings for different situations.

Plato's interlocutor, Socrates, instructs his listeners on the importance of controlling the types of musical instruments as well. Many of the popular instruments of fifth century Athens are suspect because they will arouse too many inappropriate or uncontrollable feelings. The stringed instruments, lyre and cithara, are considered relatively safe to allow. This discussion is part of the larger context of control and censorship. Citizens must have their experiences censored *for their own good* by those who are informed enough to know what is needed and for whom. Certainly education has often been depicted as all about controlling information. What are children ready for? What ought they to know and when? What ought we to keep from children to protect them, preserve their innocence or avoid confusion? This debate remains a lively one today and we will return to it later. The key notion to recognize in Plato's account is the importance that music can play in eliciting and subsequently teaching young people proper emotions at proper times. But a misuse remains a serious danger.

Plato also argues that art, by its very nature, is imitative, thus deceptive, and must be carefully scrutinized. As a copy of the physical world, art is twice removed from the nature of true, unchanging reality and in its ability to seduce our senses, we must be aware of its inherently duplicitous nature. This renders the arts suspect, even in their positive pedagogical function. In Plato there remains an ambiguity as to the nature and function of the arts within society. Their power can be used for proper instruction but can veer too easily in a direction which can be deceptive or outright damaging.

Aristotle: Music in Education

Aristotle offers an extensive argument for a positive role for music within his larger educational project in *Politics*. In Book VIII, he points out that the value of music could be seen in three ways:

> for the sake of amusement, entertainment, relaxation: this justification sees music as a way to relax after the hard work of learning but as such it is really an interlude, not educative in its own right. Music is a form of play.

Music can lead to better character, to virtue: in this sense, music is not mere play but can "form our minds and habituate us to true pleasure."[6] This idea that we must learn to appreciate good pleasure, or, rather take pleasure in the right things, is central to Aristotle's ethical theory. One of the key justifications for early education in virtue is to form deep-seated tendencies to enjoy what is right and feel pain at what is wrong. This second role is clearly a practical application of music in character education. Music can contribute to the enjoyment of our leisure time and further our mental development. This last view suggests that music serves as an enrichment of the human experience and its function is broader than simply that of character development or mere play.

After Aristotle presents these three possible functions of music within education, he systematically examines each one. While Aristotle always argues for a certain amount of play or amusement as necessary for a good life, he refuses to make it the purpose or end of a happy life. We relax and play so as to refresh ourselves for better work; we do not live for vacations, as seems to be the contemporary view of one's work life. Music for amusement's sake is not dismissed but is ancillary to other functions. But even so, he will go on to argue that music can play a much more important role than simply that of entertainment. It can clearly have deep influences on our character and "soul" since we see that music inspires enthusiasm and we find our feelings, both physical and spiritual, moving in time with the rhythmic beat of a piece.[7] Since "virtue consists in rejoicing and loving and hating aright" educators must pay particular attention to this seemingly innate power of music to evoke certain feelings and cultivate musical taste which helps the young person live a more virtuous life through exposure to the right kind of music.[8]

What can music express? "Rhythm and melody supply imitations of anger and gentleness, and also of courage and temperance . . . and of the other qualities of character, which hardly fall short of the actual affections . . . for in listening to such strains our souls undergo a change."[9] Music can help to mold one's ability to feel in a certain way. Aristotle sees the emotions derived from the experience of music as fairly close, but perhaps not quite identical, to the emotions that occur in our practice of living. However, the similarity is strong enough to render them powerful tools in character formation. (An interesting question is what that difference might be.) Since character is made through the practice of virtue, any tool which can help us experience-and thereby practice – feeling certain ways, has a vital educative function in the cultivation of good character.

Following Plato's analysis, he also considers the different musical modes as each connected to or evocative of a distinct range of feelings. The Mixolydian is again associated with sad occasions and clearly sounds to our ears as a minor key. The Phyrgian mode is associated with enthusiasm, action, the stirring up of emotions. The most ethical mode is claimed to be the Dorian since it offers a moderate and settled sound (moderation being the key to determining the nature of virtue for Aristotle.) Aristotle adds that it is not simply the modal personality of a piece that determines its emotional tone but the rhythms can also affect character formation. Is the piece a lively one with a quick tempo and staccato and/or syncopated notes? Or does the melody flow with sustained and legato passages?[10] These brief suggestions all pertain to the act of listening to music or music appreciation as a spectator aesthetic and moral experience. What role should the performance of music play in the education of a citizenry?

Aristotle argues that children should learn to perform music and not simply become passive listeners. However that is not to say that children should become professional musicians or even attempt to move in that direction. Children should learn to play early but then stop when they reach the point at which the technical demands require professionalization. Musicians were regarded as a servant class, not in the exalted post-Romantic echelon that we consider them today. With that in mind, music should be incorporated within the education of young people in careful ways with specific musical pieces and instruments being included while others are decidedly excluded. Such instruments as the flute and harp, which are claimed to require professional degrees of expertise, should be avoided.

It is the accessibility and its universal appeal that make music such a powerful educative force for Aristotle. If educators pay careful attention to what modes, rhythms and instruments are introduced, it can have an enormously powerful positive effect on the ethical education of young people. Aristotle specifically mentions such feelings as those of pity, fear, enthusiasm and even a "mystic frenzy" as all aroused by certain musical examples. He concludes that the Dorian mode is to be much preferred for its sense of balance, which, again, is a key ethical notion in Aristotle's theory of virtue. While he does not mention music or the arts specifically in *Nichomachean Ethics*, he does devote a chapter in Book II to the importance of early ethical education in helping children feel pleasure and pain in the appropriate things. It we fail to develop a right appreciation of what is pleasurable as a youth, we will have a much harder time achieving virtue throughout our life since we will be overly attracted to things which are of less value or outright damaging to our character. This function of music is distinct from its role as edifying or enhancing human experience.[11] This third strand of musical function, that of edifying the human experience, separates Aristotle from Plato, in that Aristotle does not share Plato's hierarchy of reality from the lower physical objects to the immaterial forms. We do not get a clear discussion of how music can enhance our experience as human beings but this thread of the Greek view has persisted in subsequent accounts of the power of the arts.

We can therefore discern three themes from these Greek philosophers with respect to music and its role in our lives: Music, and by extension all of the arts, are somewhat duplicitous because they present intense, fleeting and, to some degree, unreal imitations of the physical world. That means there is always an element of falsity about the arts that must be guarded against or, at the very least, carefully acknowledged.

Music's power to elicit and shape our emotions is assumed. Because of that assumption the Greeks articulated for it an important role in the education of the young as music allows them access to emotions that they might not be able to control in practical life; within an aesthetic experience, these emotions can be felt, examined, and to some degree, controlled. Good emotions can be repeatedly experienced, thereby allowing the person to practice feeling the right emotions for the right reasons at the right times. As such, music assists in teaching young people how they *ought* to feel about certain situations.[12]

Music can simply enrich our human experience and offer us new and creative ways to experience the world around us. It expands our limited vision by taking us on an aural journey into the human heart. But, as it is linked to emotions, the element of irrationality must be consciously recognized. This could render the arts a second class of human experiences in a world where reason dominates.

Western Music: Snapshots or Skipping Stones

The influence of Plato and Aristotle on later philosophers view of the arts, and specifically music, is significant. Hundreds of years later, in the *Confessions*, Augustine will admit to enjoying music in church[13] as potentially edifying and re-enforcing of the relationship with God but also dangerously close to arousing inappropriate emotions and misdirected attentions to sensuous feelings. This ambivalence expressed in the late fourth century extended throughout the Middle Ages as church music began as a simple unadorned melodic chant on which to tone a liturgical verse but evolved into elaborate polyphonic pieces whose musical intricacy and ability to fascinate threatened to dwarf the liturgy's intent as worship. The definitive writing on musical theory prior to the fourteenth century was that of the sixth century Latin philosopher, Boethius, whose ability to read Greek, rare at the time, allowed him to translate and interpret earlier Greek musical theory. Unfortunately, he made some basic misinterpretations and the medieval concept of the musical modes are quite different from those of the pagan Greeks, although they share the same names. Periodically the church authorities would rule on the place of music within one's spiritual life and insist upon its corralling or stringent control.[14] While there was a lively body of secular music, most of this was considered of low repute and such musicians were regarded as bad characters all around. Even court music was considered suspiciously as a source of vice or unbridled feeling. By the time the Renaissance blossomed, music had freed itself from the tyranny of the church and had achieved a more respectable status which returned to a source in the Greek and Roman ideals of music as a divine art of inspiration.

In the Baroque era music appears equally in church and court with extravagantly powerful pieces being written by such creative geniuses as J. S. Back, George F. Handel, C. Gluck. However, even into the Classical Period (eighteenth century), musicians were still regarded as servants and however divinely inspired they might be, their music was a technical creation and ordered at will. Alexandra Kertz-Welzel, in her article "The 'Magic' of Music"[15] contrasts the ideas of music in the ancient and pre-Christian eras with the development of what today we label "classical music" and claims that "the aesthetics of Western European art music, especially since the eighteenth century, tends to eliminate this sensual "magic" of music only to replace the more ecstatic ways of experiencing music with an intellectual approach. " The craft element dominated over the inspirational one as composers were ordered to write music with such and such a theme or for a particular occasion. Despite that claim, the notion of music and its power over the emotions does not depart completely from Western aesthetical theory and if we fast-forward to the Romantic Revolution that began in the early nineteenth century we discover music's power to evoke and represent our emotions was again front and center as composers and their audiences discovered an antidote to the overwhelming Rationalism of the Enlightenment. "The movement of the *Empfindsamkeit* explored the ability of music to create extremely different moods that celebrate the individuality of the subject."[17]

This viewpoint claimed that as music informs emotions, it transforms them into objects of contemplation, a contemplation suffused itself with feeling and even a sacred sense. Emotions are not second class human experiences of the Rationalists but forms of knowing that rival or even transcend the mind. As Blaise Pascal put it, "le coeur a ses raisons que la raison ne connait pas. " By this comment he intended to defend a fideistic approach to religion but we can also see its importance in shifting authority away from reason and logic towards the "logic of the heart. " As the nineteenth century raged forward, the power of music to evoke genuine feelings became its defining characteristic. During this period we no longer used music in a utilitarian way to educate one's emotions so much as enjoy and immerse ourselves in feelings made readily available through the power of musical expression.[18] Music's ecstatic power had again emerged and offered us a way of engaging in deep sacred feelings "but there is some doubt whether they are a reflection of the human soul itself or a sign of god."[19] Kertz-Welzel concludes that "The Romantic artist is, like a priest or shaman, a vehicle of communication between the divine and the human, and he uses the power of music to travel from one realm into the other."[20] Music's power has reachieved the status of being magical but as such, it also runs the risk of being beyond the scope of mere mortals and perhaps even secretively manipulative. This recognition of the potentially "darker" side of music, as recognized by Plato and Aristotle, returns but as a seductively desirable outcome. Music evokes emotions and frees us from the tyranny of the rational. But what has happened? Has music become a form of Dionysian exuberance?[21] And is that to be commended and reveled in or carefully noted and controlled? And most importantly, we find in the nineteenth century aesthetics the beginnings of the challenge: in what way can we even say music is emotional? The twentieth century would witness a range of answers to these questions from Stravinsky's *Rite of Spring* to Arnold Schoenberg's twelve tone compositions to late century electronica.

Music and the Emotions Revisited: A Twenty-first Century Exchange

So, how *does* music express, represent, evoke, emulate emotions? And what place should it have in our lives and in our educational systems? As we move into a new century we find we are still struggling with the questions raised by Aristotle in the fourth century BCE and despite the enormous developments in science, technology, the fertile outpouring of artistic creativity over the ensuing centuries, we are still flummoxed by how music does what it does and what that means or ought to mean to us today. This has been a major conversation among twentieth century aestheticians. As a way to exemplify this complex, multi-voiced exchange ranging over the past 100 years, let us center on an representative sample of this discussion. Within the last several years there has been an ongoing dialogue about emotions and music in the journal *Philosophy of Music Education Review*. I would like to share some of the ideas that have been developing here and then weave some connections to a model of aesthetical education from the Philosophy and Children movement.

In a carefully crafted essay, "How can Music seem to be emotional,"[23] Kingsley Price takes us behind the assumptions of music's emotionality and analyzes the exact nature of this relationship between music and emotions. Despite their ready pairing, what precisely are we claiming when we claim that a non-sentient "thing," – a piece of music – expresses or communicates feelings and emotions? How is it that music "*seems* to be emotional?" Price specifically considers instrumental music. Price focuses on the notion of seeming or appearing versus being. Since music is not a living creature upon whom we can predicate feelings and emotions analogous to our own, what is the nature of this appearance? Perhaps it lies in our perceptions of music. While music is definitely real, it cannot actually *be* happy or sad. However, while we can directly predicate loudness, key tonality, or even poor performance to a musical experience, in what ways can we say that a symphony is "sad" or a sonata "cheerful?" But since an appearance is precisely that: something which *appears* to be but isn't – that is, it would seem to belay reality – and yet in listening to a musical piece, the emotion as perceived *seems* only *real*:

> There is only real joy; or better, just joy unqualified. And the seeming emotionality of music heard cannot be understood as emotionality that is made seeming by some additional audible characteristic. No factor internal to music heard can be a seeming factor; the distinction between seeming and reality can apply to none of them. For that reason, we cannot understand how music heard can seem to be emotional by considering the perception itself.[24]

The *seeming* of the emotionality of music does not reside in the direct perceptual experience (that is very real) but perhaps in some connection external to it. Does music designate or in some other way *mean* feelings? Price introduces the theory of meaning of Suzanne Langer and considers her claim that "music means emotions in a way that parallels, but also contrast with, the way in which language means things other than emotions."[25] He goes on the examine this claim that while words and sentences can designate or mean intellectual claims about the world and its state of affairs, music renders accessible the meaning of emotions which cannot be so translated into linguistic discursive units. Langer claims that music shares a *form* with emotions that render them meaningful through the medium of sensuous sound. The key common term here is temporality. As emotions have a form of "a pattern of motions and rests, of tension and release, of agreement and disagreement, preparation, fulfillment, excitation, sudden changes,"[26] these selfsame characteristics are found in musical form.

Price will find this analogy of the meaning of music with that of language as failing. While linguistic units of sentences can represent states of affairs about the world and thus "mean" them, music does not mean anything in this discursive fashion. Labeling them "presentation" or "non-discursive symbols"[27] does not really answer the question of how a particular musical passage can mean a feeling which exists in all of its specificity within a person. To claim that it means "emotions in general" simply impoverishes the original claim. Price then briefly considers Langer's later theory as found in her text *Feeling and Form*. Here he reads her as claiming that "music means felt time and presents what language cannot show; that is, how time in its passage feels as it is experienced in inward life."[28] But this seems to simply expand the problem: now the mystery of how music means feelings is expanded to include how it might mean time. Curiously enough, Price ends his reflections with a reluctance to abandon the identity of music with emotions. Indeed, somewhat reminiscent of Socrates' conclusion in the *Meno*, he states:

> We are left with the view we are trying to explain-the view that music seems to be emotional and, if I am not mistaken, the seeming emotionality of music is an absolute, unfathomable mystery or a par, almost, with the Trinity.[29]

That doesn't really help us at all, but we can certainly see that the relationship between emotions and music is not an easy one to decode. Let's take another approach to considering this relationship of music to emotion.

Bennett Reimer, a well-respected scholar and music teacher, offers a personal anecdote to sharpen our analysis of musical affect. In an essay entitled "Once More with Feeling"[30] he explores the ways in which performers and audience experience music musically. As a young man, he was first chair clarinctist in a premier New York City high school band. After performing a solo, the conductor simply commented that he would like him to do it again but "with more feeling." Reimer did precisely that and received accolades. Now, Reimer asks, what did that mean? One interpretation places affect or feeling within the piece itself and a good musician can "speak" that emotion in playing the notes: "Musical feeling is contained within, or is a function of, the way the notes in a melody suggest because of established expectation for how that particular melodic system functions as a culturally determined artifact, the ways they can properly interact within that system."[31] Here the emotion resides within the music itself as written by the composer and as decoded, if you will, by the performer, but it also emerges as representative of a particular cultural context. It is the interrelationship among the sounds that generate the emotion. Reimer offers a number of phrases which capture this notion of musical affectivity: "intrinsicality, immanence, presentational form, significant form, innateness, incarnation, indwelling, interiority."[32] Another quite different viewpoint of musical emotion is that of "delineation. " Here sounds convey emotion or tell a "story." Another name for this is program music: music which is clearly intended to convey a human emotion or experience or even some event in the world.[33] Is music properly delineative (its meaning pointing outward) or inherent (its meaning proper only to itself?) Some theorists see it as one or the other while others allow both, either in the same musical example or as appropriate to different compositions.

Reimer accepts that many musical compositions are overtly delineative and to claim that all such projections are in fact projections by listeners with an agenda (philosophical, cultural, political) is to ignore the obvious. And yet, we can also respond to music based strictly on its intrinsic presentation of sensuous sound, without having to "paint pictures" of what the sound means. The point of confluence here is the musical emotion. Reimer pairs these models together as he claims:

> The affective experiences music offers, I submit, are necessarily functions of what sounds are made to do that add inherent meanings to any and all delineations, or to put it differently, that transmute delineations into musical inherence while also including the delineations as a dimension of that inherence.[34]

How one balances a model of music as delineative with a model of music as inherent meaning is an open question but one with some interesting implications for music education. One can present music as a form of story-telling, picture painting and emphasis to students that they connect the aural experience to these extra-musical images and ideas. One could instead eschew any thematic content whatsoever and insist that musicality is its own separate form of expression, independent of other human experiences, including those of emotions or feelings. Reimer's own position is stated thusly:

> in engagements with music in the many musical roles cultures make available and for all students no matter their age or level of achievement, musical teaching should include attention to delineative aspects but not be content with them along, separated from what inherence creatively does with them.[35]

It is worth noting that Reimer approaches this question of the emotionality of music from the perspective of performer. Even so, he recognizes that performers are not actually in the throes of the emotion that they might be expressing in performance. We will return to this distinction between performer and audience and the question of emotion below.

Interestingly enough, Reimer argues that this question of the nature of musical emotion should itself become part of music education which he envisions as including a rich foray into aesthetics itself as integral to the performance and appreciation of music. He insists that the philosophy of music is a much needed component to any thriving program in music education. But as he ends this article, he leaves open the manner in which we might best achieve this new dimension in education. What we do see clearly is that the relationship of music to emotions which has always been recognized, if still considered to be mysterious and opaque, stands as a philosophical puzzle in its own right. Students who are studying music can benefit from exploring this conundrum, both from the standpoint of an intellectually rich project but also as a way of developing as musicians and appreciators of the arts, in this case, the musical arts. In other words, why not engage students themselves in a meta-inquiry about how music affects our selves? This question represents a slight shift of focus here from the aesthetic question to the question of aesthetics, but let us follow this thread for a bit.

This urgency of considering a place for aesthetics, for active reflection on the nature of music within human experience, was the subject of a symposium held in 2004 and reported on in the Spring 2005 issue of *Philosophy of Music Education Review*. The lead speaker was Bennett Reimer who argued for philosophy within music education programs in three ways: as essential for all students in general or introductory music classes, as a component of any music elective, and finally as featured elective in its own right to allow for more in-depth exploration. In his address, he wonders if children will be able to handle such an esoteric undertaking as philosophy, especially given its challenge to seasoned adult practitioners. But if we expect even young children to tackle such intellectualized subjects as mathematics and history, surely we can include philosophy, he muses. Curiously he bemoans the lack of any history of fostering philosophical interactions with children but rejects the public view of philosophy as irrelevant and inaccessible by stressing its presence in everyday life and its direct relevance to the musical experience.[36] He invites the seminar participants to develop some strategies for incorporating music philosophy with the school curriculum.

One respondent to Reimer, Sandra L. Stauffer, approaches the problem from the perspective of education as a form of enriching experiences.[38] As such, "the richer the experiences, the richer the philosophy"[39] which stems from them. A teacher who models philosophical curiosity to his students will encourage them to engage in "mindfulness" (an idea she borrows from Ellen Langer). Stauffer characterizes this idea as including "the continuous creation of new categories, openness to new information; and an implicit awareness of more than one perspective."[40] (This is reminiscent of Aristotle's third strand of justification for the arts: a meaningful use of leisure time for self growth.) Stauffer wholeheartedly supports the inclusion of a philosophy of music within music education; she also acknowledges that the challenge will be the preliminary transformation of teacher preparation to help undergraduates engage in their own learning about education and philosophy as future teachers, not as the students they still are. Secondly, she insists we must expand such training to include philosophical reflections on the nature of childhood and the ways in which children are engaging in music (and any of the arts.) Ultimately she wants the classroom experience to be that of co-inquirers into what music means as teacher and students engage in mindful dialogic explorations of what music *means*. She ends her essay with the promising call that:

> Rather than teach philosophy as a subject, I would aim for practices that bring into the open questions drawn from the curiosity and imagination of children and students of all ages, questions that may lead to the kinds of conversations that focus on values and beliefs. I hope for mindful music educators who can provide children with rich musical experiences and help them develop their own philosophical habits of mind.[41]

At this juncture it is time to move into a more explicated version of what such a music philosophy would resemble. Luckily we are not quite as bereft of models as Reimer and his associates seem to suggest as we can use the rich resources of the Philosophy for Children model that has blossomed from Matthew Lipman's program and taken root in creative and open-ended ways in the works of others around the world.

132 *Talking to Children About Responsibility and Control of Emotions*

Crafting Philosophical Inquiry in Music and Taking Account of Music's Emotive Role

As I suggested above, we can see a felicitous coming together of a number of thematic strands:

Music and emotions: we need to explore *how* music means or expresses feelings, if indeed we wish to argue that it does. This invites a recognition of the urgency of aesthetic education along side of traditional models of music education.

However, because of this connection between music and emotions we can also explore the idea of integrating music into a program of emotional and ethical education. This has its roots in the Greek notion of music as educative of the emotions but we must enter this topic with a certain degree of reservation. We need to engage students in meta-reflection on the nature of music and its place within their lives as a form of personal enrichment.

In a previous article, I have offered extended exercises and discussion questions to facilitate students exploring such diverse musical examples as Schubert Lieder, Chinese composition for strings, and mediaeval chant.[42] In that article I invited the reader to develop strategies for helping students explore the ontological status of music, the nature of performance and of the act of appreciation, that is, the aesthetic questions that we can ask of music. Here I would like to shift our focus to that of the theme of music and feelings and the potential for an educative connection.

Our culture has tended to bifurcate intellect and emotion, privileging intellect as the work of the mind in its search for truth. This move originates in Platonic theory where it is abstract thinking which can best grasp what is true and good, as well as beautiful. The arts exist in the shadowy realm of an imitation of the physical world (which itself is a mere imitation of reality), as unchanging abstract theoretical truths. Because of the variability and fluidity of emotions their status as forms of knowing, and perhaps even human experience, are of less value than that of certain abstract and objective knowledge. This position underlies the suspicion against music in particular, and the arts in general, which runs through Western history. But if we recall the Greek approach, particularly that of Aristotle, we can see strong arguments for the arts as helping us form correct feelings, which can then influence our will towards making correct choices and perhaps offer us a better way of understanding the nature of reality. The Greeks could not ignore the ways in which music can sooth or arouse our emotions, often in quite appropriate ways. The myth of Orpheus illustrates the nature of music as a force of goodness even as the story of the maenads of Dionysus show its darker side. Even in an Eastern tradition, if we consider a Taoist world view, we find an ontology and ethics which sees the relationship of knowing and feeling as flowing into one another, as complementary, not adversarial.[43] Here the aesthetic experience of the world is both affective and cognitive in ways which Western scientific thinking has precluded and is directly linked to the ethical world as well. We can thereby investigate ways that music, both the performance and appreciation thereof, can help us become more reflective and aware human beings. This opens up a role for music in helping us form "life worlds," ways of being in the world, creating meaning and enriching ourselves.[44]

With these ideas in mind, let's see how we might engage students in philosophical inquiry through music into the nature of music and emotions. How can music factor into a program of ethical education, the project of coming to know one's self and the search for values? In setting up some preliminary proposals and sketching out some strategies, we can begin to address the questions of the nature of music vis à vis the emotions as well as chart some concrete ways in which we can respond to Reimer's challenge to develop a philosophy of music within music education.

Philosophical Inquiry with Music: A Collaborative Effort

If we wish to expand the role of music in education to move beyond the categories of entertainment, personal enrichment, and a source for aesthetic reflection into the realm of moral education, we have a serious challenge. There is no intuitively obvious connection between one's ability to appreciate or perform music (or create any art, for that matter) and one's ethical life, the Greek view not withstanding. The history of the arts is full of creative geniuses who were scoundrels. One way to approach our task is to frame the issue as a matter of using music as a "text" which can generate reflective dialogue about the emotions, their role in human experience and their consequent influence on one's actions, the praxis of moral life. We will label this "the philosophical inquiry model. " Another tactic is to explore the nature of the musical experience as formative of the emotions themselves; with this approach we might draw some clear distinctions between performance versus appreciation. This is called the "emotion educative model. " If we wish to explore the role of music and the arts in moral education, I propose that both perspectives be used in complement to achieve that end. Let us explore what each might entail. We will begin with the former tactic, the method of philosophical inquiry.

Instead of adopting the traditional engagement with a written text, our philosophical inquiry will begin with an experience of listening to a piece of music. As part of the notion that education should offer us opportunities to enlarge our world, we must choose pieces that, while accessible, are not obvious nor overly familiar to the students.[45] This means that popular music, so often used in music education programs because "the kids like it" might not be the best choice, precisely because of its ease of access and familiarity to the children. Let's challenge the educational old saw that children need to start with what is familiar to them. Recall any kindergartener's fascination with dinosaurs or pirates and we can put to rest the position that children are incapable of appreciation the alien.[46] So, with that in mind, let us choose pieces of music that meet the following criteria:

They offer an experience of novelty and mystery to the children, thereby demanding attention and reflection to render them meaningful; this is not their everyday, familiar musical experiences.

The examples are engaging and have layers of meaning such that repeated performances do not bore but rather enrich the listener's experience in kaleidoscopic ways. They can also invite the teacher or facilitator to stretch his imagination and affective modes of thinking; that is, the teacher's comfort zone can likewise be challenged! The community of musical inquiry will focus on the affective tonalities of the pieces and engage in both ethical inquiry and aesthetic inquiry. Hence the inquiry is at least dualistic in that we explore how music means and how our emotions fit into our experiences.

Assumed in everything that we have said up to now is the direct availability of music to children. While children may lack the extensive background knowledge of music history of styles and periods, the intrinsic experience of music is readily accessible to them. Since we are confident that Reimer's concern about the accessibility of philosophy to children is not an issue, we can move forward, convinced that musical philosophy is both desirable, achievable, and a potentially rich form of educative experience for children. Music can indeed be decoded by children for its delineative and intrinsic meanings.

Consequently, our model of philosophical inquiry can be developed from two directions. One way would be that of choosing musical examples which demand focused, thoughtful, and affective attention from the listener. We might dip into Western musical history and choose pieces as plainsong, medieval contrapuntal motets of Guillaume de Machaut with their ordo and talea strictures of composition, the Renaissance polyphony of Carlo Gesualdo with its tortured harmonics, a Bach fugue, a Mozart aria such "Dove sono." Let us also consider examples from world music and whether we choose Indian ragas, contemporary Bollywood, Chinese folk tunes, classical music from Japanese Kabuki, African drumming chants, reggae, Indonesian gamelan music-here too we want to offer examples which will discombobulate the listeners into a true engagement with novelty, but a novelty which entices as it troubles us to dig deeper to mine its meaning.

A second direction in developing our program would be to consider emotions or even character traits and choose pieces that we deem representative (in a delineative or intrinsic fashion). Let's choose some emotions and consider what musical pieces might offer access or insight into them: courage, bravery, love, care, sorrow, regret, humor, anger, fear, jealousy, sorrow, longing, gaiety, excitement.[47] This project can itself become a source of inquiry since some music, while emotive, does not seem to directly generate commonly agreed upon judgments of emotions. For example, play the Chopin Etude in F minor, Op. 10, No. 9. The theme of melancholy or anguish is overwhelming. But a canon by Guillaume de Machaut (for example, "Mon fin est mon Commencement") may not elicit any particular feeling tonality at all.

Regardless from which direction we proceed (or combination thereof) so as to engage children in philosophical inquiry, we will need to attend to the basic differences between music with words and "pure" music, that is music with no lyrics to offer textual content. Clearly lyrics parallel literature as offering clear opportunities for moral reflection. Music without words or any reference to a "story" is unique among the arts as provoking a focused attention on the pure aesthetic experience and hence exploring its affective component might be more problematic.

However, for now, let us shift focus to consider the "emotion educative model of inquiry." This model echoes Aristotle's contention that involvement with music through listening and performing can itself help to shape one's character. But how can music offer us an acquaintance with emotions, actively felt but also reflected upon as detached from lived real life experiences? Can that musical experience really "educate, " or transform one's emotive life? Let us first consider the process from the viewpoint of the audience or listener: by listening to a piece of music we begin to acquire a "vocabulary" of feelings, emotions and we are able to examine them from a distance. The aesthetic experience entails a form of physical mimicry (a function of the sounding of notes and rhythms which engage our physical selves as breathing, heart-beating, foot-tapping creatures.) Try not to respond to a particular piece of music that beckons our bodies to echo itself! But we also find a form of aesthetic knowing which renders the emotion cognitively available to us and yet protects us from the effects of an actual lived affective experience. This might be a version of the famed notion of "psychical distance"[48] and as such it guarantees the audience an opportunity to "experience" an emotion but in a safe mode wherein no real life consequences need be of immediate concern. This aesthetic intellectualizing of an emotion is made possible by the potent ability of music to convey such powerful eidetic models of these feelings.

We can also trace how the composer circumscribed the feeling so as to "enflesh" it in audible structures which, while sharing the ragged open-endedness of lived emotion, demonstrate adherence to a clear formal set of compositional rules. Even seemingly non-tonal music is notated in some form so as to guide the performers in realizing its meaning.[49] Conversations which make explicit these ideas and explore their problematic implications can help students become more self-aware of their own emotions and their "shape," or flow and ebb. As a musical composition offers a model of "controlled emotion," so too we can begin to reflect upon ways to control our own live emotions. Through feeling with music, we might be able to better practice feeling in life. The efficacy of such an approach needs to be tested but the potential deserves consideration.

Another way to explore the ways in which music and emotion intersect is to engage our student as performer. This performer can be an accomplished musician or a fresh novice. The performer has a unique relationship to the emotion within the musical piece. She must interpret and communicate that emotion or feeling tone through tonalities without herself becoming overwhelmed by it. An example can be found in the opera, *Pagliacci*; the main character is a clown whose wife has been unfaithful to him and he must pretend to laugh even as he sobs in anguish. A singer cannot cry without destroying his voice and so opera singers must convey the emotion without directly engaging in the emotion itself. It must be aesthetically realized and in ways which ring honestly even while it cannot be metaphysically realized as true for that performer. The expression of emotions may seem readily accessible in song but even with words, a singer's real meaning is embedded within the musical notes themselves; the words make the feeling overt and authenticate the feelings conveyed by tonalities, melodies and rhythms.[50] Performers offer us unique models of persons who must be able to intellectualize emotively while mastering complicated physical techniques of performance: a controlled presentation which can nevertheless offer an air of abandonment, musical "frenzy," an emotional absorption and outpouring into the musical composition. Neither technique or feeling alone will suffice to make a successful performance. None of this is possible without an enormous degree of control of one's body and one's emotions.

Whether we are inviting children to listen and search for meaning in that experience or we are asking them to perform along with us, we must focus their attention on these aspects of control and abandonment, intimately conjoined together in the musical experience. Thus, when we introduce music to students of any age, we ought to focus – among many things – upon the nature of music as expressive of feelings about which we need to learn, reflect upon and engage in practical inquiry.[51] We can seek ways of doing this as audience members and as performers, even as non-professional ones. This echoes Aristotle's point that children should learn to play an instrument as well as learn how to enjoy music and experience it for its edifying force. However, we need not commit to professional mastery for realizing the value of such learning nor need we eschew such learning.[52] A philosophical inquiry into music and emotions will help us recognize feelings, explore what they mean and how they affect us and our actions and perhaps provide a form of practice of controlling them. This reiterates a dimensions of music's role in ethical education and links the two themes that we have been tracing here. The key ingredient is the reflective piece. Music training alone, whether in aesthetic listening or in technical performance will no more elicit moral behavior than viewing or playing a sport will. The necessary middle term is the conscious and communal reflection thereon. But we might also be able to build a case that the experience of music itself can afford us with opportunities to *feel* in ways that we might not be able to safely do within our ordinary experience.

We might also wish to question whether music might not have a *damaging* effect on our affects. Are there examples of music which might be deemed dangerous in the ways about which Plato and Aristotle cautioned their educators? If yes, then the educative power of music becomes even more acutely recognized. Some possible pieces to consider might include contemporary rap music by such artists as Eminem, 50 Cent, and European artists such as MC Solaar.[53] Violent Rap music is often blamed for inciting an atmosphere of moral abandonment and the glorification of violence. This is surely an ethical lesson of the negative sort. Of course, not everyone agrees that even the most misanthropic or actively misogynistic music can really cause such behaviors. Perhaps the interest in such music is a symptom of an already existent pathology of hate or alienation. But this connection can lead us to ask whether the exploration of such potentially dangerous musical examples might not equip us with a better understanding of vices, the damaging emotions or perhaps the damaging effects of any emotion inappropriately felt or expressed. In bringing conscious, communal attention to the lyrics or rhythms of music which accompanies violent emotions, we might be able to make explicit the implicit and thereby encourage an attitude of reflection in the fans of these types of musical compositions. This can lead to a serious introduction of contemporary popular music genres in a problematizing fashion. Here their familiarity may quickly engage the students as they are eager to experience that which they know and listen to outside of the classroom. Another benefit might be in opening the teacher/facilitator to listen to music that might be unfamiliar and rejected by virtue of its provenance. In a classroom community of inquiry, we might find the most felicitous opportunity for mutual instruction. What is valued about such music as that of Black Eyed Peas[54] or 50 Cent?[55] How does contemporary popular music claim to be a critique of a "sick or ailing" culture as much as it might be a produce of one? Why do young people enjoy music which defines itself as rebellious or other than the music of the adult community? And to what extent is this a phenomenon of the modern capitalistic society? Is music actively violent, can it cause violent emotions or can we listen to even the most aggressive piece with detachment and aesthetic appreciation? This tactic provides ways to help us appreciate the aesthetic quality of the works and recognize their ethical dimensions yet,in the act of that conscious recognition, avoid the argued need for censorship.

Some Beginning Discussion Plans: Music and Emotion

These two models, the emotion educative model and the philosophical inquiry model are clearly not exclusionary and must function in tandem. Once we have chosen some exemplar pieces of music (or art), we need to develop some questioning strategies to encouraging young people to engage in philosophical reflection along with the felt engagement with the musical experience. Here our main theme is the exploration of music and the emotions. I offer the following bank of questions which can be adapted for different musical (or in a broader sense, artistic) examples and for different grade levels through adult conversations as "seed" questions:

Composers and Their Compositions

What feeling does this piece seem to convey, suggest, make you feel? How are these three experiences different: music as suggesting, conveying or causing feeling?
How does the composer achieve this "communication?"

Does a composer have to be in love to compose music which expresses love? Or other emotions?

How is composing music a craft? How is it a talent or gift? How is it a mystery?

Does every musical composition address a human feeling, emotion or experience? If no, what musical pieces do not appear to be imbued with any feelings?

Do feelings mean differently in different cultures, places or times?

Is emotion a universal language? Is music?

What is the difference between music and sound?

Performers

What role does the performer play in "speaking the language" of music to us, the audience?

Can a performer convey an emotion if she has never experienced it herself?

Can children perform as well as adults in terms of expressing the feelings within a piece of music?

To perform well, must musicians experience the feeling as they play?

The Audience: Music Appreciation

Can the same piece of music mean differently to different people? Why or why not?

Does the listener's emotional state affect how the music sounds? Why or why not?

How can we distinguish between personal connotations of music and intrinsic connotations of a musical composition? Is such a distinction even possible?

Can we recognize a feeling even if we have never experienced it in lived experience ourselves? Or have all of us experienced every feeling at some point?

Does listening to a piece of music that conveys anger make you angry? What about other feelings?

Do children/young people have different feelings than older people and vice versa?

Can listening to certain kinds of music make one a better person (more patient, loving, kind, etc.) or a worse person (short-tempered, mean, cruel), or does music really have no effect on your personality and character?

Feelings: are there good feelings and bad ones? What makes an experience an "emotive" one instead of a cognitive one?

The types of musical compositions

What role do soundtracks play in movies or on television shows? Would a movie be as convincing without the music? Is the soundtrack music meaningful without the accompanying film?

What does music add to the words in a song? What do words add to music?

Is instrumental music more "pure" than vocal music? Why or why not? What does "pure" mean here?

Are different genres of music better at expression than others?

Summary and Suggestions for Further Direction

Having explored some conversations on the nature of music as expressive of emotions and connected that to the search for a more reflective experience of music within a school setting, I have offered some reasons why music's power over our feelings is so persuasive and yet also acknowledged its aesthetic function as a form of distancing ourselves from lived experience. This has not ruled out the possibility of using such engagements within a program of moral inquiry in which we seek to better understand the nature of feelings and their role in our practical lives. We do not want to erase the aesthetic experience or reduce all listening to a prelude for philosophical inquiry (ethical or otherwise), but the opposite danger is more prevalent: that we will ignore these opportunities for aesthetic and moral growth that a communal exploration of our rich world musical heritage can offer. As in life, we cannot neatly compartmentalize our aesthetic and moral categories of experience.

Notes

[1] In fact, music might be the most problematic art to cast in the role of educating the emotions since it is often wordless and story-less. Literature, drama and representational art can more readily be seen in their role as instructing us about the right (and wrong) ways to live.

[2] Plato, Republic, III, 401e from the *Collected Dialogues of Plato*, edited by Edith Hamilton and Huntington Cairns, Princeton University Press (1961), p. 646. (All subsequent quotes from Plato are from this edition.)

[3] Modes are earlier versions of what we today call "keys," and as such, each mode has a distinctive sound.

[4] For a quick access to technical information about the nature of the Greek modes and how they differ from those of the Mediaeval period which share the same names, see John Opsopas' page on musical modes: http://www. cs. utk. edu/~mclennan/OM/BA/MT. html For a scholarly treatment, consult *The Modes of Ancient Greek Music* by David Monro, Kessinger Publishing (2004).

[5] Hence the powerful highland bagpipes were played during battles. Their sound was said to terrify their enemies. The less strident versions were more for communal amusements.

[6] Aristotle, Politics, VIII, 1339. From the Basic Works of Aristotle, Richard McKeon (editor,) Random House, 1941, p. 1310. All further references to Aristotle are from this edition.

[7] "enthusiasm is an emotion of the ethical part of the soul," Politics, 1340a, p. 1311.

[8] ibid.

[9] Ibid. , 1340a, p. 1311.

[10] These terms date from much later period in music history but as familiar to the modern ear, can capture the ideas that Aristotle presents when he speaks of rest and motion.

[11] Later in the Poetics Aristotle will argue for a psychological value of the arts as a way of expressing or even discharged emotional forces without real life risks.

[12] We recognize the controversial nature of this claim and will return to it below.

[13] Augustine discusses music in Book IX: "How I wept during your hymns and songs! The sounds flowed into my ears and the truth was distilled into my heart. This caused the feelings of devotion to overflow." As found in *Confessions*, Oxford Press, 1998, p. 164. By Book X he adopts a more cautious attitude towards music's influence over the soul and its potential for distracting one from God.

[14] One interval, an augmented fourth was labeled the "devil's tritone" and forbidden in all musical compositions as so jarring as to be a tool of Satan himself for disturbing our spirits.

[15] *Philosophy of Music Education Review*, 13, no. 1 (Spring 2005), pps. 77-94.

[16] A. Kertz-Welzel, op. cit. , p. 78.

[17] Ibid., p. 80.

[18] Peter Kivy details this shift from music in its utilitarian role of accompanying ceremonies and entertainments to "pure aesthetic enjoyment" as beginning in the eighteenth century concert hall. See his Introduction to a Philosophy of Music, Oxford University Press, 2002.

[19] Ibid., p. 84.

[20] Ibid., p. 86.

[21] Consider Frederich Nietzsche's view of music's ultimate power to free ourselves from fallacious ethical restraints.

[22] While I have chosen to narrow my focus to this particular exchange medium, I recommend the text, Music and Emotion, edited by Patrik N. Juslin and John A. Sloboda (Oxford University Press, 2001) as a definitive source for a cross-disciplinary exploration of this theme. Another excellent source for a review of this debate is Peter Kivy's *Introduction to a Philosophy of Music* (2002.)

[23] Found in the *Philosophy of Music Education Review*, 12, no. 1 (spring 2004), pps. 30-42.

[24] Kingsley Price, op. cit. , p. 33-34.

[25] Ibid., p. 34

[26] Price quotes Langer from her *Philosophy in a New Key*, 228, in his article, p. 36.

[27] Op. cit., p. 38.

[28] Op. cit., p. 41.

[29] Op. cit., p. 41.

[30] *Philosophy of Music Education Review*, 12, no. 1 (Spring 2004.)

[31] Reimer, op. cit. , p. 5.

[32] Ibid. , p. 6.

[33] Reimer offers such examples as Beethoven's *Eroica Symphony*, Debussy's *La Mer*, Chopin's *Pathetique Sonata*, Mendelssohn's *Danse Macabre* on p. 8. We can easily come up with many other examples of music which is labeled as a form of discursive expression or storytelling.

[34] Ibid., p. 12.

[35] Ibid., p. 14.

[36] Bennett Reimer, "Philosophy in the School Music Program," *Philosophy of Music Education Review*, 13, no. 1 (Spring 2005,) p. 34.

[37] In addition to Reimer, the participants included Sandra Stauffer, Randall Allsup and Mary J. Reichling.

[38] "Toward Mindful Music Education: a Response to Bennett Reimer" in the same issue as cited above.

[39] Stauffer, op. cit., p. 136.

[40] Langer, as quoted by Stauffer, op. cit. , p. 136.

[41] Stauffer, op. cit., p. 138.

[42] As offered in the article, "The Mirror of Aesthetic Education: Philosophy Looks at Art and Art Looks at Philosophy," *Thinking*, Vol 15:

i. example of Arabo-Andalusian music, c. ninth century, inshad-baitain, nouba: Rash Ad Dail insiraf darj (rhythm) nouba: Raml Al Maya, *Musique Arabo-Andalouse*, Harmonia Mundi HMC90389, track 1

ii. *Mukamu, Free Melody, and Dance Music*, Uighur folk song (15th century, China), *China Time to Listen*, Ellipsis Arts CD3594, track 5

iii. *Salvator mundi, Domine*, plainsong from the Sarum Rite (7th-12th century), hymn for compline of Christmas Day, *Sarum Chant*, Gimell 454917-2, track 18

iv. *Der Leiermanni*, song by Franz Schubert (19th century) from *Winterreise*, Winterreise, EMI Classics 56445

v. *Symphony No. 3*, Henryk Gorecki, Opus No. 36 (1976), third movement with voice, *Symphony No. 3*, Elektra Nonesuch 979282-2, track 3

vi. "Prelude" from *Cello Suite No. 1*, J. S. Bach (18th century), the first movement of six for solo cello, *Inspired by Bach*, Yo-Yo Ma, Sony 52K63203, track 1

vii. "*Fas et nefas ambulant*" (Right and Wrong go walking)-from the *Carmina Burana*, twelvethcentury, the Boston Camerata, Erato, 0630-14987-2

viii. *Kanon*, Pachelbel, Classical Music for Peoiple who hate Classical Music, Pro Arte CDM 834

ix. "In the Hall of the Mountain King," Edvard Grieg

x. *Die Walkure prelude*, Richard Wagner, *Heavy Classics II*, Angel 7243-5

xi. "Der Vogelfanger bin ich ja," W. A. Mozart, *Die Zauberflöte*, DG 410967-2.

xii. ""Der Hölle Rache kocht in meinem Herzen," Mozart, *Die Zauberflöte*, DG 410967-2.

xiii. "Sampi Wenpeng," Chinese Deep South Ensemble from *China :Time to Listen*, Ellipsis CD 3594

[43] While we do not have the time to develop this theme extensively, I recommend the text, A Philosophical Translation of the Dao De Jing by Roger T. Ames and David L. Hall, Random House, 2003. In their introduction they offer the following comment: "Concrete feelings, the real site of knowing, become selectively abstracted and impoverished when they are resolved into the rational currency of names, concepts and theories without adequate deference to the affective ground of their cognitive superstructure" (p. 26).

[44] See Eva Alerby's and Cecilia Ferm's article, "Leaning Music- Embodied experience in the life-world," in *Philosophy of Music Education Review*, no. 13, no. 2 (Fall 2005).

[45] We will consider below that option of using popular music but I want to suggest that introducing children to a rich variety of music can have wider benefits since these experiences can contribute to the wider educational goal of "enlarging a self." (This phrase references one of Matthew Lipman's characteristics of the function of education.)

[46] This idea is borrowed from E. D. Hirsch, Jr. and his argument for a rich content-based education in his The Schools we Need and why we don't have them, 1999.

[47] See some suggested musical samples below:

While I have included here a number of examples with lyrics which could clearly be understood to express certain feelings, the emotions are not dependent upon the language for expressive reality. In *The Disciplined Mind*, Howard Gardner engages in an extended analysis of the first act trio from Mozart's *Le*

Emotions felt	Sorrow	Anger	Love	Longing	Gaiety	Fear	Excitement
Sample musical piece	Franz Schubert's "Gretchen am Spinnrade"	W. A. Mozart's *"Der Hölle Rache kocht in meinem Herzen"*	Prokofiev's Romeo and Juliet ballet	R. Wagner's Prelude to **Tristan und Isolde**	L. Beethoven's Symphony # 6, second movement		R. Wagner's "Ride of the Valkyrie" From **Die Walkure**
	Goercki's Symphony # 3						

Nozze di Figaro in which we find fear, jealousy, malicious humor, self-righteous priggishness . . . all in the space of 5 minutes of music.

[48] See Edward Bulloch's "Psychical Distance as a factor in art and as an esthetic principle," (1915) quoted in excerpts: http://www. csulb. edu/~jvancamp/361_r9. html

[49] Again, I reference the excellent discussion by Peter Kivy on the nature of emotions in a formalistic theory of music in his text, cited above.

[50] Or, in some cases, the music can directly belay the meaning of the words. For example, listen to the lyrics and music of Bob Marley's "I Shot the Sheriff."

[51] Thus, we are suggesting a pairing of Aristotle's didactic use of the arts for character education with Reimer's invitation to engage children themselves in reflecting on the nature and role of emotion in music. We must be careful not to treat music as simply a utilitarian tool for moral education and it certainly cannot suffice on its own in any carefully crafted moral education program. We do not want to destroy the aesthetic aspects of the art experience but that need not preclude a conscious recognition of the role of arts in the practical realm of human valuing in choice and action.

[52] Unlike Aristotle, we may not see this as inappropriate for our students as some sort of trade beneath them. Since the Romantic era, the artist has been considered as an exalted soul, not a mere technician on par with one's slaves, the Greek flute girls.

[53] Whether rap music, specifically "gansta rap" really does lead to immorality is an actively debated claim with extensive literature, both of the scholarly and popular nature. A thorough review of this issue is beyond the purview of this paper but may be a project to consider in the future. The fall 2004 riots in France which involved a disenfranchised North African youth were claimed to be predicted by or perhaps even incited by certain rap artists who sang of the disconnect of these youth from French economic and social culture.

[54] The song called "My Humps"" by the Black Eyed Peas could be used to examine misogyny and the materialistic values of young men and women as it might also be a source of dance hall exuberance.

[55] "I'll Whip your head boy" is a song which glorifies violence, but many of 50 Cent's songs could be examples of such music which stirs up a wide range of negative and antisocial feelings or perhaps serve as ironic commentary on a decadent and unjust society.

Discussion after Wendy Turgeon's Presentation

Michael Schleifer: Paul's question was: is the sadness we feel listening to music the same as genuine sadness? If I get angry, really get angry, me getting angry at something that's made me angry, I agree that's one thing. And if I listen to a play, watch a play or get involved with a story, and really get involved with a protagonist that things are happening, I also get angry. I remember however, that Aristotle made a differentiation, but why it's not the same, I'm not sure. One guess I have is that I can be angry and it's my anger, but when I listen to a play, or get involved with someone else's anger, it's in fact somebody else's anger – it's more like what we were talking about yesterday. It's being able to be empathic, and pick up the other's anger. Now I don't know if that's the way you were going to go, because you said you didn't quite want to accept that the sadness, that we all say, but there are pieces that we all say, it's universal. Children can say, that's sad and how do you feel. They say, "we're sad." There is this unanimity.

On the other hand, we all lose a loved one, and we're also sad, and so on. Well okay, we're dealing with emotions, are they of the same kind. Well, you weren't quite ready to go there yet, and this because the sadness we feel in with the music is something like the sadness I may feel with somebody in a play or movie. Something's happening, I still feel sad and I cry, but it's not my sadness, it's empathic sadness. Is that it?

Sharon Bailin: I was going the same way, because I think we have to distinguish amongst the three cases at least. I mean, the sadness of the music, first of all, you are exploring the idea of music expressing an emotion, and the problems in that, because it doesn't express the way a person expresses, or is it a relationship one of representing, does the music represent or imitate an emotion, does it imitate the dynamics of an emotion, and so and so . . . I think those are different possibilities in terms of looking at that relationship, but I think one of the oddities of music, is that it seems like it's a case of emotion without an intentional object. That it's not music about something. And I was thinking back to Catherine's question yesterday. Is there pure emotion, well I don't know. Maybe the anger you feel, listening to a piece of music is closest to pure anger than anything else because it doesn't seem to have an object, so that could be it.

But the theater case, I think is a little different because you do have an intentional object. I mean, the theater case, you're representing a real human situation, and you're putting yourself in that situation to some extent. So there's some object, you could say "why?" Well, I'm angry because this character did this to that character. But nonetheless, this still seems different from the real case (a felt emotion), because you know it's not real. So there's an element in which you're feeling it, but you're not going to go up there and hit the villain, or you're not going to run out of the theater because you're frightened. At some level, you know it's not real and this isn't happening, they're actors but you still feel something.

Wendy Turgeon: There are also multiple events going on in a play where there isn't in the music.

William Arsenio: When you played those pieces, I was able to label a few, but I didn't feel. There is a difference recognizing what the emotion is that the music might elicit, whether I actually felt wistful, pensive, or whatever.

So there's kind of the recognition of what the emotional content is and then there's that extra stuff that happens sometimes, that you feel that emotional content. It's like a cold cognition or a hot cognition, an awareness with emotion. I'm not sure if that connects.

Wendy Turgeon: The Carl Orf piece, the one that I've played extensively with the xylophone in it, I played the whole thing because I can't stop it once I get started. It's music Vekenda. He wrote these pieces for children to play, and there's a sense that when I listen to that, it makes me happy.

Michael Schleifer: I wrote playfulness.

Wendy Turgeon: That's a good call. But there's a sense there in which you don't know if you feel the emotion, and you're right. There are some pieces and people will listen to rap music and actually be angry at the end of it. Others will say, no it doesn't make me angry, I just listen to it because it's expressing anger.

Phil Guin: I seem to hear two things. On the one hand, you're saying the music brings about emotion, expresses emotion, and on the other hand, you're saying music causes emotion. And I'm just wondering, I keep thinking of the movie *Clockwork Orange*, which is taking a causal view of music in such a way, that you can't pin down any reaction to music, it can make you into a Napoleon, it can make you into a Hitler or it can make you into a peace loving citizen.

Wendy Turgeon: That's the associative power though. I mean, something awful happens to you when listening to a particular piece. There was a movie where this guys was torturing this woman, and playing the Schubert song, and yet it was just a . . .

Phil Guin: What was that? I just saw that too.

Wendy Turgeon: It was awful.

Lee Londei: I found in a lot of the pieces, I was associating visually something that the music as a sound-track too, an image that I pondered. I was picturing someone walking in a forest, or whatever it was, I don't know if that's to be learned. I associate a certain kind of music with a movie I've seen, and I look for those images but that's one thing I wanted to say.

But as much as the music evokes a representation or an emotion for me, so does a novelette or a story, or a scenario, it's like a tool that can bring about the same questioning.

Wendy Turgeon: And I wasn't trying to argue that it could do better.

Cynthia Martiny: I was thinking of vicarious empathy, you know when it happens in groups of men. When one person tells a story, the other one will capture a story that somewhat is triggered by the story, the content by the story, feels the emotion and can share on an emotional level, but not necessarily on the content level. And so that's a little of what I was thinking when you talked about real emotion or not a real emotion. I was wondering what Michael meant by, is it possibly that if someone else's anger, when you're the one who's feeling it. How can it be someone else's, and yet it goes in length of projective test and projection.

Michael Schleifer: I think when I am empathic, it's not the same, and cannot be the same, as my own anger. If we agree with that, then the parallel of it's true. For example, let's say I really get involved with a story or movie, and I'm feeling sad; my grand daughter and I are crying, these is some level at which we know this is a movie, and therefore it's an analogy of some sort, it's not quite the same. It's complicated that the two states are not identical.

And with music, it's more complicated. That's why Martha Nussbaum devotes a huge chapter, using all these groups, still puzzling it out. I don't think she has a solution either. And Jennifer Robinson has a book I just read too. They all claim this is a huge puzzle. I haven't seen anybody who's given the answer yet. Because music, precisely leaving beside the ones that have a story, they usually do, but there is music that has no story, and yet in some miraculous way, we kind of all agree. Barry Levinson of Maryland wrote an article about Mendelsohn's Hebrides overture. And he claimed that even a complex emotion like hope, many philosophers said you could have sadness or anger, but you could never have hope. And I read that, and said I don't believe that. How could someone listen to it and hear hope.

Well, I played the music for my grandchildren, and I asked your question, what are you feeling? My grandson said, I don't know, kind of happy. My granddaughter, who was 9, said "that's hope." So she did a little mini experiment on her friends. So I referred this to Barry Levinson, and he said oh well, that's empirical data, thanks very much. He's a philosopher.

So that's what I meant, that there's an analogy to your question on empathy, that I think you would agree that your anger that you feel as a therapist, or the sadness you pick up in your client, you have to distance it. Well, there's some distancing nevertheless in the anger, or sadness emotion I'm picking up in watching the play. But as Sharon said, it gets even more complicated with the music because in music it doesn't have a plot. And we are all feeling sad. And why are we feeling sad. For me, it's still a puzzle. I haven't seen a solution for it.

Cynthia Martiny: So we recognize what's foreign inside us, it's not our emotion but somebody else's . . .

Ann Sharp: But isn't it a question of going back to what Phil said? Its one thing to say what the music is assigning, but it's another thing to say that what we are actually feeling. For example, during the oriental music, I could see people write down "happy," "cheerful," or something like that. But I wasn't feeling happy or cheerful. There's two things going on here emotively: us and the music.

Michael Schleifer: Some of us always feel it and label it, like me. In other words, I was trying to play the test. I was listening to the music and saying "okay, what do I feel?" And when I didn't feel it I didn't label it and I left it blank. I don't divorce it, as Bill was saying, which you're saying as well. I think you asked a question of what is this music supposed to make me feel? What does she want me to give as an answer?

Ann Sharp: You actually knew what I was feeling. I was puzzled because I was trying to figure out and I was having a very difficult time.

Cynthia Martiny: As if there's a narrow response.

Wendy Turgeon: Paul, I think it was in your paper where you modified Wordsworth, and spoke about emotion recollected and tranquility. That sort of captures what we're trying to get at.

Music is emotion recollected. So, it's experienced emotion that is not experienced because it has an object (I'm mad at this person, or I'm happy about this situation). Or it's the other person's happiness or sadness, but it's not just a cognitive recognition, "oh, he's mad," there's some experiential personal experience there, but its not the same thing as feeling happy or feeling anxious. It's a hybrid in some way.

146 *Talking to Children About Responsibility and Control of Emotions*

Or maybe it's its own category, which I think. Isn't that what your question was about then? What's it saying in-between it is emotion, or it seems to be emotion but it really isn't.

Paul Harris: I'd like to deal directly with that particular question.

I do think there's a distinction to be drawn between the way music expresses emotion, and the extent to which it does evoke emotion (although it seems to me what it expresses is roughly correlated with what it evokes most of the time). That's why one of your grandchildren, Michael, said it was hope and the other one sort of expressed hope himself, so to speak.

The question I have, I think is in some sense much more blunt. It seems to me, irrespective of the genuiness or authenticity of the kind of emotion that music either expresses or revokes, that ,so what; in what sense has this anything to do with education? How could it possibly be a contributory factor in the education of the emotions?

I can see that it could be a contributory factor in increasing children's aesthetic sensibility with respect to music. I'm just so totally skeptical that it's got anything to do with education of the emotions. So maybe you can convince me otherwise.

Wendy Turgeon: It's a hypothesis, but it's a hypothesis that it's been around for centuries, and music provides me with an opportunity to experientially reflect upon a range of emotions without me being in danger or in trouble, or even just emotionally exhausted because I'm going through these range of emotions. I think music has a potential there to help children, and adults, for that matter. To better understand themselves and their feelings by giving them an opportunity to explore what those range of human feelings are like.

Paul Harris: But couldn't one just say, at best, it plays the keyboard of the emotions. Perhaps a little bit intensely, perhaps in a safe environment but, I mean just in the same way as certain chocolate liqueurs, can give you a little bit of alcohol. So what, nothing more.

Wendy Turgeon: Well, if all you do is listen to it, then you're right; nothing educational is happening.

Ann Sharp: But you were thinking of using it as a trick.

Wendy Turgeon: That's correct. It would have to be discussed, it would have to be explored and I'd have to think about "well, why in that I felt this, when you felt that?" How is that different? What would make this music sad? So it does have a cognitive component where you have to discuss and explore it!

Paul Harris: I certainly acknowledge that you could do that, and I would think you could have an interesting discussion. But in the end, it would be nothing, but the aesthetics of one's response to the music. I can't that see it's got to have anything to do with, for example, how you deal with the complexities of ordinary life. I don't see that just by having a more nuanced and differentiated sense of what your emotion is vis à vis somebody else's, with respect to some playing song that somehow or other you are going to go out into ordinary life and be sensitized to the variation in our responses to emotionally drastic situations. It just doesn't work.

Phil Guin: That's been an argument against the arts in the school.

Paul Harris: I'm not erecting an argument against the arts. What I'm trying to erect an argument against is the claim that you justify the arts in terms of the education of emotions. You justify the arts in terms of the arts. Period.

Introduction to Ann Sharp's Paper

A little history: in the last couple of years, I have been involved with Pierre, Catherine and Alexander, in devising a program in philosophy for children with a very focused purpose: the prevention of violence, and in particular dealing with child abuse. I did not find this very easy at all. I decided in both novels that I use, to go through the philosophy of body. I couldn't figure out how else to do it. Now I've been asked if I would devise a program that would not so much deal with violence and child abuse but in general, the education of the emotions. In the philosophy of emotions and we have come up with rough drafts of 10 short stories that will be designed for middle school children as well as a manual that will explore and focus on various emotions (including emotion identification). As I mentioned earlier in the conference, naming is only half the job. The other half of the job is to try to become conscious, if we can, of the beliefs that underlie our emotions, to bring them up on the table and then submit those beliefs to public inquiry (whether they are valid or not valid, whether we think we can find evidence for them, do other people have different beliefs, and then we would share those beliefs, etc.). In the process we hope to foster caring thinking, which includes another way of saying the same thing, and fostering of a kind of a relational consciousness so that I begin to think of myself as a being in relation to all of you.

"In daycare Mr. Williams says there are only 2 rules in this daycare center," says Jessie. "One is that we always tell the truth and the second is we have to treat each other as persons. Well we asked Mr. Williams what those words meant and he said you just wait and see, we'll find out. So in a sense the whole story is about trying to figure out what he meant by this. . .I have problems with persons because I think my doll is a person and Roller is everything to me, she's just everything to me. But I also have problems with my peers because they don't like me to bring my doll to the daycare centre and they taunt me and they are mean. I can't understand why they would do that and maybe it's because I'm a boy, maybe, but I don't think so. My mom she's better, she works all the time, you know and I'm in a daycare center from 7 till 4 in the afternoon 'cause my mother has to go to work early and comes home late and she is always tired., I don't know why, but she is always tired. So what was I telling you, oh, I have Roller and she's my best friend. And she's a person and she's real. So person and real and you have these rules about truth and then you got to respect all those – I know you got to tell the truth. I'm conscious of those words. Mr. Williams uses them and we use them in school.

"Very often, here I'm working out of people; Iris Murdoch and Simone Veil and people like that, Nussbaum of course. This normative thinking that I'm involved in is going to mean that I have some capacity, some skills in decentering. I know you think it is easy but I don't think it's easy. I'm the center of the world – my world revolves around me and that's very hard in the daycare center because I'm not the only one there. Do you know there are 15 kids in my daycare and Mr. Williams says you are one, you are important as a person but you are 1 among many. Of course you have to understand, when we bring our dolls we have more than 14 persons. Another thing in this normative thinking is that we are supposed to learn how to overcome this kind of narcissistic way of going about things and to learn to put our egos in perspective. Now Mr. Williams does not say those kinds of words, but I think that is what he has in mind. So we learn to ask ourselves certain kinds of questions and in the daycare center when things happen, for example, Ramona came to school when she had this gorgeous doll, it was beautiful and she had on a ceremony dress and it had beautiful colors and I said that is a lovely doll, what kind of doll is that? She said it is a Hopi Indian doll and I didn't know what that meant but I thought it sure is nice and could I play with it? No, she said. So I said could Roller (my doll) play with it? And she said No, Roller can't play with it either. Well, I was just so disgusted! So I said to her, that's very selfish. I know that word. She said to me, it is not! My doll is very expensive. I don't know what that had to do with anything but I didn't say anything and then she said and there is not many like it in the world, or something like that but I didn't really understand that. I said to myself, there is only one like that? What is she talking about? But I let it go.

"Then Mr. Williams said hey, we're going to do something else now – how many of you would like to go out and play in the playground. So guess what, they all went out to play but I didn't. Romona did go out and left that Hopi Indian doll sitting right there. So what happened, well I don't know how it happened to tell you the truth, I think is was Roller, I really do think it was Roller, but all of a sudden there I was walking across the room with this Hopi Indian doll in my arms and in the daycare center we have a little house and we have little tea table and chairs and stuff like that and I stood in front of the house and said I wonder where the Hopi doll will be happy and I thought about putting her in the living room and then I thought oh no that'll be too busy and then I thought about putting her in the kitchen oh no, that's not right and finally Roller said to me – why not put her in the back bedroom. Well that made sense and we put her there, so we put her in the back bedroom and all of a sudden, did you ever feel like someone is standing behind you, it's really odd, and I look around and guess who is there, Mr. Williams and he says to me Jess, what are you doing? I said, well Roller thought it would be a good idea to put the Hopi doll in the back bedroom of the doll house so that we could play together. Did Romona say you could play with this doll?, Yes. Will you be very long? Well, it will take me awhile. And then, all of a sudden, people coming in from the playground and I hear this scream, a big scream, Where's my doll? Where's my doll? Well I've never been so disgusted, that girl was acting like a real baby and finally Mr. Williams says, well, I know where your doll is Romona, calm down, she's very safe and he went over in his lovely hands he took the doll out of the back bedroom and gave it to Romona. Well now you see I have a real problem, because number one, I think I have lied, I'm not sure about that and then Mr. Williams suggested I didn't treat Romona as a person because then he asked me how would you feel if someone took Roller away from you like that.

"So anyways I went home that night and in terms of normative thinking, I got into bed with Roller, we always sleep together and she said to me, no I said to her, Well Roller, what kind of a day do you think this has been? And she said not so good. I said what do you mean? Well, how would you like to live in a world where everybody lied and nobody told the truth. And how would you like to be in a world where people didn't treat you as a person and that they stole your doll and stole your bicycle, etc. And so I had a lot to think about that night."

One more thing – one of the things we are trying to do in this community is to foster a sense of connectedness among the children, and we do that by hopefully building this community of inquiry. If you ask what is a community of inquiry I'd say it's a place where we learn how to inquire together. How do we learn that, because the teacher models it for us in the beginning and then we internalize it. We are very good at it now. "Mr. Williams has us make, I don't know what you call this thing but you put it over your head, it would be an R or a C or let me see E and so when you want to ask for reasons R would step forward, when you want to ask for a counter example C, evidence (E) and we play it very well. That's what we do in the community and we talk about things, very controversial things. I didn't know they were controversial by the way, I thought of a simple term like friend – what could be simpler than that? I mean Roller is my best friend and everyone knows what a best friend is. When we started talking about friendship and do you know there were people in my class who said that someone could be your best friend and they never played with them physically, now, how can that be? How can that be? How can you have a friend who you didn't trust? Or how could you have a friend you didn't think was going to back you up and be loyal? No, that's impossible.

"We've already decided that there are examples when someone can be a friend and you don't play with them, for example, if he has a sickness one kid said and he has to stay in bed and you can't play with him but he's still your friend, you know. Anyways we are on about our business trying to figure out what friend is and he has his hand up and when we call on him he brings us all the way back to the beginning of the conversation. It's like he hasn't heard anything and that's really hard. Then we have to start all over again and explaining to this kid what we have done. So following the inquiry where it leads, it has something to do with letting your own thoughts go for a while and listening. These are some of the things we try to do in our community. Most of you have seen those over and over again. We are coming to rely on each other though. That's something we learned from Vygotsky. Of course no one mentions that. When we came together for the first time, I was very good at giving counter examples, Mr. Williams said so and Alexander was very good at asking questions. I'm not so good at asking questions. And Lee, she was great at saying, that doesn't make sense to me. Pierre would say, what's going to happen, what's going to happen if we do that, in other words he was asking for consequences. Then there is always Michael. Michael is forever saying, well did you ever think of, and couldn't you look at it from another perspective, but he doesn't use the word perspective, couldn't you look at if from another side and then we have engage in his alternative. Well once in awhile, Michael has a very good idea and then we follow the inquiry that way. We are beginning to rely on each other and we are beginning to see that some of us are much better at some of these skills than others are. We practice everyday, and we practice. Sometimes we talk about stealing, sometimes we talk about lying, sometimes about what is it to be afraid, or whatever. And sure enough Alexander is asking the question, he's noticing the bad inferences and Michael's giving the examples but, you know, one day I might have to go home and I might have to make a judgement at home and what am I going to do guys. Here I am at home, I can't call you all up and say, come on over to my house because I have to make a decision or a judgement about something. So Alexander I need you to ask the questions and Lee I need you to do this – no you don't do it like this, you remember what Alexander did and then you start asking yourself the questions and you start questioning your own inferences, etc. So, internalization hopefully will take place. That doesn't mean you stop relying on each other because no matter how many ideas I have I always find out that the community had more. They can always generate more ideas than I have and I find that very, very helpful. You know what, they really care about me, they want me to grow. I have a few problems, I sometimes jump to conclusions, now Pierre is forever – now there she goes again he says, I'm getting a little better every day and I owe it to Pierre.

"Another thing is as we are talking about all these things I am beginning to understand that a lot of people don't think the way I do about friendship, they don't even think the way I do about the self, they don't think the way I do about a simple question like, what's a family. We started talking about the family the other day and you won't believe what some kids think what a family is. I'm learning how to listen, it was hard for me in the beginning but I'm doing a little better, etc. I'm learning not only how to take into account other perspectives, but to put myself in the place of Pierre so I can help him find reasons for what he is trying to say. He's not too good at it. The reason I can do it this is because I can get inside and I can do it from his perspective now. In one way I'm getting more confident because I am practicing these skills. In another way I am getting more humble because I realize how interdependent I am, how much I need others in order to really reason well.

"In the beginning it was hard for us to even understand what each other was saying. It's not that we don't speak the same language, we speak the same language but we have to keep saying, what do you mean by, and is this what you are saying. Could you say that again in simpler words, etc. We are learning how to take turns. It's was hard, in the beginning because we all wanted to talk at once and we couldn't hear each other so Mr. Williams said well if we do that what are we going to do, so now we are learning how to take turns. In the beginning we were raising our hands but we don't do that any more, now we are learning, we just can tell, you watch each other's body and then you learn to give a little and you can see he wants to talk.

"Not only are we learning to appreciate each other's strengths, but we also realize with time how fragile we are. A lot of us don't have nice home lives and a lot of us cry and a lot of us sometimes when we come to school don't feel very nice because there has been a big fight at home right before we left. We are learning how to take care of each other and to recognize we are all vulnerable in some ways and we can take care of each other and make each other's lives full of wonder and curiosity and good things. Ultimately as the Beatles say, with everyday we are getting a little bit better, just a little bit better at making better and better judgements, even about our emotions."

I was going to tell you more about good judgement – there is one important thing that Berlin says, that I think we should remember in our discussions, somebody who has good judgement, doesn't just have a cognitive understanding of the situation, he has almost an emotional feel for the data because he's been soaked in it day after day. He's participated in a community of inquiry, and it is a form of life. Emotions have been part and parcel of learning how to identify emotions and take care of emotions, learning to justify our emotions to each other. This is the way we go about our daily work with inquiry and in that sense there is no way that you can divorce the education of the emotions from the education of good judgement.

Chapter 7
How to Educate the Emotions in the Context
of the Classroom Community of Inquiry
Ann Sharp

Introduction

In this paper I would like to show how the transformation of traditional classrooms into classrooms of communities of inquiry can bring about not only better thinking on the part of students but also a growth in emotional maturity. The classroom community of inquiry fosters the growth of three kinds of thinking: critical, creative and caring. Although equally important, caring thinking is crucial in making possible the democratic dialogue essential to communal inquiry. It focuses on the building of solidarity and the preservation of values and relationships. It enables the child to deal with the relationship of self to other, learning how one can put one's ego in perspective in light of the other's views, interests, and concerns. Caring thinking attends to the feelings of students as well as their thinking. It aims at preserving, cherishing, and celebrating that which they value and fostering the courage to let go of that which no longer serves the growth of the self in relation to the other. . It consists in the sharpening of numerous skills of translation involved in the understanding of different world views and the making of new meanings. It relies on communication, translation, empathy, compassion, understanding, and dialogue. When it is embedded in communal dialogical inquiry, it constitutes an education of the emotions, a necessary constituent of global intelligence. Caring thinking aims to foster relational consciousness, dialogue, understanding and inquiry while at the same time helping children to tend to the reasonableness of their emotions in given contexts.

What is Caring Thinking?

Lipman has written extensively in *Thinking in Education* of the role of critical and creative thinking in making better judgments. Critical thinking aims to help children make better judgments by helping them become conscious of criteria, paying attention to context and developing dispositions of self correction. Creative thinking, with its focus on creative judgments, aims to develop a finely tuned sensitivity to context, a consciousness regarding criteria and fostering dispositions of self-expression and self-transcendence. Caring thinking is quite different.

Caring thinking fuses of emotional and cognitive thinking when it concerns matters of importance. In ordinary language, we use terms like "thinking with your heart" or thinking in terms of your personal values. Caring thinking empowers students to establish a sound value system from which to make sound, compassionate judgements. Expressions of caring thinking are as much judgments as expressions of critical or creative thinking. Caring thinking is what enables us to pick out what we think is important in a particular context (ethical, aesthetic or scientific) it determines what we focus on. In many ways, it is caring thinking that determines our moral and aesthetic perceptions. As with any other judgment, we should try to justify our caring to ourselves and, if asked, to others. Caring thinking expresses itself in prizing, esteeming, cherishing, healing, consoling, nurturing, empathizing, sympathizing, valuing, appreciating, celebrating, and responding to the other. Elgin calls this *understanding that comes to us through empathizing from the inside*. It tends to approach the other (person, object, environment, etc.) from the inside and like, Rodin creating his works of sculpture, it works from the inside out. It is caring thinking that is responsible for the fostering of a relational consciousness in children. Rather than viewing things atomistically, the caring thinker tends to focus on the relationships between things; this results in deep understanding. Caring thinking arises from our perceptual, sensual and emotional lives and determines how we act in a situation. (Think of the caring doctor versus the doctor who treats your body like a piece of meat.). While empathy, compassion, emotional intensity and deep sensitivity are at the core of caring thinking, Lipman (1994) sees caring thinking as having four distinct, but interrelated, aspects.

Valuational Thinking: To value is to highly appreciate or prize. It has two parts. One is about valuing or appreciating concrete things for their sensory or aesthetic appeal, rather than monitory worth, such as appreciating nature, art, or objects (including seeing the value or beauty in the often unacceptable – beauty in the ugly). This may be expressed by being overcome by the sound of a particular piece of music, the sight of a whale rescued from the beach and making its way to sea, or being awed by the oddities of nature such as shafts of sunlight through a forest or reflecting on the ocean. Children frequently are long term collectors, prizing objects for their feel, colour or shape, e. g. feathers, pebbles, minerals. The other aspect of valuational thinking involves valuing the abstract, e. g. valuing attitudes, behaviors, and personal qualities. Here, one can look widely at the different values of different societies, or clarify personal values by examining what things mean to you, or your attitudes and behaviors. The importance of valuational thinking lies in the fact that it underpins the establishment of ethical principles and moral modes of inquiry. Valuational thinking firstly involves thinking through a clarification process of choosing, prizing, and affirming. Students who have developed heightened sensitivity and emotional intensity have particular strength in the valuational thinking side of caring thinking. They are committed to giving reasons to oneself for one's values

Affective Thinking: To experience strong emotional and cognitive response to an offense. This is the emotional response to a wrongdoing by a person having a clear understanding of right and wrong, and a strong sense of justice. Attitudes and emotions of others have a strong impact on these caring thinkers. They feel intense empathy and will respond with indignation that injustice has been done to an innocent person or creature. Their response shows great depth of commitment, clarity of thought, willingness to articulate the case in terms of right and wrong, and strong determination to see justice done. This is genuine altruistic or other-regarding behavior which only occurs in the presence of empathy. At a very early age, children are able to interpret body language and the emotions in the tone of voice. They often realize subtle implications, or read excess meaning into ordinary statements, jump to conclusions, take offense, or reject statements or attitudes out of hand. offense to themselves or others (particularly other children) is taken seriously. They seem to suffer even more than the victim. Affective thinking consists in acknowledging these feelings and working through ways to deal with them in a non-violent manner. This includes becoming familiar with the rights of the individual and the processes that preserve these rights (e. g. giving each student opportunities to participate in making class decisions and creating classroom, communal inquiry and playground rules). It is important that children learn how to discuss all sides of an issue, taking into account the different perspectives of the group, focusing on how individuals are affected by another's words or behavior. This practice helps children to see the complexity of situations and avoid wrong thinking. Children become highly conscious of context, criteria, and the importance of seeing things from different perspectives. The key characteristics of a caring thinker may be summed up as: a strong sense of justice coupled with a commitment to non-violence and an intense sensitivity to the feelings of others.

Active Thinking: To passionately care about and be involved with a cause. Peter Singer, in *How are We to Live? Ethics in an Age of Self-Interest*, suggests that "in promoting the concept of an ethical life we need to be strongly motivated to act in ways which will contribute to making the world a better place for all of its inhabitants." This exemplifies higher order thinking. Such thinking is about using language, gesture, planning, and/or action to support a cause or belief. Children come to learn how to attend to what they can do about a situation, rather than being overwhelmed and feeling helpless. Emotional intensity manifests itself in the on-going dialogue, demonstrating a depth of sincerity and passionate commitment to caring about something. The key characteristics of a caring thinker are: highly conscious of the other, passionate commitment, inner locus of control, and a disposition to improve the situation compassionate.

Normative Thinking: To compare the actual with what could be. This is about knowing the reality of the situation but having a vision, or sense of idealism, of how things should, or could, be. School children frequently become distressed by news or documentaries relating to adverse situations because of this evident discrepancy. The anguish felt is compounded by a concern for humanity as well as a yearning for fairness and justice. Intellectual, emotional, and imaginational intensity are equally involved. Normative thinking may be on a local or global level. Often children are concerned with universal laws and principles, global issues such as preservation of the environment, human and animal rights, in such a way that rises above the usual provincial and personal ethical concerns of most people. To do so requires decentering from egoism. Caring thinking embodies three fundamental ethical tools: empathy, moral imagination, and decentering. The following philosophical questions involve normative thinking: What kind of world (society, community) do you want to live in? What does it mean to be a person of the world? What values ought I commit myself to? How should I attend to the other? The key characteristics of normative thinking may be seen as: sensitivity to inconsistency between ideals and behavior, ability to conceptualize and offer solutions to society's problems, and deep concern for humanity and global issues. A serious issue for students is that their early concern for value issues is at a high cognitive and deep emotional levels whilst their ability to cope and act to right these situations is beyond their control. Lipman's viewing of caring thinking as an essential aspect of intelligence acknowledges not only the affective traits of caring thinking but also its manifestation in an over-all intensity and commitment to act. This intensity, in turn, acts as the motivating force affecting all aspects of thinking and behavior. Fostering caring thinking addresses the intensity of feelings, compassion, sense of justice, and empowers students with strategies to respond at a dialogical, constructive, and non-violent level.

The Fostering of Relational Consciousness

To engage in caring thinking is to foster a relational consciousness in one's everyday life. Relational consciousness is knowing and feeling oneself intimately connected with and part of everything that is, and it also means coming to act and relate out of that awareness. It is experiencing oneself not as an atomistic ego but as a self in relationship to the other. Some have called this consciousness the we-consciousness. The question is, "how big is your we?" (1996, Monk Kidd). Children's future on this planet may hang on how we come to answer that question. For a long time we have lived under an illusion of separateness. We have lived as detached egos, unaware that we are part of a vast fabric of being, and communal oneness. Now we are learning from the new sciences that the universe has actually be constructed as a *we*. Everything in creation – oceans, whales, mountains, human, eagles, roses, giraffes, and viruses – is a dance of subatomic particles. Fields of energy flow and mingle together. They are all stitched into the cosmic quilt, which underlies and give rise to everything. Connectedness is the crucial factor in relational consciousness. Feeling connected to the other. Jean Houston talks about her work with dolphins, pointing out that they have evolved millions of years more than humans, that they don't have wars or attack each other and that they don't experience the levels of anxiety we do. She said dolphins do real work, use language, play using a high degrees of whimsicality, and even seem to reflect on death, exhibiting high concern when one of their members dies. Further, there claims to be evidence that dolphins are beaching themselves out of despair when caught in polluted water. Imagine dolphins despairing, weeping over what humans are doing to their waters. Imagine what it is like to be a dolphin. Imagine swimming in waters with all sorts of netting, filled with billions of tons of toxic waste, oil and sewage (1993, Monk Kidd). Relational consciousness allows children to enter an elusive place where consciousness overlaps and boundaries dissolve. Susan Griffin in *Women in Nature: The Roaring Inside* Her writes of a red-winged blackbird and says: "I fly with her, enter her with my mind, leave myself, die for an instant, live in the body of this bird whom I cannot live without . . . because I know I am made from this earth as my mother's hands were made from this earth." As children practice caring thinking they find the illusion of separateness crumbling and begin to feel their connectedness with the earth, their compassion for it, even if at times a raging empathy. They begin to realize that they are connected with everything in a deeper way than they have imagined and in so doing they free a new valuing of the force that moves us into relationship with everything else.

Emotions as Judgments

No aspect of our mental life is more important to the quality and meaning of our existence than emotions. They are what make life worth living, or sometimes ending. So it is not surprising that most of the great classical philosophers – Plato, Aristotle, Spinoza, Descartes, Hobbes, Hume – had recognizable theories of emotion, conceived as responses to certain sorts of events of concern to a subject, triggering bodily changes and typically motivating characteristic behavior. What is surprising is that in much of the twentieth-century philosophers of mind and psychologists tended to neglect them, perhaps because the sheer variety of phenomena covered by the word emotion and its closest neighbors tends to discourage tidy theory. In recent years, however, emotions have once again become the focus of philosophical concern. It is common to speak of emotions as interferences, something to be overcome with our reason because they are disruptive to good judgment. We tend to associate them with irrationality, something that overwhelms us. "We speak of judgments being disturbed, warped, heightened, sharpened and clouded by emotion, of people being . . . emotionally perturbed, upset, involved, excited and exhausted" (1972, Peters). Yet there are philosophers today who subscribe to the view that emotions are judgments, de Sousa, Solomon, Amelie Rorty and Nussbaum among them, who argue quite the contrary, that each emotion entails a cognitive appraisal, that these appraisals are central features of the various emotions, and that emotions are therefore a type of cognitive activity. To be angry is to make a judgment that one has been wronged; to be delighted is to judge that something beneficial has happened. Since emotion is inextricably linked with judgment, emotions are forms of cognition (2002, Lipman). From this it follows that emotions should not be disregarded in the making of good inquiry. It makes a big difference if I respond to the praise of a classmate for a leadership role with anger, sadness, jealousy or benevolence. Although over time the intensity of one of these emotions may diminish, both my immediate and considered actions will likely hinge on how I judge the praise of my classmate in relation to myself. Judging it as evidence of my being discriminated against or not appreciated, I am likely to be angry. 'Seeing' it, on the other hand, as resulting from my own weaknesses, I might be sad, but not angry. Resenting that my classmate received praise can result in all sorts of counter-productive behavior such as aggressive violence.

Emotions as Perceptions

How I feel or how I see, a situation means, in part, what I have determined to be salient to my own interests. From among the information that constantly barrages us we decide from moment to moment what to attend to. Logic alone cannot solve a dilemma of how a child will decide when confronted with a popular but environmentally injurious measure. It is a question of how the student 'sees' the impending decision. She may be delighted or even elated at the opportunity to win favor by deciding in favor of a popular view and thus further her popularity. Or, if she is ecologically conscious, she may find herself challenged to speak out against the popular view, eager to help her peers, or understand how the measure could result in consequences that would hurt the environment. Her choice of action is likely to be driven by her determining which is the stronger of the two emotions. Even the scientific acquisition of knowledge rests on judgments of salience. DeSousa writes that "the most important areas of indeterminacy have to do with what subjects to investigate and what inductive rules to adopt. No logic determines *salience*: what to attend to, what to consider important, what to choose to inquire about." This is not to deny that emotions can lead children astray. For example, we can imagine a classroom community of inquiry making a bad decisions when the children have been swept up either by excitement or fear or anger at a perceived threat. Some might feel that violence is justified. Within weeks or months it becomes evident that the decision was an error, that the resulting violence exacerbated the situation instead of solving it. In retrospect, what happened is all too clear: the atmosphere of the deliberation was ardent but not disciplined. Bold statements were made but not subjected to serious inquiry. No one asked for assumptions or possible consequences; no one posed counter examples. Carried away by emotion, the children overlooked important considerations.

Consider an alternative scenario: Suppose that the teacher and children were persons who love serious discussion and derive satisfaction from digging down deep into the essential elements of a problem. Suppose the children had asked each side to justify their positions with reasons and their judgments

156 *Talking to Children About Responsibility and Control of Emotions*

with criteria. And suppose these reasons were assumptions and possible consequences. Suppose one or two children had suggested an alternative position to violence which when analyzed held much promise. Had this been the case, it is not that pure cognition would have prevailed, but that a passion for inquiry and reasonableness – a practice in critical, creative and caring thinking – would have prevailed. Love of dialogue and inquiry, commitment to reasonableness (rationality tempered by good judgment), and cooperative, collaborative inquiry; these emotions *direct the attention of the students*. Yet the communication of salience, rests on a judgment of salience. Only a judgment that something before us is worth noticing and acting upon. Why? Because we find it puzzling, threatening, saddening, initiating feelings of wonder, curiosity, anger, compassion or indignation, and so is worthy of our communal inquiry.

Moral Perceptions as Emotions

If the function of emotions is to assess salience and to communicate it, then emotions have particular relevance to those interested in moral education, for it is an emotion that in the first place will 'see' a moral problem as a problem. A person weak in moral emotion is unlikely to notice or become 'preoccupied' by the moral dimension of a situation. Upon seeing a hungry child asking for money on a street, one child is disdainful of the child's appearance, another finds herself compassionate and a third child is indignant that this situation exists within the context of a wealthy country. The three emotions – disdain, compassion and indignation – rest on a common judgment, something like: "This kid is in a miserable condition; I'm not, but I could be someday." One child, threatened by the stark recognition that that such a condition could overtake any of us, experiences disdain or disgust as a means of dealing this terrifying thought. The second individual, perhaps with a sense of the same threat, experiences compassion, and by helping the child attempts to combat the threat itself and the third child might very well be moved to bring attention of others to the injustice of the situation. The emotions in the above case are indeed judgments – judgments of a particular nature of salience, and a communication of it, with a characteristic tonality, timbre and register. Rarely does knowledge of moral norms or the capacity for moral reasoning alone prompt a child to recognize the existence of a moral problem. It is usually our emotions, which simultaneously suggest actions, that motivate us to distinguish what is significantly moral in a situation. The perception of a moral need in most cases rests on an emotion, one that can be described as a moral perception. Moral perception, understood this way, takes the form of preoccupation – a caring from the inside. There is invariably this displacement of interest from one's own reality to the reality of the other (1984, Noddings). Noddings, following Simone Weil and Iris Murdoch, describes a quality of active receptive attention to the other. Noddings posits that that the memory of caring that we ourselves have both received and given (such as one student for another in the process of communal inquiry) leads children to extend caring to those who are in need.

There is no reason to doubt that children can become engrossed with the needs of others with whom they do not have a personal relationship. Remembering their best moments of being cared for, the feeling of the need to respond is most reasonable. When communal inquiry leads to a recognition that caring for another often conflicts with fulfilling our own egoistic needs, the community can reflect on the image of our ideal selves as caring people. Reflecting on that image often yields a decision to act. Thus the substance of the care we have received from others is converted into an ethical caring What Noddings calls caring is an emotional judgment (i. e. an assessment of salience communicated through feelings);

Lipman calls this term caring thinking in the second edition of *Thinking in Education.* caring thinking, a fusion of the cognitive and emotional taking the form of prizing, nurturing, empathizing, appraising, and cherishing. Were it not a judgment, it would be difficult to explain why one person allows herself to become involved and another ignores the situation. It is precisely this assessment of salience – the judgment that this person or this issue is worth caring for or about – that motivates children to act, even if it negatively influences their own self-interest. To recognize a problem as a moral one is a judgment; to recognize a moral problem is also a moment of caring thinking. Remove the emotion and it is doubtful that cognition on its own would notice the presence of a moral need, much less bring it to consciousness, and act on it.

Education of the Emotions in the Classroom Community of Inquiry

If one wants to educate children to make good judgments, one must attend to the education of the emotions. When children come to class they come as persons: persons who can think and feel. Some come with a repertoire of cognitive skills gained in the family setting; others with positive emotions toward the world of others as a result of a sense of trust established in the home. But some come with little cognitive skills and a host of emotions that suggest a mistrust of the world around them. A classroom community of inquiry is a group that is willing to deliberate together about matters of importance, build on each others' ideas, help each other detect assumptions and anticipate consequences. Each member must also come to identify with the world of the group, learn and practice the art of self-reflection, and learn how to put one's ego in perspective. All of these characteristics assume a gradual mastery of critical thinking, creative thinking, and caring thinking. It follows then that in addition to practice in critical and creative thinking, a classroom community of inquiry, should provide the opportunity for children to:

Identify one's emotions: I might experience a sensation, such as what seems a pain in my stomach, but if I cannot put a word to the sensation, e. g. jealousy or envy, there is a real sense in which I cannot reflect upon it. Just as there is a specific vocabulary identify with the cognitive life, so such a vocabulary exists with regard to the emotional life. And somehow children must master this vocabulary. Here the world of literature can help immensely. Teachers and children can attend to the emotional characteristics of literature. It has often been noted that, without the necessary language, many complex emotions may not be experienced. Nussbaum points out that a function of literature is not only to express our emotional experience but to broaden it by providing it with language.

When discussing a story, for example, children can learn to attend to the specific language used to describe the character's emotions. They can encourage each other to identify the nouns, verbs and adjectives that describe emotions. Taking the role of facilitator, the teacher can then help students refine their understanding of the nuances of difference between, for example, being angry at a friend and being disappointed with her or being sad and being depressed, or feeling joyful and feeling excited.

Ferret out the underlying belief of an emotion If a child is angry, she might have good reason. For example, she might have discovered that her bicycle was returned with a flat tire. Thus the underlying belief of her anger is that the person to whom she lent the bicycle knowingly returned the bike with a flat tire. If she were to discover that her friend did not know the tire was flat, this would mean that her belief was invalid. Once she discovers this, it could be that her anger toward her friend will be lessened a great deal.

Identify a procedure for justifying emotions: If a child is happy, she might or might not have good reason; if she is sad or fearful she might or might not have good reason. Children should be encouraged to explore the beliefs that underlie their emotions. If the beliefs are submitted to inquiry, and, through dialogue, are not deemed valid (or downright incorrect), then children should be encouraged to reflect on the unreasonableness of the emotion. Self-correction based on a broader understanding of the situation might take the mode of substituting one emotion for another or learning how to put one's emotions to use in a constructive rather than destructive way.

Let go of unjustified emotions: Children wonder why they are feeling jealous, indignant, guilty or resentful, why they feel repulsion, disgust or shame. Once they uncover the underlying belief of these emotions and submitted the belief to inquiry, they may discover that the belief is invalid. I could be angry with you because I thought you betrayed me, yet I could discover through dialogue that I was wrong. What now happens to the anger? Will I be able to let it go? To what extent can the other members of the community help me to let the anger go and replace it with benevolence or humility.

As Peirce reminds us in his *Evolution of Love*, emotion is the other side of reason and the education of both is essential in bringing about a better world. one's life. The classroom community of inquiry is more than a pedagogy: it is a *way of life* involving the instilling and perfecting of cognitive, emotional, and behavioral habits. It is these habits that eventually come to characterize how the child goes about the world. The consequences of such practice are many: fostering of critical, creative, and caring thinking, learning how to make better judgments and internalizing a dialogical methodology. These consequences constitute an internalization of a form of life that also fosters the education of the emotions.

References

Averill, J. (1982). *Anger and Aggression: An essay on Emotion.* Spring-Verlag. New York.

Baier, A. (1995) *Moral Prejudices. Essay on Ethics.* Harvard UP. Cambridge.

Beane, J. (1990). *Affect in the Curriculum: Towards Democracy, Dignity and Diversity.* Teachers College Press. New York.

Bennett, J. (1974). The conscience of Huckleberry Finn. *Philosophy, 49.* 123-34.

Ben-Ze'ev, A. (2000). *The Subtlety of Emotions.* MIT Press. Cambridge.

Blackburn, S. (1998) *Ruling Passions.* Oxford Un Press. New York.

Boler, M. (1997). Disciplined emotions: philosophies of educated feelings. *Educational Theory, 47* (2) pp. 203-225.

De Sousa, R. (1980). The rationality of the emotions in A. Rorty (ed) *Explaining Emotions,* Berkley: University of California Press

Gardner, H. (1983). *Frames of Mind.* New York: Basic Books

Goleman, D. (1995) *Emotional Intelligence, Why it can matter more than I. Q.* Bantam. New York Greenspan.

Griffin, S. (1978). *Women and Nature: The Roaring Inside Her.* New York: Harper and Row.

Kidd, S. M. (1996). The Dance of the Dissident Daughter. Harper, San Francisco. Kidd, Susan Monk 1993) "Weeping with Dolphins, " in Pilgrimage: *Psychotherapy and Personal Exploration* (May-August.)

Lipman, M. (1994, July). Caring Thinking. *Paper presented to the Sixth International Conference on Thinking*, Massachusetts Inst. of Tech., Boston MA

Macy, J. (1989). *Awakening to the Ecological Self in Healing the Wounds: The Promise of Ecofemnism.* (ed) Judith Plant. New Society Publishers,

Nussbaum, M. (1992). "Emotions as Judgments of Value", *The Yale Journal of Criticism, I*(5).

Nussbaum, M. (2003). *Upheavals of Thought: The Intelligence of the Emotions.* Cambridge UP. New York.

Patricia S. (1988). *Emotions and Reasons: An Inquiry into Emotional Justification.* London: Routledge.

Peirce, C. Evolutionary *Love in the Collected Papers of Charles Sanders Peirce.* (eds) Paul Weiss and Charles Hartshorne. Harvard UP. Cambridge, Mass.

Peters, R. (1972). The education of the emotions in R. Deardon, *Education and Reason*, London, Routledge and Kegan.

Philadelphia M. I. (1992). *Metaphysics as a Guide to Morals.* London: Chatto and Windus.

Pollack, W. (1999). *Real Boys: Rescuing our sons from myths of boyhood.* New York, Owl Books

Rorty, A. (ed) (1980). *Explaining Emotions.* Berkely: Univeristy of California Press.

Singer, P. (1981) *The Expanding Circle: Ethics and Sociobiology.* Farrar, Sraus and Giroux, New York.

Singer, P. (1993). *How are We to Live? Ethics in an Age of Self-interest.* The Text Pub. Comp. : Melbourne.

Singer, Peter (2002). *One World: The Ethics of Globalization.* Yale UP, New Haven.

Scheffler, I. "In Praise of Cognitive Emotions." *Teachers College Record.*

Solomon, Robert (1983). "Emotions as Judgments," in The Passions. Notre Dame Un Press, Indiana. Wallace, Kathleen. Reconstructing Judgment: Emotion and Moral Judgment. *Hypatia. 8*(3), 61-81.

Zambylas, M. (2002). "Structures of Feeling," in Curriculum and Teaching: Theorizing the Emotional Rules. *Educational Theory*, 52 (2).

There is an entire elementary school curriculum revolving around teaching for non-violence within in a community of philosophical inquiry which has been developed in Quebec and published by the University of Laval Press in Quebec City Novels: (kinder) *Nakeesha et Jesse* A. M. Sharp, translated by Sylvia Dekyndt, PUL, 20 (Second grade) *Gregoire et Beatrice* P. Laurendeau, PUL, 2005 2ndade Fabienne et Loïc Pierre Laurendeau, PUL, 2005 Third grade *Mischa* Nathalie Côté, avec la collaboration de Michel Sasseville, PUL, 2005 Fourth grade *Romane* Nathalie Côté, avec la collaboration de Michel Sasseville, PUL, 2005 Fifth and sixthgrade *Hannah* Ann Margaret Sharp, translated Sylvia Dekyndt, PUL2005 Manuals: Kinder *Chair de notre monde* Ann Margaret Sharp, traduit de l'anglais par Sylvia Dekyndt, PUL, 2005 First grade *Apprivoiser la différence* Pierre Laurendeau, PUL, 2005 Second grade *Faire face aux tempêtes de la vie* Pierre Laurendeau, PUL, 2005 Third grade Le fil de Misha Mathieu Gagnon et Michel Sasseville, PUL, 2005 Fourth grade *Le fil de Romane* Mathieu Gagnon et Michel Sasseville, PUL, 2005 Fifth and sixth grade *Rompre le cercle vicieux* Ann Margaret Sharp, traduit de l'anglais par Sylvia Dekyndt, PUL, 2005

Discussion after Ann Sharp's Presentation

Sharon Bailin: Back to the beginning when you were talking about caring thinking and one of the things you said there was that thinking from one's own values, that that was important.

Ann Sharp: It is thinking in such a way that you express your values.

Sharon Bailin: But then the rest of what you have listed under caring thinking express particular values, so it is normative, if I'm a nasty person and my values are not caring values then my values are not going to be thinking in the kind of caring way you are describing.

Ann Sharp: We do have one guy at the daycare center who is not very nice. The other day when I came to school with Roller, he said why do you bring that ugly doll, why, get that doll out of here, that's what he said to me. So I didn't know what to do, so I went in there and after a while, Mr. Williams, I think he overheard Stefan say this to me and after a while Mr. Williams said that we were going to have a little sit down and talk about ugly and pretty and stuff like that. So we did, we had that discussion. In the process he asked Stefan if he could give some reason why he called it an ugly doll. He gave reasons, he said first of all he didn't like its face. So he asked him why he didn't like his face. He said because it's a different kind of face. Look at our face, they are all different. We kept questioning Stefan, he's very strong by the way, he was right there arguing all the time. At the end though Romona said to him you know you've given us reasons but you haven't given us good reasons for what you said to Jess. So, in answer to your question, we listened to Stefan, he's part of the group, we inquired with him, he is kind of mean, but we worked with him.

Sharon Bailin: The only part that jarred me was the thinking through one's own values because the rest are normative and that's kind of descriptive of what one's values are which may or may not be caring values.

Ann Sharp: That's kind of where I start in order to be part of the group, I mean here I am following Dewey, values I think are important, what I care about. Obviously in Stefan's world, I guess, in his world boys don't bring dolls to school, it's just obvious. That's where we started.

Sharon Bailin: The starting point is to get people to be more caring.

Ann Sharp: Hopefully, and I did have problems with the novel because I did put in the 2 rules to start with because that's a prescriptive and I debated about that a lot.

William Arsenio: I have a political question, years ago we taught the Kolhberg Community Work. I remember the idea of trying to arrive at values and ethical standards when and then have a group discussion level and working that out and all the ups and downs and the history of that and I remember one of the problems that a lot of the people had including William Bennett, the former secretary of education, and others, they didn't like in the end this kind of critical focus. They saw it not just undermining authority but they saw it as undermining the purpose of school which was more in their model the transmission of, we know these things and you don't ask kids, and so the best thing we can do is to

162 *Talking to Children About Responsibility and Control of Emotions*

efficiently transmit these things to you and this inquiry stuff not only gets in the way but it also makes you disruptive of our goal here.

Ann Sharp: Bennett was very, very successful in stopping our funding for a long time. So yes, there is a political problem there. However, we've been around for 30 years and we are in 50 countries. In the story there is a lot of inquiry that takes place in the daycare center and there are rules too. I might not know what the rules mean and I might have to really discuss that. It's not like anything goes in Mr. William's daycare center.

Alexander Herriger: Yes I think there is a political problem. What we can see here in Quebec is the transformation of this political problem. A few years ago we had a minister who introduced a reform and said that the schools should place more emphasis on developing competencies; not only transversal competencies, not only philosophical competencies or mathematical competencies but competencies that would be good in any field.

Michael Schleifer: Like judgement for example, was what the minister actually said, and brought me in at one point and asked how do you do that.

Alexander Herriger: Yes how do we do that, and I would argue at transforming our classroom into a community of inquiry. Not everybody would answer like that. The thing is that we cannot absorb the change in this political problem which is from not fighting. It is still a problem in many countries but here in Quebec we made steps, one little step.

Ann Sharp: It is an important step because at least the word is on the books, at least you can talk about it openly.

Alexander Herriger: The problem is that now the teachers don't know how to develop these competencies and they don't even know how to identify them.

Paul Harris: Pursuing this theme a little bit, if you look at developmental psychology, whether it's Piaget or to some extent Vygotsky and other educators like Montessori, the notion of the child as able to be relatively autonomous or at least collaborative, then gradually draw out good conclusions is central. This is also true of Kolhlberg, who was a neo-Piagetian. Somewhat paradoxically Piaget didn't think that was terribly likely in the domain of morality. But if anything you could draw the ironic conclusion that he was wrong about that because, especially in domains such as discussion of what was good, children could do that. But then it seems to me, developmental psychologists have neglected I guess, what is Bennett's issue, which is there are vast areas of knowledge where children aren't in very good position to figure things out for themselves. So it is not obvious that 4 year olds are going to reconstruct Darwin's theory of evolution, it's not obvious that they are going to come to conclusions about the shape of the earth. So I guess my question could be boiled down to the following, although I think it has larger ramifications; would you say that this particular pedagogic mode is especially appropriate for certain domains or do you think of it in some sense as a cross-disciplinary pan-situational mode?

Ann Sharp: That's a question that has been agonizing philosophy. In many countries right now, some want to argue that you can go across disciplines with the community of inquiry. Others argue that in domains, say as science and mathematics, it would be very problematic. Others then come back and say, no, I had a class in mathematics and it was conducted in pure inquiry and it was very, very successful and as a matter of fact, the children were far more advanced when they finished, etc. I really don't know. I think that this might have to work itself out in the real world by test and experiment and one thing is for sure, it seems to work with philosophy. I think it works with philosophy because the controversialness of the subject matter. But when you get into the hard sciences, I don't know. I'd have to talk to people in those fields to see how much open inquiry is possible in the early years when you are trying to get into the discipline itself. If you remember, some of you in the late 70's the natural science foundation where they were trying to rework the science program, to be more and more open inquiry, collaborative inquiries, etc. How successful they were I don't know, well compared to traditional learning the text, learning the book.

Michael Schleifer: We have an experience here in Quebec in two ways. One, there are people in mathematics who you mentioned (Louise Lafortune and others and I have collaborated with them), who believe you can create these kinds of materials in doing this kind of approach with math and science. The end result is mixed. There are many people who think this is wonderful and there are others, particularly the teachers who experimented say: "I am cut into two halves, when I am there to do my mathematics I do my mathematics and then there is privileged time while I do this thinking about, well what does infinity mean. In one way, it is really mixed because the teachers tell me the good point about doing philosophy is the kids love it, it is like a free period. There is no exam, no testing and they love all that, that's the good part and the teachers have a good time for the most part. The bad part is it interferes with them because after all the child has to know how to subtract in grade 2 and all the rest of it has to be done, there isn't that much time. Many schools in Quebec love this philosophy but we have no time to do it and we try to bring it into the year. It is also interestingly political because it is part of the reform. Now that the ministry had a group look into history, not just math and science but every single subject, children are supposed to reflect about it. This came from above because they picked up this idea, not necessarily doing Philosophy for Children, just in general, and it came from what the people have read, some of the people from the ministry have read among other things, Jerome Bruner. Going back to Sputnik back in 1958, where the Americans said the Russians have a Sputnik we got to do something about it, because we are not creating real scientists or mathematicians. Let us revise the education system to get them to reflect and we have to start young so we just don't want to teach kids that in fact this is what happens about planet or Darwin. Let them get into being an historian or being a scientist. Well, it's a mixed bag. It came from above and so now you are supposed to not just say here are the facts of history, you are supposed to be a bit of a historian. You are not just supposed to just give the scientific or mathematical facts, you are supposed to get them to be a little bit of a mathematician. So the teacher says, "how am I supposed to do that, nobody has told me how to do that. I don't have time to do it, and I am supposed to make the students able to do it by the end of the year!"

Ann Sharp: I think one of the reasons why it doesn't work in the other fields is that, it is not so easy to reconstruct a discipline so that you bring the child into controversial paths, the constituents of that discipline, in a language that he or she can understand and at the same be faithful to the discipline. From experience, it's not that easy and you make lots of mistakes. That's what needs to happen in science, math, and history if it needs to be done it needs to be reconstructed so that the child is invited in at the very basic level which also happens to be usually the most controversial aspect of the discipline. So in a sense he is picking up the skills as he goes on inquiring about the philosophical dimension of that discipline.

164   *Talking to Children About Responsibility and Control of Emotions*

The philosophy of history or the philosophy of science or the philosophy of math and if that's the case, God help us because it's not easy.

Sharon Bailin: An example from BC, I was involved in a project on critical thinking, it isn't Philosophy for Children but it shares a lot of the goals and focuses on thinking according to criteria and a notion of community of inquiry broadly conceived, not necessarily, but centrally to the notion of inquiry. The project revolves around the development of what we call critical challenges. It is infused into many subjects across the curriculum and instead of subject matter knowledge, some of it may be philosophical, a lot of it is disciplinary, but these kinds of critical challenges or problems that are built into the inquiry and the disciplines so it's not just accumulating the knowledge, but the students need to gather the knowledge in order to deal with a specific issue or challenge some of which may be practical (e. g. building an insect habitat you have to think according to criteria and you are being creative but you need the knowledge). Two more philosophical challenges in language arts you may deal with some of these philosophical issues or in history, secondary history in dealing with issues of bias, maybe looking at different accounts of the same historical event and try to understand what a fair minded account might be. So it is a kind of a way dealing with the subject matter and it's actually been quite a good project.

Ann Sharp: Does it work?

Sharon Bailin: There haven't been a lot of studies but teachers love it and feel that they can do it.

Part V:

General Discussion

Topic #1: Emotion and the Arts

Sharon Bailin: I'd like to follow up on the arts education issue.

Michael Schleifer: We'll call that the challenge from Paul Harris. Talking about music that's great, we love that. Talking about emotions, we love that, but so what? And to our surprise, Sharon is allying herself with Paul.

Wendy Turgeon: First, I'm not saying we shouldn't do aesthetic education in its own right, it certainly is valuable, and I don't think we should see music or any other art as the answer to moral education, it can exist on its own. What attracted me to using music in this certain way, it's really an act of emotive reflection and reflective feeling, and I want to see these as paired together. I don't think they're bifurcated. I don't think our emotions are over here and our intellect is over here. And Sharon said much the same thing. The sensuous, aesthetic nature of music reminds us of this fact, that emotions and thinking are a unified whole of experience. Every thought has a feeling tonality and every feeling has a cognitive dimension to it. While lived emotions are contextual and intentional, at least in some cases, in other words, I'm mad because I was pushed off this swing and I'm mad at you because you did it. Those factors are there. I think it's possible to have feelings disassociated with events . . . I have a vague sense of sadness, but nothing sad happened to me. The emotions in music offer us a unique opportunity to separate out the emotion from the context. And I think in an intellectually and aesthetically enriched way. And I think this can affect moral education, first as a way to acknowledge the power and richness of emotional life. Contrary to the deontological model, where morality is all about rules and the principle in doing one's duty and as Kant would say emotion should have nothing to do with a moral life. I think in real life, it has a lot to do with it. My moral choices and actions are definitely influenced by emotions. And so I think music can acknowledge that these are intertwined, not compartmentalized.

Secondly, I think it might offer us, and this is a hypothesis, an opportunity to practice feelings, but in a very non-threatening, safe milieu, and maybe even give us a vocabulary of feeling, by listening to music and by talking about and reflecting about what that music means, or why I thought is was foreboding and you thought it was calm. I think that might help me to expand my vocabulary of feeling. And vocabulary implies a sort of intellectual component here, it's not the same as real life foreboding or real life calmness. But if we use music in this way, always remembering that it's using music as a tool . . . We want to make sure we're not abusing music or "text-booking" an art object. We don't want to lose the aesthetic perspective, then I think if we're encouraged to reflect on that experience, the aesthetic experience can be transformed into a component in educating ones moral life. It's a hypothesis, but I don't think it's completely out there, because there's an entire field called music therapy that uses music in some kind of interventional or educational perspective, usually targeted at adults or children with problems, or pathologies and this would be simply saying that all of us could learn something from this reflection. You just can't play the music and have it happen. So I could be aesthetically, extraordinarily knowledgeable and I might be an awful person. That's certainly possible – it's not inevitable. It's a circuitous route –

168　*Talking to Children About Responsibility and Control of Emotions*

certainly not solitarily causal. Introducing music into a moral education program isn't going to turn them all into great children . . . or adults for that matter. But I think there's that potency there, that it might help us do that. Ann's talk confirmed that in my mind. It's still on the board there. . . Isn't beauty good? And isn't goodness in some way beautiful? And while we tend to separate them out, (throw truth in there too), as nothing to do with one another . . . I'm not so sure I've experienced that they aren't intertwined.

Sharon Bailin: I also was thinking a lot about this after and trying to sort out exactly what my position is because I absolutely loved your paper and I was with you all the way until you talked about moral education and that's the point where I'm not sure. And I want to believe that; I'm an arts educator amongst other things but I haven't found the justification for myself that I feel happy, so I was trying to sort that out by coming at it from different angles, Do arts educate morally or is all education morally education? I think the case of literary arts, including film and theatre and dance, that portray human situations are a special kind of case because that's like expanding our repertoire and our experience and probably in a particularly potent and helpful way because the artist, by the way they've structured the situations, really focuses us on the dynamics of the situation. In regular life lots of other things get in there, but the work of art's really focused on those issues, so the viewers get a little bit of distance on it so it's a really good context for reflecting on how people react emotionally and so on. But I think that's a kind of a special case, and music (has got be) different from that.

Let's make a claim more generally about arts education having to do with education of the emotions. It's plausible that there's a connection, because the arts have a connection to emotion and I think emotion is somehow kind of a necessary condition to interaction with the arts at some level. That is, you can do science or math without having strong emotions. We would like students to get excited about it, but you could do science or math without getting excited. We wouldn't say "you solved this outstanding problem of mathematics but were you excited? No, oh well, then that's not valid." Emotion is not considered a necessary condition to these disciplines, whereas if we were never moved or never had an emotional reaction to any work of art we would say something's wrong here. There seems to be that connection; at least on the face of it. So what's the nature of that connection? Looking at the case of music, which is interesting because it doesn't have the representational contents. There's just sort of that pure form, at some level. I think it's true that we may interpret certain pieces of music in terms of certain emotions and we did that; it was an interesting consensus on some of the pieces we heard yesterday, we would say this was an angry piece. In terms of aesthetic experience, I'm not sure that what the emotion we're hoping people will get by listening to an angry piece is anger. I think it's something else. It's some aesthetic emotion; it gets really tough to characterize what that is but the language gets very mystical . . . talk about transcendence or you start talking about language like that, it's hard to know what that means, but I don't think it's anger, I think it's something else that I think we're hoping people get out of the experience with the art works, kind of an aesthetic emotion.

So, where does this education come in, and in what sense is that education of the emotion? What I ended up thinking about was the idea of educating sensibility, and although that's kind of fuzzy, it's hard to pin down what that might mean but I think it would include things like close attention, attention to form, noticing not just content but how things mean what they mean, attention to perception, and a kind of openness to letting the artwork work on you. And so aesthetic education is knowledge about the work and all that, I mean that's crucially important, but it's more than that. And as you said, if people could just do an analysis that wouldn't be enough. We want their sensibility to be educated. And I think the kinds of question that you have for discussion at the end are wonderful in terms of trying to illicit that and educate sensibility in some sense. So that's the kind of connection I see as arts education as an education of sensibility. Now whether that has moral implications, I don't know, maybe in the broad sense. Is there any transference, or, if you are open to aesthetic experience, are you going to more open to other people?

One more point on practicing emotion. I think what I was resisting, both for the audience and even for the performer, is that they're not necessarily practicing the emotion. The musician playing the angry piece is not necessarily angry or the actor acting an angry part is not necessarily anger. There are different schools of thought about. There's an apocryphal story about Dustin Hoffman and Laurence Olivier in Marathon Man. Hoffman is a method actor and there's a scene where he's tortured by Olivier, so that day on set Hoffman comes out and he looks terrible. He's ragged, so Olivier says "what's the problem?" Hoffman replies "well I haven't been sleeping, I haven't been eating, I'm trying to get myself into this place of someone who's tortured." Olivier responds: "my man. haven't you ever heard of acting?" Olivier may not have been practicing any of those emotions but he was a wonderful actor.

Cynthia Martiny: In therapy we often use the arts to recreate the family, so that's a little bit acting, role-playing, we use listening to music in order to relax, and then to allow visualizations to come, guided visualization. Sometimes there's photographs that are brought in to talk about, but it's mostly a stimulant to evoke an emotion. The re-education would be to restructure the thinking around what the person projected into the act, to try to talk to somebody differently in this situation that was created. But the troubling part of what I felt when I was listening to the music is that I was thinking, many things can happen, but if I just write the emotion, identify it, label it, there is no educational content for me. If you had asked me afterward "where do you think that came from that you heard anger in that piece, I would have to say "Well it was the music that was rolling in such and such a film, or perhaps it was because that's the kind of things I heard in the background when something happened or I heard that in 1981 when I was listening to something on the news." But that's where I'd take it. Just identification of the emotion, as in therapy, is not enough.

Michael Schleifer: On the question of music as such, it is a puzzle. I have some ideas about this and Martha Nussbaum takes many of the people you quoted, plus others, puts them altogether in all the possible explanations and then, as if they're all no good, comes up with her own, which I think is also no good. Jennifer Robinson's latest book also thinks it's no good and so on.

Ann Sharp: What do you mean by "no good."

Michael Schleifer: It doesn't explain it. We don't quite understand how music evokes emotion. Yes, music is sad, but why?! What is it about the music that is sad? And it's ambiguous, of course, saying the music is sad, or it makes us sad, or we all agree it's sad. We talk about emotions, and talked a little, Paul mentioned, about moods. Emotions and moods, Martha Nussbaum thinks, are very different. And I think they overlap to a great degree I think music does touch us directly; we get sad or angry. We don't just label it. Now maybe not everybody does, but I was intrigued by Paul's other question: "there's the sadness you feel when somebody dies or the anger of a situation. that we've been talking about it, and then there's the sadness where we said, oh that's sad music, but those are two sadnesses," maybe so, maybe not, I have to think about that one. For me, that's the same sadness. When I listen to Schubert I get sad . . . I have to think a lot about that.

I don't think anybody has come up with the answer. I'm talking about where the content, or the communication or the language has . . . There is music, of course it has a certain language or the composer helped it but sometimes Schubert just wrote it, we all listen to it, and we all say, "wow, that's sad." It's universal, nobody doesn't say that's sad but now, people like Levinson go into the actual work: the harmony, the rhythm, the instruments used . . . He claims that when you have, for example, clarinets playing the theme, and then the violins take up the theme, *that* intrinsically, neurologically hits the brains of any human being.

Cynthia Martiny: There's empirical evidence to that?

Michael Schleifer: Yes. I really wanted to say something much closer to our topic, moral education and aesthetic education . . . to which you really do think, there's more of a link, Wendy, and to which Sharon has a question. I believe that when we're talking about the emotions including those in music, we are doing moral education. But let me be the devil's advocate with beauty and good. You were saying beauty might be good and good might be beautiful. Now we've taken those two values and beauty with aesthetic education and goodness with moral education; but here's two counter examples:

I love Schubert, I listen to him, he's my favorite composer. But I'm told that there were people who ran concentration camps and killed people who also loved Schubert. Schubert brought the exact same emotions to them. So I think they share it. I think there are people who share the beauty, but not necessarily the goodness. Another example is discussed by Richard Hare in *Freedom and Reason*. He gives an example (I don't know if it was true or not) of some Roman emperor who had an aesthetic theory about colors. He worked it out and he was really into it. Aesthetically educated. . . He was into not just sensibility, but he could write things like, for example, why green and red were important. He decided to do an experiment and so he had a green field and he killed some thousands of people to see their the red blood.

So, aesthetic education would deal with the redness and the greenness and the philosophy and the theories, yet, like Sharon says – and here is the challenge – what does that have to do with morality? Beauty is beauty and goodness is goodness, sure that's terrific, but will it help us in some way with our sensibility or to do the right thing or the altruistic good? So, I'm talking for the devil here, I'd like someone to show me that beauty and goodness are more close together with these counter examples in mind.

Ann Sharp: Perhaps if judgment should be brought in here because it seems to me that we know emotions can help us make good judgments, but we also know that emotions can send us off on the wrong track too. I'm wondering if what music gives us is a kind of sensibility and a kind of a feel for the texture of a situation. I don't know how to say that; Dewey talks this way, a tertiary quality or something. And when I'm making a judgment, it's important that I feel that quality. I could go wrong, certainly, but I sense that this sensibility is something that you pick up. Berlin, in the making of good judgment, says that people who make very good judgment calls are people who have this feel for the overlapping of the data, overlapping of the emotional surface, etc. Now I don't know *how* music helps us pick up that texture of experience, but I think it does. It has something to do with its richness, complexity, overlapping emotions, and stuff like that. It's hard to talk about but I think it's very important if you want to say that you're educating for good judgment because practical wisdom is in a sense relies heavily on that feel for a situation. And where do you get that? How do you educate for that? We can barely talk about it. And I think that music is one way in; art is way in.

Wendy Turgeon: It's not inevitable. I make a point of saying that you could have an incredibly developed aesthetic sense and be a Nazi torturer. Absolutely. There's hundreds of examples. Kathleen Battle is an absolutely, gorgeously, phenomenally beautiful soprano, but I've heard she's a witch in real life. However, that's not what I'm saying; I'm not saying that if you educate in aesthetics that will automatically make people good. It's more what Ann's suggesting, that art can be an element of moral education, if it's brought to their attention and they're allowed to reflect on it.

Michael Schleifer: But art is neither necessary nor sufficient, I mean to use those terms . . .

Ann Sharp: Ahhh, I wouldn't go that far.

Michael Schleifer: You would think it's necessary?

Ann Sharp: I don't know how you're going to get this feeling that I'm talking about except through the arts. But somebody who is a real bore, for example, and comes in and says the wrong thing at the wrong time . . . there's something missing. And if you were going to try to help that person, it makes kind of more sense to turn to the arts.

Lee Londei: I'm going to bring back this idea of the pure emotion because I think music can bring forth this pure sense of emotion. When you say sadness when it is evoked through music and sadness that I experience because of a concrete situation, because I can see the antecedent; I think it's the same thing. Basically, the emotion we experience through music is the pure emotion, but less of an intense emotion, because confounded with triggers such as cognitive situations and stimuli make it such that we experience it more intensely, but I think it's just a continuum of the same thing. It's just when you put in the cognitive element, it makes it look different. And I do agree with you Ann about the idea that there's this sense of the emotion that music or the arts can bring us to. There's something there worth investigating.

Cynthia Martiny: However you are evoking a thought about the shutting down of the cognitive process. We talk about left brain and right brain, but there is at one point in therapy when you stop rationalizing and you're forced to concentrate and take the flow of consciousness you're using. Then there is the possibility of bringing up the emotion whereas if you're thinking, you can block the emotion out. So art could serve somewhere, in that way. I know that is one of the reasons therapists use the aesthetics to help a person stop distractive reasoning, the thinking so they can concentrate on the other free-flowing thinking, which evokes emotion and feelings.

Lee Londei: Why is emotion confusing, because we try to understand it . . .

William Arsenio: I'm just gonna say some simple minded things from what we've talked about. Music is not intentional or representational or whatever you want to use to describe it, at least music without lyrics (I listen to rock music so I have a different sense of how music works). The fact that music is not about something means, perhaps, that when kids and adults are listening to it, that it involves them rather than trying to figure out what this is supposed to be about, what does it represent, what is this person feeling in this situation, it's up for interpretation in a way. How does this make me feel? No one can argue with how that makes me feel because that's how I feel, and maybe that forces a different kind of label on understanding your own emotional experience. An important part of stuff with kids is that you don't always have a simple readout and you're able to label your emotional experiences. It's surprising how hard

172 *Talking to Children About Responsibility and Control of Emotions*

it is to put words, and how long it takes to construct that link between emotional events and the labels that go with it. Maybe one thing that music can help with, it's just got a different way that it makes that leap. . .

Michael Schleifer: Leonard Bernstein has written several fascinating books on this puzzle, which are along the lines you picked up. He suggests that you've got to make an effort with music, that many of us already know what the emotion's supposed to be. Then there's stuff where the composer helps us out. So Bernstein says, and he knows with the harmony and the rhythm that this music is supposed to be sad and he says, ignore all that and just react. Mahler is the same way, but Nussbaum says the trouble with Mahler is he gives us a bunch of hints, the poetry was this and then you have the music . . . even if we haven't read that, we know a little bit, everybody's picked it up about Beethoven and Mahler, so it spoils what you were intuiting as a kind of pure . . . Nevertheless, there's some kind of insight here that I'm feeling which is interesting about that.

Sharon Bailin: I think there's something to that, that one would be thinking about, "what am I feeling, what does this make me feel?" I think an important part of it is, the focus not just on my feeling, but on the object. It comes back to Ann's point. One thing you need to do in the arts is to focus on the aspects of the experience, to really pay attention to it. I can go in and no matter what the music I can feel angry because of what just happened. But what I need to do is be open to, focus on, pay attention to notice the formal, the qualities of the object, and be open to what that does. . . Things like perception here, might be related to what Ann is talking about, getting a sense of the qualities, paying attention to the qualities of an experience, not just the inward, but also, "I've gotta engage with what this is giving me . . ."

Ann Sharp: Not only do I think it's some kind of a perception but it has something to do with learning a subject, learning something about what to do with your ego when you're trying to attend to something. If you project all your anger there is a sense in which you're not listening . . . you're missing it, you know. So you have to learn how to get out of it, so that you can really attend to the piece. And, of course, that in a sense is very educative because this lovely man here is not just a projection of my needs, he's a person in himself, with his own reality and what have you. So if I'm constantly seeing you as "oh there's the lady, she's head of the education foundation department she might be able to link me to this . . ." There's a sense in which that's not right to do that . . . Where do I learn how to de-center this ego and really pay attention to the arts? And I think the arts teach us that.

Wendy Turgeon: That's the performer aspect of it, so it's not just music as appreciation, or listening as audience, but there's also children and adults performing music and what that entails, in terms of inter-pretation, in terms of objectifying and understanding and recognizing, but also in terms especially of a community, of a group performance, of how I have to work with others. It might be somewhat analo-gous to playing sports on a team. It certainly doesn't always result in ethical behavior, that's another good example where we know that doesn't always happen. But interestingly enough, there's a major argument in the States for the ethical efficacy of team sports and maybe in its good sense, it does instill ethics.

Alexander Herriger: I'd like maybe to come back to Ann's point and the link between seeing others or using others as a means – considering him as a person or as a end. This is Kant's big morality principle. I was wondering how does art make this possible and I was thinking, I don't know if any art makes this possible, but I was thinking of music especially. One link I could see maybe is the faculty that it helps us to listen and I think the first step to consider the other as a person is to listen to him. And I think music can help us to learn to listen. I see this when I'm working with children: one difficult thing is just to get them to listen to each other. And this is a whole learning that takes weeks and years, so I think in this way music can help moral education in some way.

Topic #2: Developmental Considerations

Wendy Turgeon: I'm wondering what the development psychologists can offer to parents, educators, therapists in terms of educating children's emotions and emotional self-reflection. What can we do to intervene when there isn't a solid attachment in early infancy, or toddlerhood, or there isn't even a psychological interaction? Many educators struggle with angry children, children with all sorts of emotional problems. Do you have any advice or directions in which we could go?

William Arsenio: For me, one of the missing pieces is: what are our models of emotion? We're talking about the fact that this a built-in part, and then there's socialization and so on. But for me, that built-in part is complex and it constrains the way in which a lot of the other things go. Some people talk about functionalist models of emotions and there's this great quote: emotions contain the wisdom of the ages. The idea that there's something that's directive in emotions and Martha Nussbaum discusses developmental stuff too. A question that I ask my students is: if emotions start out being functional, according to all these theories, then how do they get implicated in all kinds of dysfunctional forms of psychopathology? There is an answer, but I think in order to do that we need some sort of grounding for how the basic emotional stuff works.

So what are the foundations? We're not going to do a tutorial or whatever . . . There are a couple of things I agree with in Paul Eckman's approach. There's a number of folks who have this general shared emphasis on the idea that emotions are to some extent biologically rooted. There's a limited subset of relatively discreet emotions. They have unique motivational properties that have been selected for over thousands of millions of years, so they're adaptive, and then as part of being social species, we have these abilities to recognize . . . there are discreet facial displays that go with certain emotions. And then there are lots of people who don't take that. That's one of hard version, so I'm probably more extreme in taking that harder "biological" version, but the idea is that emotions are inherently adaptive to begin with, and they serve evolutionary needs and it really fits with the way attachment works. So I can't think of attachment as emotions. . . I mean they're separable, but they're part of one unified system in a deeper way. But the other part is that people like Eckman, very early on, made it clear that he was using a neurocultural model. Even though he's always associated with the idea that there are meaningful universals, and I actually share that view, he argued for the fact that cultures can do very different things with these hardwired pieces. So emotions are not strictly biology unfolding, end of story; the biological piece is significant, but cultures do incredible things on top of the biological piece.

Very simplistically, one thing is that cultures emphasize different display rules for emotions. What are the emotions you can and cannot show in different situations? What's appropriate, what's not? That's the idea that you have an emotion, and then you decide whether to show it or not. Other people emphasize, in opposition, the idea that you could have culturally different appraisals. If part of what goes on in emotion is evaluating a situation, "is what you just said to me a threatening thing?", then from that appraisal I have an emotion. You can actually have some cultural influence (to some extent) on the appraisals that people make so it's not just what I show, it's how I evaluate things. It's not completely flexible but there's some flexibility, and then different directions from the appraisal and this play piece. That's where I start from. To me it constrains what you can do later, but I'm reevaluating that idea in relation to all the things that we've talked about . . . Maybe it does and maybe it doesn't. I think the heart of the start is that emotions are initially functional whatever that means in a human sense and adaptive. It's probably not quite that clean and simple (you know is anger really as adaptive as it used to be), but as a package, they're more adaptive than not. So if you're going to talk about developmental or psychopathology or individual differences, that's where I need to start.

Paul Harris: Just to pick up from where Bill left off so to speak, the work of Eckman is deeply, deeply influenced by Darwin, in some ways, Eckman's life work is an elaboration on *Exigesus*, Darwin's book on facial expression of men and animals. I actually think that the vision for a model of human emotion, both with respect to the cultural input for appraisal and the cultural input for a mode of expression, is deeply superficial and deeply problematic. The main problem with it seems to be, the problem is already in some sense, intrinsic to Darwin's formulation, the main problem with it, is it's essentially a continuity thesis, it's a thesis about the similarities between man and animals. And indeed, if you go back to the reasons why Darwin wrote it, it was indeed to drive home a larger evolutionary story that he was trying to tell. Why do I dissent from that? Well it seems to me that once you introduce human language and human communication, you dramatically change what it is to experience, express, and share emotion.

And if anything, I think, of the work that's been going on in the last twenty or thirty years with respect to the capability to increasingly make sense of their emotions as an exploration of that theme and I'm buoyed up by that thought in the sense that it's increasingly evident that the individual differences we see among children are intimately connected with the child's language ability and the language in the home and the kind of conversations that the child has. Just to drive the point home a little bit more, once you ground human beings' language, and the kind of self awareness that language confers, it seems to me that you end up in a very different place from anything we see in our nearest cousins, the non-human primate. It doesn't seem to make a great deal of sense to inquire about the extent to which the chimpanzee is aware of its emotions or thinks about the conditions under which its emotions might be attenuated. That whole self-consciousness just seems to me to be conceivably present, but it's so embryonically present that it still doesn't bridge the gap between what's going on in the non-human world and what's going on in our world. So to that extent, I would say even with the additions that Bill emphasized, the role of culture with respect to appraisal and the role of culture with respect to expression, I would still end up saying that's not enough of a re-conceptualization of a sort of Darwin program. Having arrived at that point then, coming back to the more specific question of what do you do? . . . Well I guess we're gradually beginning to be able to specify what the landmarks of this self-consciousness are. We're gradually beginning to be able to specify the conditions under which that self-consciousness can be brought about. And in the next ten, twenty years maybe we'll have some better guides for our therapists and clinicians who have had to in some sense re-direct a child who's gone dramatically awry from what we take to be a fairly canonical developmental path, even allowing for the kind of cultural variations which I'm sure we would all want to emphasize.

Cynthia Martiny: And how are you going to do that?

Paul Harris: How will we do the research or how are we going to give you advice?

Cynthia Martiny: Where is research going that will be helpful for us?

Paul Harris: Let me give you one or two of the kind of research that's going to be important. A lot of the work that's going on at the moment is looking at ordinary children in their biological families to understand the kind of discourse that goes on in that home, as well as its impact on the child's self-awareness and emotional standing. A problem we've found is that we don't know about the extent to which some of the links we're seeing are biologically driven, as opposed to being dependent upon the language and socialization that the child is receiving. But there are already some straws in the wind, so for example some very interesting work going on, both in Britain, and in New York. It's being conducted by Howard and Myriam Steele, and they're looking at adopted children. Once you look at adopted children, and you sort of eliminate the biological link between the parents and the child. One of the things they've been looking at is if they interview the parents before the child is adopted, to what extent does the self-awareness and mode of talking of the parents have an impact on the child; specifically, they investigate to what extent is the child's emotional well-being and emotional adjustment facilitated by the kind of home into which the child is adopted (given that these are often children who have been in difficult circumstances and are therefore up for adoption). And they're really getting some intriguing results about the fact that child's emotional development and emotional wellbeing and emotional understanding will vary as a result, dependent upon the family into which the child is being adopted. I find that very provocative – the power of certain kinds of parenting. Now, I only know of one such study, but given the number of adoptions that are going on . . . I just look around me, my hometown of Newton . . . many, many adoptions, of children all over the world . . .

Michael Schleifer: There are emotions in my view that animals do have, but there are emotions that they cannot have, and to a large degree it has to do with language, and for example, notions of the future and time . . .

Topic #3: Research on Educational Interventions

Michael Schleifer: Some of us who work in intervention, we work with groups, we work in conversations, indeed, but not as parents, although many of us are parents and grandparents. We encourage conversation, dialogues, and discussions hoping to take up exactly the parallel to what Paul was just talking about. But, having said that, what methodologically is the other side of the coin?

We say research is a fruitful area. but what do we also do, in terms of intervention, counselling programs and so on. Paul, for example, you said: "let's be careful, because if we're going to evaluate our programs to see what really doesn't have an impact, let's at the very least be careful with our control groups, let's just take that part." Okay, so we know that, we try to say, we are convinced some of the time (even before we start our work with the classroom conversations) that our work is having an affect. But showing this affect is not easy. Paul put it as dramatically as this, when you work with a group of kids and education, you may say "A, B, and C are the factors hindering education, but there's always going to be D, E, F, and G and that's just the way it is."

For example, let's take the research that we all are involved in doing. We're working in Quebec on using some of Ann's materials in classrooms. We're using some of our material and over the course of the year we work very hard, the teachers work very hard at having discussions. At the end of the year we would like to show, not just state, that our program had an impact on the development of emotions. Alright, so we all use control groups, but that's hard. For example, you take the same school, so at least there's two classrooms in the same school exactly, and we may match them and so on, but it may not be the same teacher. Even if it's the same teacher, we say "you're going to do philosophy of your children with the "formation" the training we give them," and then we say "don't do it, just do your regular curriculum and so on." This is human research, it's not physics, we're never gonna control D, E, F, and G. This is my second question: Can you help us do better research? I don't mean the developmental research, but intervention research, because we're never going to control all the variables, even though we try hard.

Paul Harris: I agree, you could never control all the variables, but there are two imperatives. One imperative is that you are very explicit and clear about what you did to these really efficacious components of your intervention. If I may say so, I don't think in this meeting it's been terribly clear what the critical ingredients are. That may be because there hasn't been time to spell them out, it may be because you think that there are a variety of ingredients and you're not quite clear which ones to emphasize and maybe you think it's a whole gestalt. . . I'm not sure. But any assessment or intervention has to be preceded by an absolutely crystal clear and explicit statement of what the alleged critical ingredients are. So, I would certainly ask you to in the future be more explicit about that. So that's the first thing.

The second thing is that I acknowledge some of the practical anxieties you have of how to run such research. But in the end, the difficulty is that those practical obstacles have to be overcome – certainly if you want to convince a broader audience. It's not as if you can say "well there's too many practical obstacles." So, you're between a rock and a hard place really.

Cynthia Martiny: Research is changing. There's a new paradigm and we have to go there. We've moved away from the era of the positivistic point of view (i. e. we're going to be statistical and we're going to use our way of proving or exposing evidence); we're no longer there anymore. There's a lot of research that we could throw in the garbage now, because it is too simplistic or reductionist ,so it doesn't mean anything. There's a huge emphasis now on qualitative data, methodologies,techniques, and the ways of analyzing data. But we have to admit that there's a new paradigm. The world is being recognized as more complex, so some of our methods are faulty. We can no longer just rely on the isolating variables as we used to because we know it's relatively impossible. Perhaps one response is to become more explicit, but that is a funny thing to hear when we're talking people, since we are already complex. When we isolate a variable are we really just forgetting something? It's not as easy as it used to be, because we're too knowledgeable now about how complex the human is.

William Arsenio: Isolating the variables doesn't always mean that you know here are seven things, like Piaget, and then take this one out and then see how the others function. Sometimes it's going to be true that things co-vary and things clump together and that may be the true and genuine nature of the intervention. One of the things that we've talked a lot about in the last couple of days is the affective and the cognitive piece of what you're trying to do. So, to some extent, it may be impossible to say, "oh if we could deliver this program without any kind of positive emotion and we just did it in a kind of detached, cold way, we'd separate out the affective piece."

Cynthia Martiny: Well the ethics committee would never let you do it anyway.

William Arsenio: There are some things that are going to be hard and undesirable to separate out, but being able to have supportable findings is always the goal.

The other thing I would say has to do with the early days of Headstart where people were trying to evaluate the educational programs. I remember there was a really strong focus in the beginning on looking at a narrow set of cognitive measures. And for awhile the interventions were deemed failures because they would raise kids' IQs, 6-8 points whatever, and then that would wash out after a year or two. And there was a lot of hand wringing for a while; people were saying, "this is a waste, it doesn't work, it's not worth the money." Headstart had another political history so it survived. And then a number of studies that were done; they were funded through universities, and they followed the kids not just for a year or two and they had a whole bunch of assessments. Ten-12 years later they would have measures from this simple intervention, and it was done by random assignment, whether you got it or not (they did all these kind of good research kind of things). And they got major effects! I think it was by Lycard and called the Perry preschool project. There are a number of projects like that . . . So I think that one of the things is that there's always a push and I understand how that works, I was in education (I still am) with young kids for years. People want to see the immediate gain. They want to know immediately that it works, and that it's real. And I think that you need to make sure you don't narrowcast what you try to assess and if you can, to be able to look a little bit more down the line, because sometimes the effects immediate.

Michael Schleifer: Our team being often called upon to say what impact philosophy has on children, have, not immediately, but over the course of a year or two, so we've done research like that. And some of it has been convincing to a degree, with the dependent variables. For example, these little tests of judgment seem to work, and we are undertaking longitudinal studies to see if this is maintained beyond the short term. But at the end of the day, my response to the complexities of cognitive and affective work and assessment is to use a design of pre and post test; we're only going to look at what effect our work may have on things like judgment or reasoning, but we're getting into other things. Francisco Pons has been one of our collaborators, he's helped us in saying, "okay, you have to look very carefully and use dimensions of comprehension of emotion." Francisco works with Paul in some of those areas and others, in a sort of multi-dimensional aspect, and we've also used one of the things we've designed . . . work we've done on cooperation, to look at some of their social skills in a certain way, using cooperation tests and so on . . . So I see that . . . we're back to dependent variables again, we're working hard on that, to try to get a picture of how philosophy for children is having an impact. But the idea of being clearer on what goes on, I don't know how to get a handle on it. It seems so multi-complex.

Cynthia Martiny: Well, maybe group counseling research is an example . . . we have to be patient. We used to not be able to enter in a room when there was psychotherapy going on, we didn't have any devices so we were just taking notes. Then we became more interested in taking tapes and we listen to the content and now we're getting video tapes, we're seeing more, and in group counseling, now we're getting more sophisticated, I have a room downstairs and we have cameras all over the place so we can have the whole interaction of a group and how they work and we can start to analyze it.

Michael Schleifer: And we're filming in philosophy for children too. I have thousands of films that we've done with permission, but an analysis of what is actually happening even when you're looking at the film, at what level are we going to say, as Paul said, this is the crucial ingredient . . . I wouldn't even know how to start.

Cynthia Martiny: But you have to do systematic observations with a specific variable . . .

Paul Harris: It's not a question of just doing systematic observation; you have to ask yourself, which of these various variables – all of this complex stuff – is having an effect. And there's no way to do that just by looking more and more attentively. It's hopeless.

Michael Schleifer: Can I directly put it to you? Would you think a research was valuable, very general, which just globally said, "I don't know. I can't do it. Here Philosophy for children was done as opposed to philosophy for children wasn't done. " And being very careful to the suggestion that you made about the dependent variable, the results are impressive and significant. Is that not good enough?

Paul Harris: So let's be clear. There are two very different issues. One issue, which you and I are focusing on is, is an intervention having an effect? And in some ways that's an easier issue to deal with because you can have your pre-test measures and your post-test measures and in some sense, provided you have a control group who got nothing, you could definitely say, probably, that this intervention has an effect. But that's the easy part – easier, relative to the other part. The other part is, "okay, we have spent months with these children, we've trained all these teachers, we believe it's a complicated life-enhancing mixture of affect and thinking and reflection, etc." The question is: what are you doing that's more effective, and in some sense different, from just regular instruction?

Michael Schleifer: But what do you suggest?

Paul Harris: In order to help you, I would have to look at the data you have on the effects you achieve. In other words, I would want to say, let me compare the pre-test and the post-test, let me see, for example, those domains where children are especially benefiting from this program. Once we've established that, at the very least we've got some clues as to what might be especially crucial to the program, just in terms of plausibility, we would backtrack. For example, if you find that the children were particularly improving in their listening skills, so they waited 'til somebody finished and they were much more likely to answer in terms of the particular point of the preceding speaker had made, but on the other hand, if you for example measure their verbal IQ, there was no shift there . . . so, in some sense, a shift in pragmatic skills but not a shift in vocabulary or semantic development, well that would give you some clues perhaps as to what might be the especially effective aspects.

Michael Schleifer: Okay, that's good, but we have another problem which of course overlaps work again. In regards to the children, we do the research of comparing the experimental group to the control group. But there's a long history . . . there's lots and lots of data which pretty well however, when we talk about variables, they tend to be reasoning and they tend to be judgment tests and even with content like violence . . . so it's comprehension. The children seem to comprehend more and they articulate more and they communicate more and so on. That's the kind of stuff . . . But, what kind of an effect does it have on their being caring people or being moral and do they cooperate more . . . It's anecdotal, and it's not that impressive. I've done the work myself and I have to say, and our stuff is always more impressive when it deals with the comprehension aspects or the articulation, understanding as supposed to . . .

Paul Harris: More impressive because that's what you measured or . . .

Michael Schleifer: More impressive because the results are clearer even when we tried to measure . . .

Paul Harris: . . . the other aspects, you don't get such . . .

Michael Schleifer: No, you don't.

Alexander Herriger: We said we have to see if it has an impact. Yes, I think, but I think we have to see if it has not only an impact, but also if it has the impact we expect, because we have to settle up what impact we want to have. Is it to control emotion, is it to freeze emotion, what kind of emotions? We have to think also of why we want to educate emotions, and I think maybe one of the answers could be that we want to prevent violence, because we see that many violence comes from emotions. And I think one point that Lipman brings up related to violence prevention is to try to handle frustration. I've observed frustration children when, for example, a child couldn't be understood by others, or he didn't express himself clearly enough so that others could understand him, so he was frustrated because I ask him questions and he couldn't explain himself clearly, and the others didn't understand him, so this came up as frustration . . . Two weeks later I came back and he said, "today I think there was no confrontation among us, but I think there was more collaboration." And I think he could handle his frustration somehow. I don't know what happened in these two weeks when I wasn't there but there must have been something. We can see it, they have to deal with frustration all the time: They raise their hands, but they cannot talk because the teacher doesn't see them or the period is over. They cannot express themselves clearly enough, they cannot be understood by the others. Is frustration one emotion that we want to educate or to freeze or to control, and how?

Phil Guin: It seems to me that you could ask this about anything in the curriculum, couldn't you? Why do you say, the impact of emotions, or what kinds of questions you might ask about emotions, whether we're trying to cause emotions, etc. But it seems to me you could say this about anything in your curriculum, what's the impact? You say it's pretty obvious with some things like mathematics (although don't know if it's all that obvious). Where do you start looking for impact? Ten years after you get out of school, or as you're going through school or at the conclusion of a class? I'm just not sure. . . I know in Philosophy for Children, and correct me Ann if I'm wrong on this, when it was being created, the idea was that it would be a free-standing program. In the sense that it had just as much right to be in the curriculum as any other thing in the curriculum. Now, you could say, that's making a pretty strong assumption, especially when you try to put the program over to, say, a superintendent of schools, or a principal, or whoever it may be who might be interested. They'll say: "look, our curriculum is full. We have no more places. What is it about your program that makes you think it deserves this place in the curriculum?" Well, I think historically what happened was, that we started looking for ways to show that the program, or philosophy for children, might have an impact indirectly in other areas. For example, what if you were to give the program and give something to a control group to compensate, the Hawthorne effect, and see how you come out say on standardized tests. And what they found was that there was a kind of a consistent significance in areas like mathematics and in reading comprehension that would be of interest to superintendents, it would be of interest to people that make decisions about what goes into the curriculum. I mean, if you can show that your kids are improving say 66%, if I remember that right, in reading comprehension, isn't that something that is desirable, isn't that something that you want in your curriculum?

Paul Harris: But there are lots and lots of ways to improve children's reading comprehension.

Phil Guin: Well alright, mathematics we're also getting about 33%.

Ann Sharp: But I think Paul's point is there are lots of ways to improve reading comprehension. Why Philosophy for Children? And I think that's what you started with . . .

Cynthia Martiny: Yet this is true with anger too. We can give guys drugs and we could put them in jail and also we could give them electro-shock and take out their frontal lobe, we have techniques. . . I'm being a little facetious, but it's true; we have tons of techniques to work on all of the issues. I think what we're looking for maybe is a technique that's efficient but that's also somewhat human.

Paul Harris: One reason or justification of teaching philosophy to children, they'll just engage in philosophical thinking more often . . .

Michael Schleifer: But what Alexander has a sense of is different. He thinks that he has helped some kids to become less frustrated, or to deal with it and so on. It may be true and I suspect it is true, maybe not all thirty in his class, but maybe two or three. I don't think that's a different one, I mean when we've tried some things, what we are trying currently, as I said, to look at interactions with certain situations, cooperation tests and various sorts which we are adapting as such and we are putting in research assistants that are blind, this is the other aspect. So they don't know when they see the kids in different aspects are they coming from control groups or experimental groups? You know, we are trying these factors which are another aspect of it. You know because there is so much of a halo affect, people want so much to believe that this is happening, that it is hard to do the research and so on. So the question of this whole seminar, controlling emotions, so lets take frustration, a good example. I think we probably could get a handle on devising a way to see if children at the beginning of the year, say understand it in a certain way, say frustration. And at the end of the year do they understand it better, and I think we can devise that. How we go about trying to validate your intuitions and the investment you have that some of the children are actually getting better at controlling their frustration and so on, I think I need another 40 years of research.

Paul Harris: The problem is even if you could, there are lots and lots of teachers out there who will come to you at the end of their year, who don't teach Philosophy for Children. Actually several of my children now handle frustration better. I am a conscientious, loving, respectful teacher and by virtue of their interaction with me and by virtue of various developmental processes, a proportion of them are . . .

Ann Sharp: Paul, why don't you just focus on the validity of philosophical thinking for philosophical thinking? You can do philosophical thinking in a number of environments, you could have the debate team, you could have the way it was practiced in university when I was growing up: get your arguments, and I'm going to shoot you down, we could do all sorts of things, and we could be snapper jack, etc. But I *don't* think we would be helping children to grow into citizens, good people. So, it's not just philosophical thinking as much as it is learning how to think about philosophy but in a community where I become slowly reflective, not just of my own thinking, but how we as a community are doing, always with the goal of doing better, self correcting, better tomorrow. As the kids say, "well we did okay today, but listen guys we could do a lot better tomorrow." You know one kid will go to the board and say, "you didn't listen, now let's try and work at that part." It is that kind of self awareness and self reflection, and there is an ethical domain to the whole thing.

Paul Harris: That does suggest, the kind of intervention, experiment, in which some children will get this more communitarian intervention, focusing on the philosophical concepts that you have emphasized. Whereas another group of children would get a less communitarian intervention but still focusing on the same concepts. If you really think the communitarian aspects are critical then we ought to see a difference at the end of the year between those two groups of children. Particularly I suspect in the kind of things you are emphasizing. Sensitivity to the point of view of the other, ability to hold back and synthesize and so forth. That seems to me, if that's what you want to emphasize clearly doable, it is plausible that you could do something along those lines.

Cynthia Martiny: And the content could change in the control group, take the philosophy out.

Paul Harris: On the contrary, I am saying keep the philosophy constant and vary the group interactions that you are nurturing.

Lee Londei: Because what's important is the way you go about creating community; it's a way of doing – it's a philosophy of being,

Cynthia Martiny: But what I'm thinking is if you compare it to a psychotherapy group, it's the same thing we do.

Wendy Turgeon: what's the difference between that and cooperative education? You need to have some way of measure the aspect of philosophy . . .

Lee Londei: But group counseling is more effective in many instances than one on one psychotherapy.

Cynthia Martiny: Yes

Paul Harris: It is an open question as to whether you need philosophy to nurture. You could imagine four groups: communitarian philosophy, non communitarian philosophy, communitarian math and non-communitarian math.

Cynthia Martiny: The question that the developmental psychologists can answer is the methodological one. The problem is more complicated than the stages of development, in which there are specific stages in life where you learn certain things. So when we want to apply at a stage level you could also have another design and continue doing this at different stages to see if there is an effect at different age groups.

Wendy Turgeon: Can I suggest that it can't be as open ended as you, Michael, were suggesting the teachers go into their classrooms and you don't know what they are doing but they've been trained. There has to be some sense in which, you don't want it to be a rigid methodology, but there also has to be some common elements in both pedagogical strategies and content teachers do.

Michael Schleifer: Ann and Mat have described this in great detail. We also have teachers tell us what they did, and what the circumstances were and what the training was and what the process was when they teach philosophy. But, I think Paul saying "okay, I can see pretty well what you do in philosophy for children in a vague way," but research is different. Yet there are two points, we want to do the research and we want to be impressive. So we must look at our dependent variables more carefully and isolate them (as Phil said). Then there is the essential point that Paul said, "what is that ingredient that is going on in Philosophy for Children?" Let's specify that element. After all the years we can specify the philosophy we do and the community that is formed. At the very least there are those two things.

Paul Harris: By the way, I said to specify the ingredient, but it may well be a cluster.

Wendy Turgeon: I think that is one of the problems with Philosophy for Children is that people say that they are doing it, but each do wildly different things.

Cynthia Martiny: That is true in group therapy too.

Ann Sharp: There is a lot of research that we have so far, that shows that unfortunately this is not teacher proof in any way. In other words, whatever results you get, whether you are looking at critical thinking or caring thinking or whatever, it is going to be dependent on the ability of that teacher to really do philosophy for children in a communal way. The weakest link of the whole project is the formation of the teachers. It is one thing if Alex does it, it is another thing for him to train teachers who have no philosophy background and little psychology background, and get the same results. We have never been able to break that problem of the teacher formation.

Cynthia Martiny: Paul, I'm sure there's a similar problem with parents. What is the skill that they use when having conversations with their children? You are probably using extreme clear cut different educational levels.

Paul Harris: They are slightly differences in the case, the people I mentioned are looking at the natural variations in adoptive parents. Whereas Ann begins with a certain assumption that you are bringing the same cohort of teachers to a certain frame of mind and a certain set of skills to, hopefully, a certain level. The problem is that you don't succeed at doing that.

Ann Sharp: Also, we've been told by the psychologists that it isn't good enough if you can do it. The point is, can you train another generation to yield the same results? And that goes to how the teachers are prepared in the first place, the culture, the things.

Paul Harris: If it is any comfort to you Ann, it is a problem that bedevils every educational innovation in the past two hundred years.

William Arsenio: There are ways to get a handle on that. There was a whole conflict resolution study in New York city that involved 10 000 or 15 000 kids conducted by Aber and that whole group. One of the pieces that they dealt with a lot was try to along with the intervention, they had ways of assessing the fidelity. They essentially knew who did a good, or not so good job, in terms of administrating. I don't remember the exact details and how they assessed that but they had a way to know, after everyone did their intervention, who did it the way they wanted and so on.

Michael Schleifer: By fidelity, do you mean to the paradigm?

Cynthia Martiny: Repeatability.

William Arsenio: Yes, who did it the right way – who did it intensely the right way. They found major consequences depending on how well you delivered (I guess that is obvious). I know a lot of people haven't done that, I guess they were able to show not only, look not only does the intervention work, but it works best with those folks who were able to deliver it in the way in which we meant it delivered. The overall effects of their study were relatively weak, but when you consider this interaction of who did it well and some other things, then you got some powerful effects. The overall program, in my understanding, was not that powerful and you know people were interested in pulling the plug, but now they are trying to figure out what to do with that I think.

Michael Schleifer: So one variable is whether or now a teacher is an experienced interveners. Then there is the fact that even the experienced ones need accompanying. We have a model called the Accompanying Model, we have people who have been there for years, but, despite the fact they are experienced, if you abandon them they may have forgotten what to do. An experienced, accompanied group do best, but not on all variables. That's the other thing, sometimes you have a whole group of novices, who are motivated, so by the end of the school year they are just catching on with everything (Ann's materials, or Marie-France's materials, and the methodology and so on). Nevertheless, even with that group, some dependent variable like for example, as I said with my judgment test, some kids got better even with a less experienced teacher, less accompanied, that's good in the sense of the dependent variable. It is less good, with Paul's question about what is the ingredient, or the combination of ingredients.

William Arsenio: I am a little less pessimistic than he is. I think maybe to help figure out what is going on you could use four or six variations on the same program, and then take out this piece or whatever. Maybe the first cut is to be able to assess broadly enough. There are lots of good measures to allow you to cast a wide ne,t in terms of assessment. You can come back and see and "well what we found is that it actually did reduce conflict, it increased emotional understanding . . ." You can get a picture, here are the things that seemed to work better than others.

Michael Schleifer: Can I take you up on frustration as a test case? Let's play the game. Say Alexander has come to me, and simply says "here is my intuition. I think this is *the* ingredient, can you do something?" So we work on it for months and come up with a model. What would you do – I know it isn't your field – to see if these children had improved control of frustration?

William Arsenio: I would have to think about it. I know what some other people have done experimentally, but we don't want to do these things. They have done things where kids play a game, either a computer game, or more provocatively a game with another person, and the game is rigged. It is rigged in such a way that they can't win. On top of that, sometimes the other child who is in it is trained to say things that are more or less provocative. She does it experimentally.

Michael Schleifer: What's her name?

William Arsenio: Hubberd. I wouldn't use that test, but one of the interesting things she found in that task is looking at aggressive and non aggressive kids. Aggressive kids could just opt out; they'd say "I am out of here, I don't want to do this." She found this reaction in an extremely high percentage of the aggressive kids. Yet, she didn't have this as an independent measure, and she should of.

I think there might be more benign versions of this test. and I would have to think about it. It is complicated, you have to figure out what you want to do. It is also a resource issue, what you want to put your time and energy into.

You are looking for measure. You have ideas about where the effects will come out, you have things that you want to look at in particular, so perhaps something called the Madson cooperation board would be useful.

Michael Schleifer: We are working on cooperation already. It's one of the ideas that has come up because of Ann's ideas, so we have added it in and we are working on it. We will show you, we have devised little tests of cooperation for young kids, some of which are inspired from others but they have to be adapted to younger age groups. So on cooperation, yes, that is somewhat different from dealing with the raw emotions that we have described. Alexander is convinced, he is probably right in my view, that he is having an effect. I don't doubt that a child, because of the philosophical conversations, becomes more cooperative. But maybe, as Paul would say, it is only due to the fact that Alexander is a nice guy and the child interacted with him; it may have nothing to do with philosophy for children. That's the problem.

Ann Sharp: Regarding frustration, let's say we are 15 kids, and we put up 15 things we are going to talk about and mine is always at the end, so we are never going to talk about mine. With time I can get pretty frustrated. I remember one kid saying to me, "we never talk about what I am interested in." Another kid said to him "ya, but no matter which one we pick it is always interesting."The first kid said "but that's because you sure participated a lot." As you practice it you become aware of the intrinsic fun in doing it no matter where you start. Again, it is back to that ego thing. That you begin to realize that we don't have to start with mine for me to really enjoy participating. But that takes time, because we really have to begin to understand that, and usually it is my friend who points it out to me.

Cynthia Martiny: In group psychotherapy it is not enough to experience it, but it has to be said. So look what you are doing now, so that a client would recognize that this is what they are learning. Otherwise, the frustration accelerates quickly, and they just get angry.

Ann Sharp: But that's what happened, this one kid said to the other kid, "but look at how much you participated", and the other kid says "ya because I really enjoyed it."

Michael Schleifer: At the very least, and maybe it is the very most that we can do, we can combine the interventions that you people do and the paradigm of coming along and making a link to what's really going on. Maybe we don't want to devise tests of the handling of frustration, maybe the best we could do is to see if the children begin to understand frustration (which is itself a concept). Let's say we have five year olds right, they know the word. They certainly understand anger right? But I don't know if your brilliant six year old would understand the emotion of frustration. I don't know if anyone has done work on that?

Cynthia Martiny: So now we are into the last question. Which is "what is the cognitive or educable part of emotion learning and decision making or responsibility?" We are moving there.

Paul Harris: I was a bit surprised by how pessimistic you are at the possibility of measuring frustration tolerance. Even though it was mentioned as so problematic, it is not such a hard thing to look at, if indeed you feel that is a major focus of the program.

Michael Schleifer: Just off the top, what would be an example of frustration tolerance that you think would be appropriate say for a group of 5 year olds.

Paul Harris: I guess before I could answer that, I would have to ask you to be a bit more clear about the kinds of frustrations that you were talking about. Life is full of frustrations, but do you want to discuss the frustration that the children feel in these group discussions?

Michael Schleifer: Yes.

Paul Harris: In that case it seems to me the obvious thing to do would be to test the child at various points with respect to his ability to engage in discussion. I don't see anything terribly hard about that.

Lee Londei: (directed at Alexander) But you are saying his frustration doesn't impact on his ability to participate? It's just impulse control, at what degree?

Alexander Herringer: I don't know.

Paul Harris: You said he improved, what is it you felt improved?

Alexander Herringer: What I felt improved is that he could participate in another way than he did two weeks ago. I think there is a big difference in what we say and the way we say it. He felt that others were against him because he couldn't express what he meant. The children asked him questions in order to understand what he said, and he couldn't respond. Sometimes he would say "oh I didn't say that, I never said that," and he would get angry about it because he was feeling like everybody was against him.

Cynthia Martiny: So he went from being defensive to open.

Alexander Herringer: Yes. Two weeks later he was participating and more open. But the context was different and the subject was different and he didn't have all these people against him. What he said at the end is "this time I didn't feel any aggressiveness but I felt collaboration again."

Paul Harris: How old is this student?

Alexander Herringer: I think he was in the fifth grade, so 10 or 11.

Michael Schleifer: Alors il aurait pu utiliser le mot *frustration*.

Alexander Herringer: Oui, mais ils n'ont pas beaucoup de vocabulaire les gens . . .

Michael Schleifer: I was saying if you talk about frustration, you could use the word "frustration," but it may not even have an impact on their comprehension of their frustration.

Paul Harris: Just to backtrack, I just want to clarify the fact that in the course of your observation this child seemed to move from an aggressive-come-defensive mode of conversation with the other children to, as Cynthia was hinting, something more relaxed and more open. If that is what you are looking at then why not just look at that. Why do we need something terribly different from that, that seems to be a goal in itself. It is tremendously valuable if children can engage, so one might want to emphasize emotionally charged and somewhat challenging topics. We would have a pretest when a child is assigned to a small group, and then you want to observe that child engage, and at the end of your curriculum you revisit the child's capacity to do that.

Wendy Turgeon: As philosophy is intrinsically contentious it would possibly lead to frustration which might be a good reason to have philosophy

Ann Sharp: In some countries they talk about self-evaluation, so, for example, we take a video of our community discussion at the beginning of the year, and then around November one of our sessions is devoted to looking at that video and comparing it to the video that we took last week. Then we ask how are we doing better, how are we doing worse, etc. Then the kids put they ways they think they are doing better and worse. What they are doing is pulling out the criteria and very often they say, "oh look how I listened." How do you know he listened? Because he repeated what he said. Test again in January and one more time at the end.

Michael Schleifer: So the children verbalize their observations?

Ann Sharp: Yes: "I didn't jump up and down like I did the first time," and other such things.

Michael Schleifer: That's interesting, because that paradigm is not one that we use, in fact most people doing research have used the pre-test/post-test design. But Cynthia, in fact, working in her groups and so on, is the expert in this field, which is to say she looks at interactions of people to measure non-verbal empathy . . . you can say it quicker than me.

Cynthia Martiny: Non-verbal synchronicity. They look at imitation behaviors, we look at things that are copied or coordinated so that we can have an idea if they are intoned, the resonance is a difficult thing to know. We haven't quite put the things in their hearts yet to find the heart beat, although there has been research that heart beats can exactly beat at the same beat.

Ann Sharp: But what I found interesting about this one is that then the kids will say "let's face it, last time we got somewhere." And so then you have to explore, and that's a metaphor . . .

Michael Schleifer: What I meant is that paradigm that I understand you have in your groups. You have your clients, working on being therapists, and then they go back and look at the films of themselves, replay, and then they talk about that, that gets filmed too, and then they have the third order discussion of the discussion they have. That is fascinating, and we have never used that paradigm.

Ann Sharp: What I liked about this one from a philosophical point of view, is that when they said they were doing better they weren't just looking at their behavior; instead, they said "look it, we got somewhere," and they began to dig down deep, so they walked away with an understanding that they didn't have before.

Michael Schleifer: Your point is important to consider, especially in light of Paul's double challenge. I need to get a better handle of what is going on with the children.

Cynthia Martiny: It is a long.

Michael Schleifer: Yes, it's long and complicated, but maybe to answer what's going on, one actually has to see what's going on. That's is where filming comes in.

Paul Harris: I have a slightly different idea of that. Alongside looking at the child's actual ability to engage in a group discussion pre-test and post-test, it would be fascinating to show the child a video of a group discussion at pretest and to get the child to comment on what was happening during that discussion and the extent to which the child was alert to and able to articulate the coherence of the discussion.

Michael Schleifer: But he sees himself though, it's his own group.

Paul Harris: No, it could be neutral, it could be a canonical discussion that every child gets to see. You get the child's narrative about what's happening. I am fairly hopeful that when you reshow those same children at the end of the curriculum the same video or some comparable video and you get the child to comment on the group processes and the contributions that people make and the point that your making about the extent to which the group got somewhere. The child having gone through your curriculum might show a lot of metacognition that the child lacked at the onset. I think that would be a very nice conjunction of these more tacit skills, since they are socially participating and using the reflective skills, which you are trying to nurture.